TRAIL BOSS'S

◆

Cowboy Cookbook

*Containing recipes
from throughout the West
and around the world.*

ISBN 0-9603692-6-0
Library of Congress 88-60338

©1985 by Society for Range Management.

SRM SOCIETY FOR RANGE MANAGEMENT

EXPRESSION OF APPRECIATION

Appreciation is expressed for the invaluable help of many who have assisted in various ways: to the Secretary of Commerce, Malcolm Baldridge, for his support and for writing the introduction; to Mary Fry, American Fisheries Society, for suggestions and contacts in getting the project started; to George Kovach for painting the book cover picture; to Don and Bettejoe Pendleton, Bobby and Shirley Williamson, Gale and Justine Wolters, Bud and Marie Rumburg, and Jack and June Schmautz for their many contributions as members of the Trail Boss's Cowboy Cookbook Committee; to J.D. Ross for help in artwork and design; to Richard and Caroll Reed for keeping and managing cookbook sales and distribution records on their home computer; to the SRM Executive Director, Pete Jackson and his staff for their invaluable help, and all the SRM members, ranch folks and friends who provided recipes and information for the book.

COVER PICTURE: The Society for Range Management is obliged to George Kovach, a Texas artist, for his rendition of *"Cowboys to Dinner"* painted specifically for the cover of *The Trail Boss's Cowboy Cook Book*. Kovach's art works are included in art collections throughout the United States and several other countries. For information about obtaining his artwork write to: George Kovach, P.O. Box 297, Blackwell, Texas 79506.

DEDICATION

The Trail Boss dedicates this book to Doug and Virginia Sellars of Fairfax, Virginia. Virginia conceived the idea and together they have been largely responsible for its development. Virginia, a high school teacher and Doug, a Soil Conservation Service (SCS) employee, both have western backgrounds including ranching and other activities. Virginia, a native of Oklahoma and Doug, a native of Idaho, met in college in Oklahoma, where she was rodeo queen and he was the college rodeo committee chairman. Along with painting and drawing western art, Doug auctioneers and as an SCS Range Conservationist, has worked with ranchers and range management specialists in Texas, California and a number of other western states.

Doug and Virginia have developed and promoted the *Trail Boss's Cowboy Cookbook* as a means of helping SRM promote the science and art of Range Management.

THE SOCIETY FOR RANGE MANAGEMENT (SRM) is the broadest, most knowledgeable organization concerned with rangeland and its renewable resource products and values. The membership interests encompass ranching, wildlife biology, hydrology, range conservation, soil conservation, students, teachers, and private industry.

The Trail Boss ©

THE SOCIETY WAS FOUNDED IN 1948 as a non-profit corporation dedicated to a more comprehensive understanding of rangeland, its ecosystems, and their use.

THE SOCIETY, CONSISTING OF OVER 5,500 MEMBERS, is international in scope, representing 50 states and 48 countries. The Society is divided into national, regional, or state Sections, encouraging active participation in specific geographical concerns.

MEMBERSHIP IN SRM IS OPEN FOR ANYONE INVOLVED or interested in the development, study, effective management and wise use of rangelands. The objectives to which our members are dedicated are:

—*to properly take care of the basic rangeland resources of soil, plants and water;*

—*to develop an understanding of range ecosystems, and of the principles applicable to the management of range resources;*

—*to assist all who work with range resources to keep abreast of new findings and techniques in the science and art of range management;*

—*to improve the effectiveness of range management to obtain from range resources the products and values necessary for man's welfare;*

—*to create a public appreciation of the economic and social benefits to be obtained from the range environment;*

—*to promote professional development of its members.*

The Trail Boss Says:
"You Have a Stake in the Range"

Management of rangelands should concern you. We all have a stake in the rangelands in more ways than one.

First, rangelands are the primary source of our meat supply. Nearly all calves and older animals that are fattened (finished) in feedlots are born and raised on rangelands. Most young cattle are not fed grain until they reach more than three-fourths of their final market weight. The majority of a steer's life is spent on rangeland, a kind of land that cannot grow food for direct consumption by humans. More importantly, a large portion of the breeding stock which produces animals for slaughter year after year spend nearly all their life on rangelands. The most efficient, economical way to harvest the renewable vegetation of rangelands is through the grazing animal. In turn, this method provides economical, high quality meat for your table. Were it not for domestic livestock, millions of acres of land might not be useful for producing any kind of food.

Rangelands also provide a home for the sheep and goats that supply meat, wool, and mohair. Livestock hides used for shoes, boots, clothing, and other goods are another important indirect product of rangelands.

Rangelands provide the vital food, cover, and water for many kinds of wildlife. Big and small game and numerous birds depend on range during a part, if not all, the year.

Rangelands are one of our greatest sources of water. They provide vast underground storage reservoirs for water used for domestic purposes, industry, and agriculture. Natural runoff from rangelands contributes water to streams, rivers and lakes.

Finally, rangelands provide many forms of year-round recreation. Whether your interests are hunting, fishing, rock collecting, hiking, horseback riding, painting, or photography, the rangelands have something to offer. Regardless of whether you live in the city, a small town, or on a farm or ranch, its important for you to have an interest in the conservation, improvement, and proper use of our rangelands. Your stake is as big as that of your neighbor!

Table of Contents

BREADS, continued

ROLLS

BISCUITS & MUFFINS

CHILI

STEWS

CASSEROLES

CASSEROLES, continued

BARBECUE SAUCE

BARBECUE MEATS

BARBECUED MEATS, continued

RED MEATS

BEEF

RED MEATS, continued

GOAT

LAMB

WILDLIFE, continued

VEGETABLES

VEGETABLES, continued

MEXICAN FOOD

THE COWBOY'S SWEET TOOTH
CAKES

CANDY

COOKIES

COOKIES, continued

COBBLERS, CUSTARDS, PIES & PUDDINGS

PIES, continued

JAMS and JELLIES

SWEETS

APPETIZERS
HORS-d'OEUVRES
BEVERAGES
SAUCES

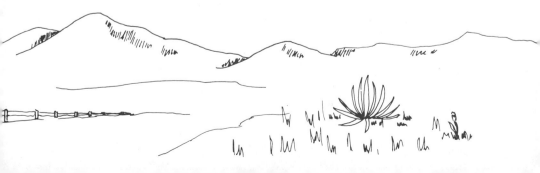

THE TRAIL BOSS

The rangelands of the world produced a unique society of people. They came from diverse lands and cultures. Each had a special reason for being there and each had a special set of skills in surviving there. This mixture of cultures and survival techniques in the rangeland setting resulted in various styles of food preparation, each unique to a particular geographical area, combination of cultures and availability of foods

The Society for Range Management, through its members is pleased to present to you a collection of "Rangeland Receipes" used on trail drives and ranches of a past century and ranches of the present day.

Also included in this first volume of the *Trail Boss's Cowboy Cookbook* you will find interesting bits of information about rangelands, their development, their present use and their value to each and all of the citizens of this land.

We all partake, in some way, from the rangeland, i.e. food, water, wildlife, clean air, recreation, fiber, energy, pharmaceuticals, industrial materials, adventure, drama, literature, music and the pride of heritage.

RANGELANDS occupy about 47% of the earth's total land area. They are the largest single land category in many countries, including the United States, Canada, and Mexico.

RANGELANDS provide:
- approximately 75% of the worldwide forage needs for livestock
- food and ·cover for wildlife
- water for many uses
- open space for beauty, recreation, environmental balance, and diversity

Here is a vast natural treasure which, with proper management and use, can contribute significantly to YOUR food supply and the quality of YOUR environment.

Wilma Newman
Fairfax, Virginia

CHEESE-RYE PUFFS

8 oz. grated sharp cheddar cheese   1 tsp. mustard
½ grated onion   ½ c. mayonnaise
5 slices crumbled bacon

Toast small rye bread on one side, spread with mixture. Broil till bubbly.

Ann Gates
Corvallis, Oregon

CRAB MOLD

1 can mushroom soup   1 c. mayonnaise
1 tbsp. gelatin   7 oz. canned crab
3 tbsp. water   6 oz. cream cheese
6 green onions, sliced   green olives
1 c. celery   parsley

Heat the soup. Dissolve gelatin in water and add to soup. Cool. Add onions, celery, mayonnaise, crab and cheese. Put in loaf pan or mold. Chill overnight. Decorate with olives and parsley. Serve with crackers.

June Schmautz
Fairfax, Virginia

1, 2, 3 HORS d'OEURVES

1 lb. sausage (hot or mild)
2 c. sharp cheddar cheese, grated
3 c. Bisquick

Combine all ingredients and shape into balls the size of walnuts. Bake on cookie sheet at 350° for 15 min. Makes about 5 dozen. Sausage balls may be frozen before or after baking. If frozen after, defrost and reheat at 350°.

Ann Gates
Corvallis, Oregon

CHEESE DIABLO WAFERS

1 c. flour
½ lb. sharp cheddar cheese, grated

½ c. softened butter or margarine,
1 tsp. cayenne

Mix all ingredients and shape in 1-inch balls. Arrange about 2 inches apart on baking sheet and bake in very hot oven (450°) about 6 minutes. Serve hot or cool. Makes about 4 dozen. Reduce amount of cayenne pepper for milder wafer.

Ann Gates
Corvallis, Oregon

CHEESE-OLIVE PUFFS

2 c. grated sharp Cheddar cheese
1 c. flour

½ tsp. paprika
½ c. butter or margarine

3 to 4 doz. small pimento-stuffed olives

Mix first 4 ingredients very well and chill. For each puff, use a generous teaspoonful and shape into a ball. Push finger into center to make a deep depression, insert olive and shape dough around to fully cover olive. Bake in hot oven (400°) 15 min., or until baked but not browned. Serve hot. Makes 3 or 4 doz. Puffs can be frozen.

Ann Gates
Corvallis, Oregon

CHEESE PUFFS

4-oz. soft cream cheese
1 egg yolk

Dash of cayenne
30 white bread rounds, 1¼" diam.

Combine first 3 ingredients and beat until fluffy. Spread a heaping ½ teaspoonful on each bread round. Put on baking sheet and broil about 8" from heat for 5 min. or until golden brown and puffy. Serve hot.

BEVERAGES

The Four 6's Ranch
Guthrie, Texas

6666

CAMPFIRE COFFEE

2 qts. cold water
8 tsps. egg*

1 c. ground coffee
8 tsps. cold water

Dash of salt

Heat 2 qts. cold water in large pot. Mix 1 cup ground coffee with 8 tsps egg and 8 tsps cold water, (*prepare eggs by beating white and yolk together; store in refrigerator); add dash of salt. Stir in coffee mixture when water boils. Return to a boil, stirring occasionally. Turn off heat and pour in ¼ cup cold water; let stand 10 min. Makes 8 mugs.

Peter N. Jensen
Lincoln, Nebraska

FLAXSEED TEA

Pour one pint of boiling water over one ounce of flaxseed and a little pounded licorice root. Place the vessell near a fire for four hours, strain through a linen or cotton cloth.

Background: From the Blue Ribbon Cookbook, 1907.

Wilma Newman
Fairfax, Virginia

HOT CHOCOLATE MIX

1 2-lb. box of Nestles Quik
1 16-oz. jar coffeemate

1 14-qt. box powdered milk
2-lbs. powdered sugar

Mix ingredients together. Use ⅓ cup of mixture per cup of boiling water.

June Schmautz
Fairfax, Virginia

PUNCH

2 bottles white grape juice '   1 bottle club soda
                    2 28-oz. bottles 7-Up

Mix ingredients. Serve well-chilled. Tastes like champagne!

SAUCES

Lewis Ranches
Clarendon, Texas

BASTING SAUCE FOR ROAST

10-12 lb. chuck or arm roast   2 tsp. salt
2 tsp. dry mustard   1 tsp. pepper
½ tsp. garlic salt   2 tbsp. mayonnaise
2 tsps onion salt   2 tbsp. vinegar
2 tsps. celery salt   2 tbsp. Kitchen Bouquet

Place unseasoned roast in roaster with 1 inch water. Cover & cook 3-4 hours depending on size of roast. Add sauce and baste. Continue to cook covered til tender. Thicken liquid with flour.

Background: One of the oldest ranches in the Panhandle, the RO Ranch was established in 1878 by three English brothers, Alfred, Vincent and Bernard Rowe. After buying out his brothers, Alfred Rowe began raising Herefords, one of the Panhandle's first ranchers to do so. In April of 1912, Rowe crossed the Atlantic in the *Titanic* and drowned in the fatal iceberg collision.

William J. Lewis had worked on the RO Ranch as an eastern-bred 14-year-old in 1896. Twenty-one years later he bought the spread for more than half a million.

Lewis managed the ranch himself, as did his son, W.J. Lewis, Jr., who became a partner in the expanding ranching and cattle operation.

After the elder Lewis's death in 1960, and his son's death a year later, Frank Kerrick, who was raised on the Lewis Ranches, and whose father worked on the ranch for 65 years, became general manager, a position he still holds.

Today, the 100,000-acre ranch raises commercial Herefords and Quarter horses.

H.F. Heady
Berkeley, California

BRANDY SAUCE

1 c. water	½ c. sugar
2 tbsp. corn starch	1 tsp. nutmeg
2 tbsp. butter	¼ c. brandy
	1 tsp. vanilla

Mix dry ingredients and then stir them into a cup of boiling water. Boil for 5 minutes and then add butter, brandy and vanilla. Serve hot over mince pie.

Archie Fuchs
Brush Prairie, WA

AF

KILLER SALZA

Two oz. pkg. dried chili pequins	2 - 3 cloves garlic
1 tsp. cumin (crushed)	1 tsp. oregano
½ tsp. salt (optional)	1 or 2 c. tomato juice
Add juice of one lemon if you are canning.	

Soak the chili pequins 3 or 4 hours in vinegar; drain. Throw into the blender with all other ingredients and blend well. Let set in the refrigerator to cool off. EAT!

Ora H. Chipman
Delbert Chipman & Son (Woolgrowers)
American Fork, Utah

ONION SAUCE

This onion sauce is original and we enjoy it with *lamb chops and leg of lamb.* We receive comments from many of whom we have served.

I use medium size white onions and finely chopped rather than grind. I add sauce which I make from equal amounts of salad dressing and mayonnaise; add a dash of salt and pepper and a small amount of sugar.

Sometimes I put a small amount of this on lamb chops, and place under the broiler just before I serve them. Otherwise I let my guests add it as they choose. It goes well with a variety of lamb receipes.

Ann Gates
Corvallis, Oregon

LAYERED MEXICAN DIP

1 can refried beans, 16 oz.   3-4 avocado*
    1 c. yogurt   1 c. sour cream
 ½ pkg. taco seasoning   grated Cheddar cheese
           finely chopped tomatoes

* Mash avocado and mix with lemon juice to prevent darkening.

Layer refried beans on bottom, then avocado; mix yogurt and sour cream with taco seasoning for next layer. Top with grated cheese. Last layer is chopped tomatoes. Chopped black olives also add color. Serve with large Frito chips. A quiche dish is ideal for this recipe.

June Schmautz
Fairfax, Virginia

SPINACH DIP

        1 c. mayonnaise   1 c. sour cream
1 can water chestnuts, chopped   1 pkg. Knorr vegetabel soup mix
  3 green onions cut up fine   1 pkg. frozen chopped spinach

Defrost, drain, and squeeze moisture from the spinach. Combine with remaining ingredients. Chill several hours. Serve with raw vegetables or serve in round bread that has been hollowed out.

John L. Merrill
Triple X Ranch
Crowley, Texas

XXX

GRANDMOTHER MERRILL'S CHILI SAUCE

1 large onion
½ c. sugar
½ tsp. salt
1 tsp. cinnamon

15-oz. can of tomatoes
½ c. vinegar
1 tsp. all-spice
2 peppers from pepper sauce
(vary with taste)

Chop onions fine and mix with sugar, vinegar, salt and chopped peppers. Cook slowly until onions are tender. Chop tomatoes and add to mixture, add all-spice and cinnamon; stir well and cook 3 minutes. This makes 4 cups of sauce. Good on dried peas or beans, boiled cabbage, etc.

Background: Recipe was first used in the family by Mrs. Sarah Antonia Merrill of Somervell County, Texas in the early 1890's. It has been a standard additive to Pinto beans and cabbage by the family ever since.

Ginny Cartwright Todd
Cartwright Cottonwood Ranch
Kaufman, Texas

LD's HOMEMADE MAYONNAISE

2 eggs
1 tsp. dry mustard
1½ cup vegetable oil

4 tbsp. apple cider vinegar
1 tbsp. Lawrey's seasoning salt

Blend eggs, vinegar, mustard and seasoning salt in the blender; add oil very slowly (steady flow) while blender continues to run. Might need to stir toward end of adding the oil. Makes 1 pint jar.

Background: The Cartwright Ranch has been in Texas since 1846. Ginny is the 6th generation. The Doubleheart brand was passed down from my great grandfather and his brother Matthew and Leondias Cartwright. The brand was designed by their sister for their ranching operations together and is about 100 years old. LD Preston was born and raised on the Cottonwood Ranch over 70 years ago.

Shirley Williamson
Fairfax, Virginia

SHRIMP CANAPES

3 oz. soft cream cheese
3 tbsp. sour cream
1 tsp. prepared horseradish
½ tsp. lemon juice
¼ tsp. onion salt
1 c. finely chopped cooked shrimp
Small rounds of toast

Combine cream cheese, sour cream, horseradish, lemon juice, and onion salt. Add shrimp. Mix well. Spread on rounds of toast.

Sam H. Coleman   *Texas Section Range Camp*
Junction, Texas

JALEPENO-CHEESE DIP — TEXAS SECTION STYLE

1 pt. Kraft mayonnaise
1 lb. Velveeta Cheese
1 onion, medium to large
5 green pickled Jalapeno peppers*
Corn chips as needed

*For variety, pickled carrots can be substituted for Jalapenos. For different effects, additional carrots and/or Jalapenos can be finely diced and added to the dip. Dip increases in jalapeno strength with age.

Use blender to liquify Jalapenos, then onion, and cheese cut in 1 inch cubes. When well blended, mix in bowl with mayonnaise. Dip will stay for 2 weeks in refrigerator.

Background: This dip was served in the 1950s-1970s in my back yard at the directors' meeting each night after the campers were settled for the night. Beer or grape soda pop was served with it. This period was used by the directors to critique the day's activities and finalize plans for the coming day. The meeting generally broke up when the first director failed to properly discard his drink container.

BREADS

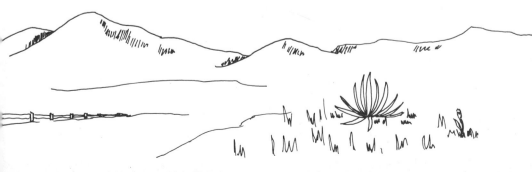

Facts

Rangeland is land on which Nature develops a grazable crop. Prior to settlement and the introduction of domestic livestock, rangelands provided habitat and forage for many native grazing animals. Therefore, grazing whether by domestic livestock or wildlife, is not a new impact on native vegetation. Grazing animals have influenced on the development of range vegetation over many centuries.

More than one-half of the world is rangeland. The well-being of many nations depends on the proper management of this vast area to guarantee a continual supply of range resources. There is more rangeland than forest and cropland combined.

While grazing is the largest single use of rangelands, timber, recreation, and watershed values also have a place on our ranges. As the Nation's needs and values change, nongrazing uses will rise in importance.

BREADS

Mr. & Mrs. John Maloney
Bitter Root Valley Ranch
Helena, Montana

HOME-MADE YEAST

Boil 6 large potatoes in 3 pints of water. Tie in a handful of hops in a small muslin bag and boil with potatoes. When thoroughly cooked, drain the water and add enough flour to make a thin batter. Set this on the stove and scald it enough to cook the flour (this makes the yeast keep longer). Remove from the fire and when cool add the potatoes mashed.
Add:

½ c. sugar	2 tbsp. salt
½ tbsp. ginger	Teacupful of yeast

Let stand in a warm place until it has thoroughly risen, then put in a large mouthed jar or jug and cork tightly. Set away in a cool place. The jug should be scalded before putting in the yeast. ⅔ of a cupful of yeast will make four loaves of bread.

Background: John Maloney, born in Ireland, came to the United States during the Civil War and to Montana during the mid-sixties, via a Missouri River Steamboat and Fort Benton. He followed the various gold mine rushes, finally settling on a homestead in the Bitter Root Valley at the junction of Miller Creek and the Valley. This homestead is still in the family. In the mid-eighties he returned to Ireland and married Margaret Dowling, returning to the Bitter Root Valley ranch with his bride where they spent the remainder of their lives, raising nine children.

The 6666's Ranch
Texas

6666

RICHARD'S SOURDOUGH BISCUITS

2 c. all-purpose flour	1 tbsp. sugar
1 tbsp. baking powder	¾ tsp. salt
2 c. sourdough starter	2 - 3 tbsp. softened lard or butter

"You might add a few raisins to keep these sourdoughs from chasin' any tumbleweeds."

Sift flour, sugar, baking powder and salt into large bowl; pour in starter. Mix to make a firm dough. Grease 12-in. iron skillet with lard. Pinch off balls the size of walnuts. Place in pan. Set biscuits in warm place 10-15 minutes. Bake in 400° oven for 24-30 minutes.

Tom and Shirley Cook
Fernley, Nevada

FRY BREAD

2 c. flour	½ tsp. baking powder
1 tsp. salt	water

Mix all to a biscuit dough. Roll out thin 6 to 8 inch round. Deep fry individually to golden brown, serve with beans, butter, jam honey or as they are.

Shelly (Jackson) Van Haur
S and J Livestock Co.
Hilger, Montana

ς

FRY PAN BREAD

2 c. flour	½ c. dried milk
1 tsp. salt	1 tbsp. sugar
2 tsp. baking powder	about 1 c. lukewarm water

Mix all ingredients together to make a thick dough that isn't sticky. Roll dough into a ½-inch thick circle. Cut into wedges. Fry in hot (not smoking) fat until golden brown on both sides.

Background: I'm a fourth generation ranch wife, raised to appreciate the range and its good management.

J.W. Bailey
Prairie Ridge Ranch
Cheyenne, Wyoming

•J•

INDIAN FRY BREAD

1¼ tsp. baking powder	3 c. flour*
1⅓ c. warm water	½ tsp. salt

*Use all white flour or half white/half whole wheat

Mix flour, baking powder and salt. Add warm water and knead until dough is soft but not sticky. Stretch and pat dough until thin. Tear off one piece at a time, poke a hole through the middle and drop into a kettle of sizzling hot lard or cooking oil. Brown on both sides. Serve hot. DELICIOUS served with butter and honey, jam or syrup (like pancakes); or can be sliced in half or used for hamburger buns or sandwich bread.

Belinda Style
Soil Conservation Service
Tuba City, Arizona

NAVAJO FRIED BREAD

6 c. unsifted flour	*½ c. instant non-fat dry milk*
1 tbsp. salt	*2¾ c. lukewarm water (apprjx.)*
2 tbsp. baking powder	*Lard or shortening for frying*

Combine flour, salt, baking powder and dry milk in a bowl. Add enough lukewarm water to make a soft dough. Knead thoroughly. Pinch off a ball of dough about the size of a large egg. Shape it round and flat with a small hole in the middle. Work it back and forth from one had to the other to make it thinner and thinner. Stretch gradually to a diameter of about 9 inches. Heat fat at least an inch deep in a heavy iron skillet. Drop thin rounds of dough into hot fat and fry to a light brown on one side. Then turn and fry other side. As it fries, the bread puffs up and becomes light. Drain each piece on paper towel. Serve hot with butter, jam, or honey. Makes about 18-24 pieces, about nine inches across.

Background: Fried Bread is a favorite among the Navajo People. It is usually served with mutton stew which consists of vegetables like celery, potatoes, onions and mutton. The Navajo have adopted the fried bread from the Spanish people who are known for their "sopaipillas".

James Newland
Greenwood Ranches
Bell Fourche, South Dakota

BASIC RANCHHOUSE BREAD

Place sourdough starter in large bowl. Add 2 cups flour and 2 cups milk or water. Let it set until spongy. Replenish starter in crock, leaving about 2 cups in bowl. To this add 2 or 3 tablespoons oil, melted butter or drippings. Add enough flour to make into a soft, kneadable dough, about 3 cups. Knead well, but do not work in too much flour.

When dough is smoothly elastic, put in an oiled bowl and let rise until double in bulk. Punch down and knead again. Form into large round loaf and set on oiled baking pan to rise. When loaf has risen, make cross design in top with sharp knife. Paint with lightly beaten egg white and put in oven at 450° for about 5 minutes, then reduce to 350° and bake for 40 to 45 minutes or until hollowish sounding when tapped. For a crisp crust, leave bread to cool on a rack after removing from the oven. For tender crust, paint the loaf with melted butter, wrap in clean cloth and leave to cool.

Fran Symms
Idaho

CHEESE APPLE BREAD

½ c. butter	1 c. peeled shredded apples
2 eggs	½ c. shredded Cheddar cheese
1½ tsp. baking powder	⅔ c. sugar
½ tsp. baking soda	2 c. flour
1 tsp. salt	

Combine butter, eggs and dry ingredients in large mixing bowl; blend well. Stir in apples and cheese. Turn into well-greased 9-by-5 loaf pan. Bake at 350° for 50 to 60 minutes, until center of loaf tests done. Cool thoroughly before removing from pan. Serve with sweet butter. This bread freezes well.

Marilyn J. Samuel
Cheyenne, Wyoming

SOURDOUGH BREAD

½ c. sourdough starter	3 tbsp. honey
1½ c. bread flour 'sponge'	1 c. wheat flour
1 c. water	1 tsp. salt
½ tbsp. butter or margarine	1 tsp. baking soda
1 c. warm milk	additional flour as needed

Combine starter, 1½ cups flour and water the night before. Next morning add butter melted in warm milk, honey and wheat flour to sponge. Mix well. Sprinkle salt and soda over mixture. Mix lightly. Let stand 30-50 min., until bubbly. Add flour until mixture cannot be stirred, place on floured board and knead 100 times or until silky mixture is developed. Place dough in greased bowl and let rise until double (2-4 hours depending on temp. of room). Punch down and form into loaves, 2 1-lb. or several smaller. Let rise again. Bake at 400° 10 min., then reduce temp to 325° for 20 min. longer or until done. Remove from pans to cool. Butter top of loaves to prevent too much crustiness. (This bread may take 16-20 hours, depending on vitality of starter and temperature of room).

Background: This recipe is modified from *The Complete Sourdough Cookbook"*, by Don and Myrtle Holm, 1976, Caxton Printers, Caldwell, Idaho. This bread has a distinctive flavor, but won't have the San Francisco "sour" taste unless the starter has that character.

RICHARD'S SOURDOUGH BREAD

1 c. milk
⅓ c. shortening
2 tbsp. lukewarm water
1½ c. sourdough starter

⅓ c. sugar
1pkg. active dry yeast
or
1 cake compressed yeast

5 c. all-purpose flour

Scald milk; add sugar, shortening and salt. Stir to melt sugar and shortening; cook to lukewarm. Dissolve yeast in warm water. Beat together cooled milk mixture, yeast, starter, and 2 cups flour. Add remaining flour to make a stiff dough. Turn onto floured surface, knead 5-10 min.; add only enough flour to keep from sticking. Place in greased bowl, turning to grease surface. Let rise until double, about 1½ hrs. Punch down, let rise again, about ½ hr.; divide into 2 balls, cover with towel and let rest 10 min. Shape into 2 loaves and put each in a greased 9x5x3-in. pan. Let rise until double, about 1 hr. Bake in 400° oven for 40 min. Turn out and cool.

Marjorie Wolters
Portis, Kansas

HOBO BREAD or STOVEPIPE BREAD

1 pkg. yeast
½ c. milk
½ c. salad oil or melted oleo
1 tsp. salt

3⅓ c. sifted all-purpose flour
½ c. warm water
¼ c. sugar
2 eggs

Dissolve yeast in warm water. Put 1½ cups of flour in large bowl. Add milk, water, oil, sugar, and salt and beat until smooth. Add eggs and beat well. Add 1 cup more of flour and beat until smooth. Stir in last cup of flour to make a soft dough. Pour or spoon batter into well-greased 1 pound coffee cans. Cover and let stand in warm place. When dough has risen almost to top of cans, place in 375° oven and bake for 30-35 minutes or until browned. Let cool about 10 minutes in cans before removing. Serve hot if desired. Makes 2 loaves.

The Four Sixes Ranch
Guthrie, Texas

6666

JALAPENO PEPPER CORNBREAD

Follow the Corn Bread recipe except: omit butter. Add 1 cup shredded cheddar or Monterey Jack cheese, 1 cup chopped onion, and ⅓ to ½ cup finely chopped jalapeno peppers. Bake at 425° for 40 minutes.

Niels L. Martin
Range Specialist
LCRD Project
Lesotho, South Africa

BASOTHO STEAM BREAD

*4 c. flour**	*½ tsp. salt*
2 tsp. yeast	*1 tbsp. sugar*

2 c. (approx.) warm water

* *I prefer whole wheat flour.*

Mix the yeast and sugar in the ½ cup of water to dissolve. Pour the yeast mixture and the salt into the flour and mix in with hands, adding more water until it makes a somewhat firm dough (if it becomes too soft and sticky, gradually add more flour until it is the right consistency). Knead the dough to develop the gluten so that it stretches and is rubbery in texture when pulled apart. Put it in greased pan or bowl and place in a warm place until it doubles in size (if it is cool outside, this can be wrapped in a pre-warmed speeling bag or floating in a larger pot of warm water, kept at about body temperature by pouring a little hot water on it from time to time).

After it has risen punch it down and cook it in a large pot prepared as follows:

Fill the bottom half of the large pot with clean rocks, pop or beer cans filled with water, or almost anything else you can find to make a platform. Fill to within about two inches of the top of this platform with water, cover the tops of the rocks, cans or whatever with plastic wrap or plastic bags and place the dough on the plastic. Grease the sides of the pot above the plastic to prevent the bread from sticking when it rises during cooking.

Boil until a knife inserted into the bread comes out clean. Slice or break into pieces and serve hot with butter.

Background: This is a traditional Southern African recipe.

Mathias Christen — Christiansen Ranch
Submitted by **Mrs. Hester David**
daughter of a Pioneer
Butte, Montana

SPOON BREAD

4 c milk	2 tbsp melted butter
1-1⅓ c. yellow cornmeal	4 tsp. baking powder
4 eggs, well beaten	1 tsp. salt

Cook 2 cups of milk, salt and cornmeal into mush. Add rest of milk, eggs, baking powder and butter. Bake in medium oven 30-40 minutes. Earthenware baking pan is best.

Background: This recipe has been used in the family for generations. Mathias Christen, Hester Davis' father, came to Montana in 1880 from Switzerland. He spent the first winter in Camas Hot Springs and in 1886, he married Hester's mother, Mary, and they made their home in Butte where he died at the age of 98.

Amby Ranch — Great Falls, Montana
Submitted by **Mrs. Elizabeth Cheney**
Pioneer, Stanford, Montana

SALLY LUNN

¼ c. shortening	2 c. flour
⅓ c. sugar	2 tsp. baking powder
2 eggs	1 tsp. salt

Mix well and bake in a rather shallow pan. Before baking, sprinkle the top of the batter with ½ cup brown sugar mixed with ½ teaspoon cinnamon. This recipe doubled or tripled and served with plenty of hot cereal, bacon, eggs, etc., provides a hearty breakfast for 8 to 10 hungry men and boys and was a favorite with the family. In ranch days, I baked it in a pan 24x24, large enough to fit the coal stove range oven. A much smaller pan is needed for a single recipe.

Background: I was born near the present city of Great Falls in 1885. I have been told that my mother and father took me to the first dance every held in Great Falls when I was only six weeks old. I married Ambrose "Kid Amby" Cheney in 1903, and I am the mother of seven sons. In 1954 I was Montana Mother of the Year and in 1963 was selected to represent Montana pioneer women in the Cowboy Hall of Fame in Oklahoma.

Cowbelle's

RANCH BREAD

BOIL:
1 c. water
⅓ c. sugar
1 c. ground beef
1 c. raisins

SOAK:
2 pkg. yeast
1 tsp. sugar
½ c. warm water

Mix and Let Rise 10 minutes:

1 c. All-Bran
1 tbsp. molasses
2 c. graham flour

1½ c. warm potato water
3 tbsp. melted butter
2 c. white flour

Yeast mixture

ADD:

3 tsp. salt
cooled beef mixture

½ c. chopped nuts
2 to 3 c. white flour

Made a soft dough. Knead. Rest 10 minutes and knead again. Cover and let rise until double. Punch down and raise 20 minutes. Shape into 3 loaves and let rise. Bake 40 minutes at 350°.

—————————————————————————————————————

Mrs. R.M. Harris
Nur Kinder Farm
Aledo, Texas

DOROTHY'S JALAPENO CORNBREAD

2 eggs, well beaten
1 c. buttermilk
½ c. oil
1 can cream corn
1 medium white onion, chopped
2-4 jalapeno peppers, chopped
(seeds removed)

1 c. yellow cornmeal
½ c. sifted all-purpose flour
½ tsp. soda
1 tsp. salt
½ tsp. sugar
Optional: ½ lb hamburger or sausage,
crumbled and browned

½ c. sharp Cheddar cheese, grated

Combine first 7 ingredients and stir. Combine dry ingredients and add to egg mixture; stir until well blended. Pour into large iron skillet or a 13x15 inch pan. Bake for 35-40 minutes in a 425° oven or 400° for glass baking dish. Recipe can be halved and baked in smaller pan.

Phyllis Simpson
Alton, Kansas

BRAIDED CINNAMON BREAD

2 pkgs. active dry yeast
1-½ c. warm milk
½ c. sugar
½ c. shortening

½ c. warm water
2 tsp. salt
2 eggs
7-7½ c. all purpose flour

Dissolve yeast in water. Stir in milk, sugar, salt, eggs, shortening and beat well. Add 3 cups flour and beat until smooth. Add enough of the remaining flour to make a soft dough. Knead until smooth and elastic. Place in lightly greased bowl turning to cover all sides of dough. Cover and let rise. Punch down and let rise again (about 30 min). Punch down and divide into two or three balls. Cut each ball into 3 pieces and roll each under hands to make a rope about 16 inches long. Dip each rope into melted butter then in a mixture of cinnamon-sugar. Braid, place in greased loaf pans or on greased cookie sheets. Let rise until double. Bake at 350° for 30 minutes or until done. Turn out onto cooling rack.

Mona Larson
Larson Ranches
Watrous, New Mexico

MEXICAN SPOON BREAD

1-lb. can creamed corn
¾ c. milk
⅓ c. melted shortening
2 eggs slightly beaten
1 c. corn meal

1 tsp. baking powder
1 tsp. salt
1 4-oz. can chopped green chiles
1-½ c. shredded cheese
¼ c. flour

½ tsp. soda

Mix all ingredients except chili and cheese. Pour half of the batter into greased 9x9 pan and spread half of chili and cheese over the batter. Add remaining batter then sprinkle remaining chili and cheese. Bake at 400° for 45 min. Serves 6-8 hungry people.

Background: Years ago, (about 35) when I was first married, my mother-in-law told me a secret about keeping a happy husband. When a meal is late because you have been doing foolish projects, or whatever, always set the table even before you put a pot on the stove. He will come in and see the table is set and pick up the latest market report and settle down to read this and will give you time to get a meal put together. It worked for Annie and MM. Larson for 56 years and I am telling my girls about it!

Shelly (Jackson) Van Haur
Van Haur Polled Herefords
Hilger, Montana

 s

SOURDOUGH HONEY WHOLE WHEAT BREAD

1 pkg. yeast	*⅔ c. sourdough starter*
1 c. warm water	*½ c. honey*
1 tsp salt	*1½ tbsp. shortening*

4 - 5 c. whole wheat flour

Dissolve yeast in 1 cup warm water. Mix yeast, starter, honey, salt and shortening with 3 cups flour. Add more flour as needed to make a stiff dough. Knead 150 strokes on a floured suface and place in a greased bowl. Cover and let rise 1-1½ hours until doubled in size. Punch down, let double again. Punch down and roll into tight loaf. Grease and place in bread pan. Let double in pan and bake at 400° for 35-40 minutes until very dark golden brown.

Background: My husband and son will eat a whole loaf if I let them! Our sourdough crock goes constantly as it did in almost every ranch kitchen 100 years ago.

Maurice & Barbara Bidart
Leonard Creek Ranch
Nevada

MB

SHEEPHERDER'S BREAD

3 c. very hot tap water	*½ c. butter or margarine*
1 c. cugar	*2½ tsp. salt*
2 pkg. active dry yeast	*9½ c. flour*
salad oil	

Combine water, butter, sugar and salt. Stir until butter melts, let cool til lukewarm. Stir in yeast and cover; let stand until bubbly (about 15 min.) Add flour and knead for 10 min. Let dough rise 1½ hrs. Punch down. Cut a circle of foil to cover bottom of Dutch oven. Grease Dutch oven & lid with salad oil. Place dough in Dutch oven and let rise 1 hr. (Lid will push up about ½") Bake in 350° oven with lid on for 15 min. Remove lid and bake another 30 to 35 min. Turn loaf out of pan.

Background: A Basque tradition of Sheepherder's—before serving, a herder would slash the sign of the cross on top of the loaf, then serve the first piece to his invaluable dog.

Shelly (Jackson) Van Haur
S and J Livestock Co.
Hilger, Montana

S

SOPAIPILLAS (MEXICAN FRIED BREAD)

4 c. flour	*¾ tsp. salt*
¾ to 1 tsp. baking powder	*2 eggs*
(use ¾ tsp. baking powder at	*1 c. milk*
higher altitudes)	

Mix dry ingredients together, mix eggs and milk together. Combine all ingredients and let rest about 10 minutes. Roll to ¼ inch thick, cut into 3-inch squares. Fry in deep hot fat (350°) until golden brown.

Background: Once when I was 17 years old Bob and Nancy Ross introduced me to Mexican cooking in Old Town, Albuquerque, New Mexico and I've been in love with it ever since. By the way, they were also chaperoning me to the Range Youth Forum at the time, along with my dad, Pete Jackson.

The Four Sixes Ranch
Guthrie, Texas

6666

6666'S CORN BREAD

1½ c. cornmeal
1½ tsp. salt
1½ c. sourdough starter
1½ tsp. baking soda

1½ tbsp. sugar
1½ c. milk
1½ tsp. cream of tartar
2 eggs slightly beaten

6 tbsp. melted butter

Combine cornmeal, sugar and salt in a mixing bowl. Scald milk, pour over cornmeal; cool to lukewarm. Add remaining ingredients and mix well. Pour into buttered 9-inch square pan. Bake in 425° oven for 40 minutes.

Historic Trail Drive Recipe

FRIED SODA BISCUITS

2 c. all-purpose flour
1 tsp. baking soda
½ tsp. salt

¾ c. buttermilk or
sour milk
Shortening

¼ c. shortening

Stir together flour, soda, and salt. Cut in ¼ cup shortening till the mixture resembles coarse crumbs. Make a well in the dry mixture; add buttermilk or sour milk all at once. Stir just till the dough clings together. Knead gently on lightly floured surface 10 to 12 strokes. Melt enough shortening in deep skillet to give a depth of 1 inch. Heat to 375°. To shape each biscuit, cut off about 1 tablespoon of the dough and form into a ball about 1 inch in diameter; flatten slightly. Carefully place biscuits, a few at a time, in the hot shortening. Fry till golden, turning once, about 2 minutes per side. Drain on paper toweling. Serve hot. Makes about 24 biscuits.

Background: The range cook shaped soda biscuits by a different method from that used nowadays. Since he did not want to bother with a biscuit cutter, he merely pinched off pieces of dough about the size of an egg. He then rolled these pieces into balls with his hands and fried them in hot grease in the Dutch oven.

Patti Dorward Fulton
Morrison Ranch
Throckmorton, Texas

P

ANADAMA BREAD

1½ c. water
1 tsp. salt

⅓ c. cornmeal plus 2 tsp.
⅓ c. molasses
1½ tbsp. shortening
1 cake yeast in ¼ c. water

1 tbsp. honey
2 tsp. butter
1 tsp. water
1 or 2 tsp. sugar
4 c. flour

Bring water and salt to a boil, remove to large bowl. Add ⅓ c. cornmeal, while stirring to avoid lumps. Then add shortening, followed by molasses. Let mixture cool to lukewarm. Meanwhile dissolve 1 cake yeast in ¼ cup warm (not hot!) water. Add yeast mixture to cornmeal mixture. Mix in 4 c. flour. Dump out mixture on floured board and knead about 7 minutes. Put dough in large greased bowl and let rise until double (about 1½ hours). Punch down, knead again for 5 minutes. Let rise until double again in greased bowl (1½ hours) Punch down, knead and make into loaves. Sprinkle with 2 teaspoons of cornmeal before last rise. Let rise until almost double (1 hour). Put in 375° oven for 30 minutes for 2 small loaves or 40-45 minutes for one large loaf. Bread will be golden brown when done. Mix honey, butter water and sugar in hot skillet and drizzle or brush over bread while it is hot from the oven.

Background: According to history, a woman named Anna made her husband nothing but cornmeal mush, day in and day out. Finally he got his own ideas for cornmeal and while kneading the bread he'd say "Anna, damn her!" — hence the name. This bread has been a Christmas tradition in our family for fifteen or twenty years.

My great-grandparents, Mr. & Mrs. E.S. Cook, homesteaded our family ranch in Throckmorton County in the late 1800's. It became the Morrison ranch in the 1940's when my grandparents, Tom and Zula Morrison, established a purebred Hereford operation. I work for the Soil Conservation Service as a Range Conservationist in Abilene and frequent the ranch whenever possible.

SOURDOUGH BISCUITS

Begin with half the recipe for basic bread. Add 1 tsp. baking soda. Knead as directed. Roll out to ½ inch thick. Dot that top with bits of butter, margarine or lard. Fold in half, roll and dot the surface again. Fold and roll once more, this time leaving the dough about 1 inch thick. Cut into rounds with 2 or 3 inch biscuit cutter. Place on an oiled baking sheet and paint tops and sides with oil or drippings. Let set until well risen and bake at 350° for 20 to 25 minutes.

Tongue River Ranch
Dumont, Texas

MEXICAN CORNBREAD

1 lb. ground meat, cooked
salt & pepper to taste
1 c. chopped onion
½ lb. grated American cheese
3 Jalapeno peppers (mild), chopped fine

MIX TOGETHER:

1 c. cornmeal	*3 tbsp. bacon drippings*
3 eggs	*1 c. sweetmilk*
½ tsp. soda	*1 tsp. salt*

Brown meat and drain off grease. Grease a 9x13 inch pan. Add ½ of batter then sprinkle on meat, onions, pepper and last add cheese. Cover with remaining batter. Cook at 350° for about 45 minutes.

Background: Owned by the Swensons ranching operation until 1976, the Tongue River Ranch was bought by S.M. Swenson in the late 1800's from the railroads. The ranch carries the Indian name for the South Pease River, which runs through its property.

   Located near Dumont, Texas, in Cottle, King, Dickens and Motley Counties, the ranch operates a cow/calf enterprise with 2,000-3,000 Herefords. Today the 80,000-acre Tongue River Ranch is owned by Mrs. Jim Barron, a member of the Swenson family, and is managed by Taylor Martin.

Mrs. Ruthann Wilson
Riverside, Washington

100% WHOLE WHEAT BREAD
First Place Winner in Washington State Grange Baking Contest
State and County Level

⅔ c. water	⅔ c. shortening
3 pkg. yeast	1 c. sugar
1 tbsp. sugar	½ c. molasses
8 c. scalded milk	2 tbsp. salt

About 14 c. whole wheat flour

Dissolve yeast in ⅔ cup of water while your milk is cooling. Dissolve 1 cup sugar in the hot milk. Stir all ingredients in large bowl, turn out and knead about 5 minutes. Let rise again until doubled in bulk, knead down again. Make into 6 loaves, let rise until doubled in size. Bake at 375° for 40 minutes. Turn out on wire rack. Add walnuts or raisins for variety. This bread freezes very well.

Background: Henry H. Wilson left the family farm in Tennessee in 1889, first going to Missouri and then to California, where he met and married Mertie Young. The came north and settled in Chewikken Valley in O Kanogan County in 1904. One of their sons was Ray who was also a twin. One of Ray's sons was Albert— who lives in the house his grandfather Henry lived and died in. Albert's sons Michael and Ronald also live on the ranch with their families.

Joyce Day
Charleville, Australia

WHEATMEAL BREAD

6 c. wheatmeal	*1 tbsp. Easybake yeast*
2 c. plain white flour	*1 large tbsp. treacle*
1 rounded tbsp. salt	*1 dessertspoon butter (optional)*

warm water to mix

Mix flours, rub in butter, add salt, then yeast and treacle. Add warm water and mix to a stiff dough. Cover basin with a cloth and place in a warm position and allow to rise (keep reasonably warm at all times). When risen, takes about an hour or a little longer, turn onto floured board and knead thoroughly. Return to basin, sprinkle little flour on top, and allow to rise once more. When well risen, turn onto board once more, cut mixture in half, knead and form into loaves.

Grease tins thoroughly, set loaves to rise before placing in hot oven (400-450°). Cook for approximately 1 hour. Makes two small-sized loaves.

Historical Pioneer Trail Recipe

SODA BREAD

1 tsp. baking soda	*2-¼ c. flour*
1 c. warm water	*1 tsp. salt*

To make dough, mix baking soda with water, add flour and salt. Knead well. The dough may be used at once or allowed to rise overnight in a warm place. In either case, flatten dough to a thickness of 1". Place on a greased cookie sheet and bake (in a 400° oven) for about 25 minutes.

Historical Pioneer Trail Recipe

FRIED CAKES

1-½ c. flour   beef fat
1 c. water   salt

Combine flour with water. Mix well with a fork. Using plenty of flour on hands and a breadboard, roll out dough to a thickness of ¼". Cut into 2" squares. Render beef fat in a skillet and add squares of dough. Brown slowly on both sides. Sprinkle with salt to taste. Makes about 20 cakes.

Historical Pioneer Trail Recipe

MORMON JOHNNYCAKE

2 c. yellow cornmeal   1 tsp. salt
½ c. flour   2 c. buttermilk
1 tsp. baking soda   2 tbsp. molasses

Combine cornmeal, flour, baking soda, and salt. Stir in buttermilk and molasses. Pour batter into a greased 9" pan and bake (in a 425° oven) for about 20 minutes. Cut into 16 squares.

To make lighter cake; add 2 beaten eggs and 2 tbsp. melted butter to buttermilk and cook about 25 minutes.

ROLLS

Ethyl Light
Renderbrook Spade Ranch
Colorado City, Texas

MRS. LIGHT'S BUTTER ROLLS

DOUGH FOR ROLLS:
2 c. flour
4 tsp. baking powder
1 tsp. salt
¼ c. crisco
¾ c. milk

FILLING FOR ROLLS:
½ to ⅔ c. softened butter
1-½ c. sugar
Cinnamon (optional)
2-½ c. milk (scalded)

Sift dry ingredients for rolls, blend in crisco; add milk and mix to soft dough; knead slightly on floured board, then roll to ½ inch thickness. Spread softened butter on top; sprinkle evenly 1½ cups sugar and amount of cinnamon desired. Roll up into long roll, starting at end slice roll ½ inch thick and place in medium sized enameled roasting pan. Cover with 2-½ c. scalded milk and bake in slow oven 325-350° for 1 hour to 1-½ hours until milk has thickened and rolls slightly browned. Serves 6 to 8 people.

Background: Established in 1881 by J. Taylor Barr, the Renderbrook-Spade Ranch was bought by one of two inventors of barbed wire, Colonel Isaac Ellwood of Illinois, in 1889 from the Snyder Brothers.

According to legend, the ranch, located 22 miles south of Colorado City, takes its name from the nearby Renderbrook Spring, so named for a soldier ambushed by Indians along its banks. Actually, however, an 1876 Army staff map shows the spring was named for a Captain Joseph Renderbrock.

The Spade Ranches today consist of three outfits: The Renderbrook-Spade Ranch in Mitchell County, the Chappell-Spade Ranch near Tucumcari, New Mexico, and the Borden-Spade Ranch near Gail, Texas.

SRM **SOCIETY FOR RANGE MANAGEMENT**

Clermont Branch
Australia

SCONES

2 c. self-rising flour
1 tbsp. butter or margarine
pinch salt

2 tbsp. powdered milk
1 egg
1 small c. milk, slightly warmed

Sift flour into bowl, add salt, rub butter into flour, add powdered milk and mix in lightly. Make well in centre of mixture, add lightly-beaten egg and milk gradually, stir lightly with knife until well-mixed.

Turn onto floured board and knead lightly, then flatten mixture to ½" thickness, and cut into shapes.

Cook in hot oven for approximately 10 minutes. (Sultanas and a little sugar may be added if a sweet scone is desired.)

Clermont Branch
Australia

PUMPKIN SCONES

2 c self-rising flour
½ tsp. salt
1 tbsp. butter

1 tbsp. sugar
½ c. cold mashed pumpkin
1 egg

½ c. milk

Sift flour and salt. Cream butter and sugar, add pumpkin. Beat egg till thick, add milk. Add to cream mixture and blend lightly. Sift in flour, mixing to a soft dough, turn onto floured board. Knead dough for a few minutes before cutting.

Greg Purvis, "Kilmarnock," Clermont
Australia

DAMPER

3 c. self-rising flour
3 oz. butter (melted)

½ c. milk
½ c. water

1-½ tsp. salt

Place flour and salt in basin. Stir in melted butter, milk and water. Mix to soft dough and place in greased and floured tin. Bake in hot oven.

Patrick Beres
Alpine, Texas

SOURDOUGH HOT ROLLS OR PIZZA CRUST

butter
2 c. sourdough starter batter
¼ c. milk
1 tsp. salt

2 tbsp. sugar or honey
1 egg
3 tbsp. oil
1 tsp. baking soda

flour

Place starter batter in bowl. In small dish mix egg, oil, milk. Stir into batter. In small dish mix salt, soda, and sugar.

Gently fold the mixture into batter. Gently mix. This will cause a foaming and rising action. Allow to stand for a few minutes.

To this batter add enough flour, plus ½ tsp. salt for each cup of flour, to form a stiff dough. Turn on floured board and knead, adding flour as necessary until it is a smooth ball with satiny finish. Place in a greased bowl, brush with melted butter, and allow to rise in a warm place for about 1 hour. Punch down, turn out on floured board and knead again, adding more flour if needed. Roll out to ¾-inch thickness. Cut with coffee cup or biscuit cutter; dip each round in melted butter, and place, just touching, in dutch oven. Cover. Let rise until nearly doubled (about 1 hour). Bake in moderately hot oven (375°) for 30 to 35 minutes. Serve hot with melted butter or gravy.

Mrs. Robert L. Storch
Virginia

WHOLE WHEAT ROLLS

2 pkgs. yeast in 1 c. water
1 egg, beaten
½ c. sugar
1 tsp. salt

1 c. lukewarm milk
3 c. white flour
2 c. whole wheat flour
½ c. cracked wheat (opt.)

Dissolve yeast in water. Set aside. Beat egg and add sugar. Beat. Add remaining ingredients, beat with dough hook or knead well. Let rise 1½-2 hours. Shape into rolls (30-36). Let rise about 1 hour or when doubled. Bake 350° for 20 minutes.

Jean M. Frischknecht
Kay Frischknecht's
Manti, Utah

SOUR DOUGH SCONES

4 c. milk or	YEAST MIXTURE:
1 c. powdered milk to 1 quart water	1 c. warm water
¾ c. sugar	2-½ tbsp. yeast
¾ c. shortening	1 tbsp. sugar
1 tbsp. salt	2 c. sour dough starter

Combine yeast mixture and dissolve yeast. Add to milk, sugar, melted shortening, and salt. Add sour dough starter. Add enough flour to make a sticky dough. Beat with a large spoon. After it has raised double in bulk, add enough flour to make a very soft dough (not too much), just enough to make dough easy to work with. Either roll out with rolling pin and cut in squares and let rise about 15 or 20 minutes, and fry in deep oil. If you are in the mountains let rise 15 minutes in pan and pinch off a small patty and fry. Makes a large batch. Serves around 20 people, depends on how many they eat.

Background: We have used this recipe on many family picnics and cooking for the workers at shearing time and docking time. We have also used them at many special parties. We cooked this recipe and fried lamb chops for our church (500 people).

Pat Seeley
Seeley Ranch
Halsey, NE

MOM'S EASY ROLLS

2 eggs	1 c. milk
2 cakes of yeast	1 c. water
½ c. sugar	7 c. flour
½ tsp. salt	9 tbsp. shortening

Heat the water until lukewarm, add yeast and let stand for a minute. Place eggs, sugar, salt, milk and 4 cups flour in mixing bowl. Add yeast mixture and beat for 4 minutes. Add shortening, then knead in the remaining flour. Cover and let rise until double in bulk. Make out rolls and let rise until double in bulk. Bake at 400° for 10 to 12 minutes.

Background: This recipe has been used on the Seeley Ranch for 4 generations. We hope you enjoy it as much as we have. Good Eating—From the Sandhills.

BISCUITS & MUFFINS

Patrick Beres
Alpine, Texas

MULE MUFFINS

1 c. molasses	1 tsp. soda
½ c. margarine	2-½ c. flour
1 tsp. salt	1-½ tsp. ginger
1-¾ tsp. baking powder	

Heat mollasses to boiling point. Remove from heat. Stir in shortening or margarine and soda. Sift together and stir in flour, baking powder, salt and ginger.

Chill dough. Roll out very thin (1/16"). Cut in desired shapes using coffee cup or gingerbread men cutout. Place on lightly greased baking sheet. Bake at 350° for 5-7 minutes. (Overbaking gives a bitter taste but makes for good hard saddle-bag cookies).

Grant M. Esplin
Esplin Ranch
Beaver, Utah

SOURDOUGH BISCUITS

flour	salt
sourdough starter	baking soda
3 c. water	baking powder*

* Baking powder can be used if needed to help biscuits rise, but I like it better without baking powder. Too much soda causes the biscuits to be yellow in color. Amount of soda needed depends on how sour the dough is. More is needed if dough is real sour.

Start sour dough with level tsp. of yeast. Mix with ½ c. of water. Add 3 c. of water and add flour and mix with a hardwood stick (oak works well as does service berry). Add flour until dough is as stiff as can be mixed well. Let rise until 1 hour before time to eat (6-12 hours). Put dough into mixing pan (new wash basin works well) with enough flour in so dough doesn't stick to pan. Knead until dough is stiff enough to make good biscuits. Before kneading, add salt and baking soda.

Make into biscuits and put in greased pan. Put in warm place (the warming oven on a wood stove works well or on top of the tea kettle full of hot water). Let rise for 15-30 minutes. If you are too hungry to wait, they can be balled immediately, but will not be as light. Bake until light brown or to taste, in a moderate stove 400°. In the old wood stove stoke the fire up good and close the damper so they will cook on the bottom too. Serve hot with plenty of butter and good jam.

Be sure to leave a small amount of dough in jug for a start! Remove dough by adding: 2 to 3 cups of water (depends on how many biscuits you want) and enough flour to make the dough stiff. Let rise and mix biscuits again. Regular mixing keeps the dough in better condition. At least once a day is better. Between mixing, leave start in jug and keep in cool place. Start can be used to make cakes and hot cakes.

Background: This ranch has been in the Esplin family for about 100 years. It has a house made of hand hewn logs, that is still used and is about 100 years old. It is an operating cattle ranch at the present time and a 4th generation Esplin works full-time on the ranch now, which is owned and operated by the Esplin Family. (Sons of Charles H. Esplin).

The ranch at one time produced hay and grain as well as grazing. My Grandmother and children made cheese and butter there and sold to neighbors and people in Orderville. Dairy cattle, beef cattle and sheep have grazed on the ranch. It was the headquarter summer ranch for 4,500 sheep and 150 cattle before the end of World War II. Since then 400-500 cattle summer there. The ranch includes 3,000 acres of private land including 400 irrigated meadow located on the headwaters of the Virgin River (North Fork) at the 7,000-8,000 ft. level. Near Navajo Lake, Kane County, 3,000 acres of private land plus BLM permits in Iron County are used in winter.

This sour dough bread has been made at the ranch for at least 55 years that I know of. It was carried in grub boxes on pack horses to tent camps away from the ranch house. It was used in sheep wagons on the forest (Duck Creek) and on the winter range on the Arizona strip 50 miles south of St. George. It is still used from time to time.

Patrick Beres
Alpine, Texas

SOURDOUGH STARTER BATTER

3 c. all-purpose flour	1 pkg. active dry yeast
2-½ c. lukewarm water	1 tbsp. sugar

Place flour in glass or crockery mixing bowl (not metal). Make a well in center and add other ingredients. Stir with a large spoon until well-blended. Then beat until smooth. Cover with a thin towel and set in warm draft-free spot for 24 hours. The mixture should show bubbles and should have a yeasty smell. (Makes 4 cups.)

Use amount of recipe needed for recipe and put remaining starter in non-metal crock with loose lid. Always keeping one cup of starter batter as base for making more.

If you want more, add 2 c. warm water, 2-½ c. flour and 1 tbsp. sugar to the 1 cup of starter batter. Mix well and let stand at room temperature overnight or at least 8 hours before using.

Irene Graves
Graves Ranch
Ainsworth, Nebraska

J-Ǝ

SOURDOUGH TRAIL BISCUITS

1 c. water
1 c. flour
1 tsp. baking powder

½ tsp. baking soda
½ tsp. salt
1-½ c. flour

To the starter mixture beat in baking powder, soda and salt (mixture will foam). Slowly beat in flour until dough is thick enough to knead. Let rise for at least 4 hours. (The longer, the stronger the flavor).

Knead 10 to 15 times, form into biscuits, and bake in 350° oven for 20 to 25 minutes. Hints: The less flour used, the softer the crust, and baking biscuits touching each other softens them. Makes good pizza crust.

Background: In the 1860's-1980's, while northern Nebraska was being settled, purified yeast was a true luxury. Cooks kept a crock of starter behind the stove in winter and in a "cool" place in summer. Many times the only ingredients available were flour and water. The starter certainly improved their palatability. This biscuit forms a hard crust yet remains soft inside, thus they were excellent for packing in lunches, especially those which had to be carried in a saddle bag all day. My starter has been passed along for over 100 years but there are commercially available strains.

Dorris & Guy London
London Hog Creek Ranch
18 mi. N.E. Throckmorton, Texas

ㄜ

CINNAMON ROLLS

ROLLS:
1 box Pillsbury Roll Mix
cinnamon
butter or oleo - 1 stick
brown sugar

FROSTING:
2 tbsp. oleo or butter
3 tbsp. milk
½ tsp. vanilla
2 c. powdered sugar
Melt butter, add next 3 ingredients.
Stir until smooth. Add more sugar.
Spread on rolls right out of oven.

Mix roll mix as directed on box. Add 1 tbsp. sugar to batter. After dough has risen, do as directed on box. Roll out thin on floured surface. Spread brown sugar all over. Sprinkle cinnamon. Cut thin slices of 1 stick oleo. Roll mixture into 1 roll. Wet fingers and dampen edge to seal. Cut into 1 - 1-½ inches. Place in buttered obling cake pan. Cook at 350° for 30 minutes. Makes 12 rolls.

Background: This ranch at Hog Creek has been in the London family for 3 generations. Guy was born on this ranch. We moved here in 1943 and are still here. When our children, Sharon London Johnson, George and Tom London were in school and in sports, ·the school had a concession stand. I would take these rolls. The people were always waiting and when I arrived, these were the first to go. I enjoy making these now for my six grandchildren and will include my son-in-law, Rhett Johnson.

Gordon L. Decker
Broadus, Montana

BEER BISCUITS

2 c. flour (all-purpose)
3 tsp. baking powder
¾ c. beer

1 tsp. salt
¼ c. shortening

Preheat oven to 450°. Sift dry ingredients together. Cut in shortening until it has cornmeal consistency. Stir in beer, knead lightly, roll out to ½-inch thickness. Makes 12 to 15 biscuits. Bake 10-12 minutes or until golden brown.

Wanda Warner
Moorhouse Ranch
Near Benjamin, Texas

C

ANGEL BISCUITS

SIFT TOGETHER:

5 c. flour	1 tsp. salt
¼ c. sugar	1 tsp. soda
3 tsp. baking powder	

CUT IN:
1 c. shortening

ADD:
1 pkg. dry yeast that has been dissolved
     in ¼ c. warm water.   Add 2 cups buttermilk or sour milk.

Mix well. This can be kept in the refrigerator for up to two weeks. Pat out desired amount, cut and bake at 400° for 15 minutes. Do not grease pan.

Background: Over 50 years old, the Moorhouse Ranch was established in the 1930s by J.C. "Togo" Moorhouse, who bought land near Benjamin, Texas, with his brother to begin a cow/calf operation. The Moorhouses had established roots in West Texas nearly a quarter-century earlier, moving there in 1907 from Kaufman County east of Dallas.

Still active in managing the ranch Togo today shares his responsibilities with sons Ed, John, Tom and Bob, who were brought into the family business when it incorporated in 1979.

Mona Larson
Larson Ranches
Watrous, New Mexico

REFRIGERATOR BISCUITS

1 quart milk (powdered is O.K.)	½ c. melted shortening
1 tbsp. salt	1 c. sugar
1 pkg. yeast	½ tsp. baking soda
2 tsp. baking powder	about 8 c. flour

Beat well and let stand in a warm place to rise. Then place the mixture in the refrigerator to use as needed. As the need for dinner biscuits or rolls arises, put some flour on a board and place the desired amount of dough on it and knead with flour so it isn't sticky. Roll and cut out, or pinch off and put in a greased roll pan. They are better if they are allowed to rise at least 30 minutes, but can be baked immediately at 450° for about 20-25 minutes.

Background: This recipe was given to me by Janie Mattice who used it for years on their ranch in southeastern Arizona. She had to be prepared for early dinners, or dinners that were late into the evening and it has made many a "ho-hum" dinner look great with hot rolls.

Laura Salisbury
Lazy Ladder Ranch
Savery, Wyoming

Ⅲ, Ⲟ̸

RANCH BISCUITS

MIX IN LARGE BOWL:
1 pkg. dry yeast   *½ c. water (warm)*

ADD TO YEAST MIXTURE:
5 c. flour	*1 tsp. salt*
½ c. sugar	*⅓ tsp. soda*
2 c. buttermilk	*½ c. shortening*

Stir until well mixed. A little more flour may be needed so dough is not sticky. Put saran wrap over bowl and place in refrigerator until ready to roll out.

Bake at 400° for 15-20 minutes. Makes about 2 dozen regular size biscuits.

Roll or pat out on well floured board. Cut with cutter of desired size. Place in well-greased pan. These will keep in refrigerator and can be baked as needed. These biscuits are halfway between rolls and biscuits and are delicious.

Background: This ranch was established in 1911 and has been in the family ever since. Right now it's a case of survival with present prices and expenses.

DAMPER & TORTILLAS

Don Pendleton

JONDARYAN WOOLSHED DAMPER

4 c. self-rising flour   2-½ c. cold water
     pinch salt

Blend ingredients together with a knife until dough leaves side of bowl. Do not knead!

Cook in a moderate oven for 45 minutes. When cooked, turn upside down to cool. Cut when cool, and spread with lots of butter and golden syrup.

June Southwood
Australia

OUTBACK DAMPER

6 c. self-rising flour   pinch of salt
1 tbsp. baking powder (soda)   warm milk

Mix flour, baking powder, salt and warm milk into a spongy dough. Shape as for a cottage loaf. Place the camp oven* on the fire and heat well before placing bread mix in the camp oven. Place the bread mixture in the camp oven and bake for ½ hour. Serve with honey, butter, golden syrup, jam, etc. while still warm.

Background: This recipe was made popular by the fact that when bread was not obtainable the cook could make damper in a relatively short while. An easy to make recipe, generally enjoyed by those camping, and becoming increasingly popular at backyard barbecues.

Camp Oven: Cast iron saucepan on three legs. Has a fitted lid. One of the most used cooking utensils in the outback of Australia. No self-respecting Drover is seen without one.

Dalton F. Merz
Unidentified sheep and goat shearing cook
Sonora, Texas

FLOUR TORTILLAS

10 c. flour	*1 tbsp. salt*
5 tbsp. baking powder	*2 c. cold water*

1 c. warm water

Mix dry ingredients then add water and mix until tough. Let sit for 30 minutes. Divide dough to make about 40 tortillas. Knead individual tortillas using dry flour to avoid sticking. Roll with roller, such as broomstick about 1-½' long. Flip each time you roll across the tortillas.

Background: This recipe for tortillas is made every meal for shearing crew in the Sonora, Texas area for about 20 men. Tortillas are about 1' in diameter and 1/8 to 1/4" in thickness. They are fried on an open wood kindled fire on a piece of sheet metal about 5' square. Beans, eggs, or meat are usually rolled inside the tortillas. The unidentified cook is of Mexican origin and has about 40 years of experience.

PANCAKES and WAFFLES

Tom & Shirley Cook
Fernley, Nevada

HOTCAKES

1-½ c. flour (sifted, if possible)	*1 egg*
1 tbsp. sugar	*1 c. milk or water**

2 tbsp. shortening or cooking oil

**If you like a sourdough taste, use beer.

Cook on a very hot, well-greased griddle. I like my hotcakes about 4-5 inches in diameter.

David R. Heydlauff
Heydlauff Ranch
Wild Horse, Alberta

POTATO PANCAKES

2 c. grated raw potato	4 tbsp. flour
1 tbsp. grated onion	1 tsp. salt
2 eggs, unbeaten	⅓ c. crisco

All measurements level. Combine grated potato with onion, eggs, flour and salt. Drop mixture from a tablespoon into frying pan containing hot crisco. Flatten each cake with back of spoon. Fry to a deep golden brown on each side. Makes about 8 pancakes.

Background: This recipe is my mother's. My father's father, who started our ranch in 1904 came to Canada with the L5L. He worked as both a cowboy and a wagon cook. My father rode on the 2nd last horse roundup in southeast Alberta, southwest Sask and northern Montana.

H. F. Heady
California

SOURDOUGH WAFFLES

½ c. starter	2 eggs
2 c. milk	dash of sugar
2 c. flour	⅓ c. oil
1 tsp. soda	

Mix starter, milk and flour in the evening and store in warm place overnight. In morning take out ½ c. of starter for the next time. Starter stores indefinitely in refrigerator. Mix all other ingredients and cook on hot iron. Oil may be melted bacon grease or cooking oil. Cook all batter and freeze excess quarters for later toasting. Makes 3 to 4 large waffles.

Mrs. Arthur D. Miles
Lazy AM Ranch
Bozeman, Montana

DM

SOURDOUGH PANCAKES

To begin with, you've gotta have "starter" which is a batch of flour and yeast that you can keep for years and years (scary when you think about it sitting there in your refrigerator).

STARTER:

½ pkg. active dry yeast   1 tbsp. sugar
2-½ c. lukewarm water   2 cups flour

Soften yeast in ½ c. water. Add rest of ingredients and mix well. Let stand in a covered bowl or crock (not metal) for 3 days at room temperature (76-80°F). Stir down daily. Refrigerate after 3 days. Now you're ready to make pancakes!

1 c. starter*   1 egg
2 c. lukewarm water   2 tbsp. cooking oil
about 2-½ c. flour   1 tsp. salt
1 tbsp. sugar   1 tsp. baking soda
2 tbsp. sugar   ¼ c. evaporated milk or cream

Refrigerate the rest.

Evening: Put starter in large bowl. Add water, flour and sugar. Mix well. (It will be thick and lumpy). Cover and leave in warm place overnight. Next morning take 1 or 2 cups of batter and put back in starter bowl. Then to remaining batter add egg, cooking oil and milk. Add salt, baking soda, and sugar. Mix into batter gently. This causes foaming and rising action. Let stand a few minutes and fry on hot greased griddle. Add a little milk if too thick. Yum—Enjoy.

Background: Our ranch is between Livingston and Bozeman Mt. (60 miles from Yellowstone Park). There was a stopover place (saloon/postoffice) here where fresh horses were put on the stagecoach before going over Bozeman Pass. You can bet lots of Sourdough Pancakes were served.

We still live in the original house built in 1870.

SRM **SOCIETY FOR RANGE MANAGEMENT**

Gordon Fredine
Bethesda, Maryland

JIM PEASE'S CAMPFIRE BISCUITS

From Hudspeth County, Texas

25 lb. sack of white flour	*Baking powder*
Salt	*Lard*
Water from the nearest cattle tank	

Jim would roll down the flour sack to expose the flour, make a cone shaped depression in it with his long index finger (clean or not), toss in some salt and several pinches of baking powder. (There was no "self-rising" flour available then (1927-28), so maybe baking powder is not needed.) Then he would add a gob of lard and work it into the flour laced with baking powder and salt. Quantities depended on how hungry we were. Then he would keep adding water as he worked up a ball of dough. He removed the dough ball with all the crumbs he could find and then close up the flour sack until next time. He divided the dough up into biscuit sizes. By this time the mesquite fire was just right. He placed the raw biscuits in an iron Dutch oven, placed it directly on the coals, put the concave lid on the Dutch oven and heaped lived coals on it, mesquite of course, and bake until done — DELICIOUS!

Background: Jim Pease was a cowboy turned boss, and hired this Yankee bum to help dig slush pits for wildcat oil rigs in the Finlay Mountain country. We used mules and horses he got for free (the use of them, I mean) in exchange for breaking them for harness. Finlay was a town then on the T & P Railroad. Now its gone. We were a rough bunch, but happy. He could cook other goodies too, like pinto beans and bacon. We moved around a lot and worked out of plank wagons carrying our Fresnos and plows.

Recipe Notes

SALADS

R anchers, scientists, educators, land managers, students, businessmen, and others formed the Society for Range Management in 1948 to promote the study, management, and use of all rangeland resources. The Society includes members in 50 states and 48 countries, divided into active national, regional, or state Sections.

The sections of the Society and geographical areas are:

Arizona
California
Colorado
Florida: *Florida, Puerto Rico, Virgin Islands;*
Idaho;
Kansas-Oklahoma;
Nebraska;
Nevada;
New Mexico;
Northern Great Plains: *North Dakota, Manitoba, Saskatchewan, east. Montana;*
International Mountain: *west. Montana and Alberta;*
Pacific Northwest: *British Columbia, Washington, Oregon;*

South Dakota;
Southern: *Georgia, Alabama, Mississippi, Louisiana, Arkansas, Missouri, Tennessee, Kentucky, North Carolina, South Carolina;*
Texas;
Utah;
Wyoming;
National Capital: *District of Columbia, Maryland, Delaware, Pennsylvania, Virginia, W. Virginia;*
Mexico;
North Central: *Minnesota, Wisconsin, Illinois, Michigan, Indiana, Ohio;*
Unsectioned.

 **SRM** **SOCIETY FOR RANGE MANAGEMENT**

Edward Frandsen
Fairfax County, Virginia

RUSS PENNEY'S SAUERKRAUT SALAD

BRING TO BOIL:
⅓ c. salad oil and ⅓ c. vinegar

THEN ADD:

1 c. sugar, cool	1 c. chopped onions
1 large can sauerkraut (rinsed)	1 c. diced celery
1 c. diced green pepper	

Let salad stand in refrigerator for 24 hours. Toss salad occasionally. Serves about 15, and stores well under refrigeration. Great with barbeque.

Background: Russ Penny, a retired BLM State Director administered range management programs in four states.

June Schmautz
Fairfax County, Virginia

SPINACH SALAD

TOSS:
1 pkg. fresh spinach
1 can bean sprouts, drained
1 can water chestnuts, drained, sliced
4 hard-boiled eggs, sliced
8 crisp bacon strips, crumbled

DRESSING:

¾ c sugar	¼ c. vinegar
⅛ c. catsup	1 tsp. Worcestershire sauce
1 finely chopped med. onion	Salt

Blend, add 1 cup oil and blend again.

Deseret Land & Livestock Corp.
Woodruff, Utah

"OUR BEST SALAD"

Bite-sized pieces of broccoli — steamed to almost tender
Bite-sized pieces of tomato
Chopped green onions
Avocado (optional)

Mix all ingredients together, when the broccoli has cooled. Refrigerate. Make ahead of time a ranch-style dressing such as Hidden Valley or Uncle Dans. Combine salad and dressing before serving.

Phyllis Simpson
Alton, Kansas

MAKE-AHEAD SALAD

1 head lettuce	½ c. green pepper, diced
1 c. celery, chopped	¼ c. onion, chopped
4 hard-boiled eggs, sliced	8 slices bacon, fried and diced
1 10-oz. pkg. frozen peas	4 oz. Cheddar cheese

Put lettuce in pan. Layer rest of ingredients over lettuce in the order given. Seal with 2 cups salad dressing and top with Cheddar cheese. Set several hours covered in refrigerator.

Phyllis Simpson
Alton, Kansas

SEABREEZE SALAD

2 3-oz. pkg. Lime Jello	2 c. cold water
1 3-pkg. Lemon Jello	1 can lemon pie filling
2 c. boiling water	1 carton Cool Whip
1 c. drained crushed pineapple	

Dissolve 3 packages jello in boiling water. Add cold water. Let set until just begins to thicken. Stir in pie filling and whip with electric mixer. Remove 1 cup of jello mixture and blend with cool whip. Set aside. To remainder of jello mixture, add pineapple. Spread in 9x13 pan and chill until set. Spread the topping mixture over top of first layer. Refrigerate.

Phyllis Simpson
Alton, Kansas

MARINATED VEGETABLE SALAD

1 20-oz. pkg. frozen California
blend vegetables
3 stalks celery, sliced
½ c. sliced pimento stuffed olives
1 small can ripe pitted olives
½ lb. fresh mushrooms, sliced or

1 can mushrooms, drained
3-4 green onions, sliced
3 tomatoes, cut into 8 wedges each
⅔ c. salad oil
¼ c. vinegar
1 pkg. Hidden Valley salad dressing

Bring frozen vegetables to a boil in small amount of salted water. Cook 2 minutes just to par-cook; drain. Add remaining vegetables; toss lightly. Combine the dry salad dressing mix with the oil and vinegar. Mix well; set aside to blend flavors, about 20 minutes. Pour over vegetables. Chill 24 hours or longer, mixing lightly 2 or 3 times during this period. Add salt and pepper to taste. NOTE: You may add other vegetables such as brussel sprouts, green pepper, etc. This keeps several weeks.

Wilma Newman
Dunkirk, Montana

BEAN SALAD

½ c. vinegar
½ c. oil
¾ c. sugar

2 tbsp. onion flakes
1 tbsp. celery seed
Salt & pepper to taste

1 16-oz. can of at least 4 different kinds of beans

Mix all together. Let stand 24 hours in refrigerator.

June Schmautz
Fairfax County, Virginia

MARINATED VEGETABLE SALAD

Fresh broccoli	*Red tomatoes, sliced thin*
Cauliflower	*Celery*
Cherry tomatoes	*Green and black olives*

Frozen Brussel Sprouts

Cut cauliflower and broccoli into flowerettes. Cook brussel sprouts until just tender and drain. Combine vegetables. Pour large bottle of Italian dressing over vegetables and cover. Turn or shake dish a few times. Marinate several hours or overnight.

Marie Rumburg

TACO SALAD

1 head lettuce	*4 med. tomatoes, chopped*
1 med. onion, chopped	*4-oz. grated Cheddar cheese*
1 can kidney beans (or pinto)	*1 bag Dorito chips*
1 large avocado	*8-oz. French salad dressing*

Hot sauce to taste

Brown 1 lb. hamburger, add can of beans (kidney or pintos) that have been well drained. Simmer for 10 minutes. Mix together lettuce that has been diced, tomatoes, onion, grated cheese and crushed doritos. Stir in hamburger, beans, avocado, and dressing. Add hot sauce to taste.

Recipe Notes

SOUPS

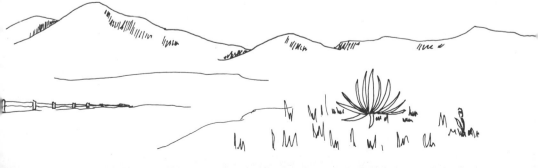

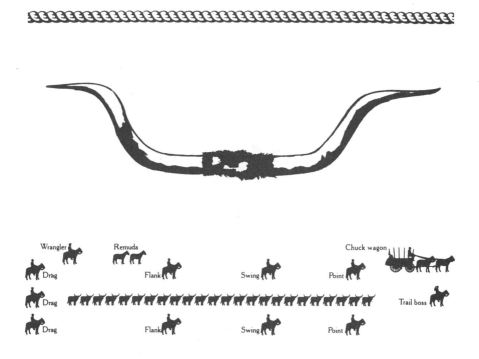

Cowboys on a drive advance in formation as shown in this diagram. While the trail boss rode ahead to scout for water and pasture, the cowhands rotated among the other positions.

SOUPS

Joan Hallman
Long Valley, New Jersey

HAMBURGER SOUP

1½ lb. ground beef	1 c. cabbage, sliced
1 medium onion, chopped	1 6-oz. can tomato paste
1 c. carrots, sliced	2 tsp. Worcestershire sauce
1 c. celery, sliced	3 c. beef bouillon

In skillet, brown hamburger and drain thoroughly. Add onion, carrots, celery, cabbage. Combine tomato paste, Worcestershire sauce and beef bouillon. Add to crock pot and stir to blend. Cover and cook on low setting for 8 to 10 hours, or high setting for 3 to 4 hours. Serves 8.

Alarik and Beth Myrin
Sleeping Lion Ranch
Teponnas, Colorado

LION RANCH HAMBURGER SOUP

1 lb. hamburger	Piece of bay leaf
Chopped onion to taste	4 c. tomato juice
1 can cream of celery soup	1 c. grated carrots
1 can cream of potato soup	1 c. green beans
1 c. water	1 c. corn (optional)
1 tsp. water	⅛ tsp. marjoram
1 tsp. sugar	¼ tsp. pepper
	Sprinkle garlic salt

Simmer 15 to 30 minutes in heavy pan. Serve with homemade bread or biscuits. Serves 8 to 10.

Background: The recipe is from a dear friend of ours. It is great to take on the trail drives — stays hot and is filling. We have a cattle ranch in Utah with summer range in Colorado. Alarik has served as President of the Utah Cattlemen's Association and is now a legislator in the Utah House of Representatives.

Gary and Dixie Mathison
A X Ranch
Laramie, Wyoming

BEEF AND VEGETABLE SOUP

1 lb. bonelss beef shank
2 chicken backs
2 carrots, pared and chopped
2 c. chopped celery
2 c. chopped leeks or onions
3 c. water
¼ tsp. pepper
4 whole allspice

½ tsp. marjoram, crumbled
2 tbsp. fine barley
1 c. chopped rutabega
1 c. shredded cabbage
1 can (1 lb. 12 oz.) tomatoes
1 tbsp. salt
½ tsp. leaf thyme, crumbled

Cut beef shank into small cubes. Place everthing in crock pot, except the barley. Cover cooker. Set dial at cooking position desired. Cook 7 hours or longer on "high", 12 hours or longer on "low". About half way through the cook period add the barley. Before serving, remove the chicken bones. Return any meat remaining on the bones to the soup. Remove the allspice. Makes 10 cups. A soup bone works equally well; at the end remove meat from bone. This is a really good soup. If the listed vegetables are not available, use whatever you have.

Background: My great grandfather, W.R. Williams, came from Nova Scotia and homesteaded this area in 1868. In addition to ranching, he freighted from Cheyenne to Deadwood and later to Montana. By 1879 he had one of the largest freight outfits in the country with some 400 head of oxen. In 1883 or 1884 he brought he first black Angus into southern Wyoming.
My grandfather, Art Williams, homesteaded our present ranch in 1909 and established the AX brand. He built our present house where my family lives from logs he cut and split himself. After his death, my father and mother, Richard and Gussie Williams, took over the AX. Today the ranch is a family corporation. I am now vice-president of Wyoming Cow-Belles and our daughter, Amber Jean, is the 4th generation to be raised in the ranching industry in this area.

John & Denzil Mills
Charleville, Australia

YELLA BELLY SOUP
(fish)

1 kg/2lbs fish	*1 potato chopped*
1 c. vinegar	*1 onion chopped*
½ c. olive oil	*Parsley*
2 c. water	*Cornflour to thicken*

Salt and pepper

Cooking time: 40-60 minutes. Clean fish. Place in dish and add vinegar, olive oil or other oil and the water. Boil until cooked. When ready drain off liquid and add potato, onion and parsley. Now thicken with the cornflour. Add salt and pepper.

John & Denzil Mills
Charleville, Australia

FRENCH ONION SOUP

1 oz. butter	*1 dessertspoon flour*
2 large onions	*3 pts. beef or chicken stock*
Pinch sugar	*Salt and pepper*

Peel onions, cut into thick slices. Heat butter in pan (you may need a little more butter); add onions and sugar and cook, stirring, until golden and transparent; they should not be dark in colour. Stir in flour, gradually stir in stock. Season to taste with salt and pepper. Cover, cook gently 20 minutes. Spoon into hot bowls. Take some slices of french bread, toast them and spinkle well with grated cheese. Place under griller until cheese melts and is golden. Put one toasted cheese slice on top of each bowl of steaming soup OR place a toasted round of French bread in base of soup plate, sprinkle with grated cheese, and gradually pour in soup. As toast floats to top, sprinkle with extra cheese. (For easier eating, some people perfer to cut the crusts from toast before putting into bowl).
On a cold winter's night, put 1 dessertspoon of brandy into each bowl before pouring in the hot onion soup. Serves 6-8.

Otto and Leona Tober
Tober Farm
Beardsley, Minnesota

GRUN SCHAUBLE SUP (BEAN SOUP)
(Green String Bean Soup)

6-10 slices bacon and/or ham, cut up	4 c. yellow wax beans
Savory, fresh or dried	(for color and variety)
3 or 4 c. potatoes, peeled and cubed	1 c. sour cream
4 c. green beans, cut up and cooked	2 c. buttermilk
Salt to taste	

Simmer bacon and savory with 2 cups water for 15 minutes, or until nearly done. Savory is a definite must for the soup. Add potatoes and salt and water to cover, then simmer till potatoes are forktender. (NOT overcooked.) Add green and yellow beans and heat until nearly to a boil. Remove from heat. Blend sour cream and buttermilk and add slowly to the potato, bacon and bean mixture. Heat until thoroughly heated. Never, never boil after cream and milk have been added. This delicious soup is now ready and is best served when prepared several hours in advance. Ummm-m-m-m. Soo-o good.

Background: Bean soup was especially enjoyed on the farm during winter months. After being out in the barn or stockyard most of the night helping with calving or pigging, a hot bowl of bean soup sure helped get the circulation going again. The more often the soup is heated up, the better the flavor.
Grun Schauble Sup originiated in Germany. It was especially popular among the low-German dialect group. They brought this traditional delicacy with them when they immigrated to America and is now dish enjoyed by their descendents. It is considered a meal-in-one, as it consists of meat, pototoes, vegtables and gravy. It is a traditional Christmas Eve speciality in the Tober household and is enjoyed by children, parent, and even by the in-laws. This recipe is for a large family gathering, so it can be scaled down to fit your family needs.

Mrs. Alfred Olson
from Julia Rock-Above, Crow Indian
Billings, Montana

BITTERROOT SOUP

Boil dried Bitterroot roots in buffalo, elk or bear broth until tender. Serve hot with pemmican patties.

BITTERROOT SAUCE

Boil the Bitterroot roots until until they are tender. Sweeten and serve.

BITTERROOT PUDDING

Use about ½ cup of Bitterroot roots per serving. Par-boil the roots for a few minutes. Drain and add fresh water. Cook until tender. Sweeten with wild honey to suit taste. Add 1 teaspoon bone marrow per serving. Thicken with the scraping from the inner side of a fresh skin.

Note: Before European cookery came West, the Indians used honey or a sweetening plant (Julie can't identify it) to sweeten the food. Julie uses sugar now.

Bone marrow was a favorite enrichment of the food but she uses butter or margarine now.

The old method of thickening was added to the scrappings from fresh skin. The glue-like substance thickened the pudding like packaged gelatin. Sometimes Julie uses flour to thicken the dessert.

Background: These recipes were given to me by Julia Rock-Above, a Crow Indian woman who tells that the way she uses the plant was handed down to her from her mother and grandmother, who in turn got the recipes from their ancestors so many years ago that the beginning has been lost in antiquity.

We know that Captain Meriwether Lewis gathered samples of the plant to take back to the states in 1806, with the botanical collection the party took back from the wilderness. The plant, of the portulaca family, was given the name Lewisia Rediviva in honor of Captain Lewis and because it revived when it was planted after being forgotten for a year or so. Lewisia Redivia, better known as the Bitterroot, was named Montana's state flower by the Legislature in 1985.

Marie Rumburg
Springfield, Virginia

SENATE BEAN SOUP

1½ lb. dried navy beans	Salt to taste
2 smoked pork chops	1 ham bone or hock
3 qts. water	2 - 1″ ham slices
1 c. minced celery	2 c. minced onion
2 cloves garlic	1 c. carrots
½ bay leaf	1 c. mashed potatoes
¼ tsp. ground pepper	1 tbsp. chopped parsley

Put water and beans in pot and bring to boiling point, boil for 5 mins. Cover, remove from heat and let steep for 1 hour. Add meats to pot and simmer for 1 hours. Add onions, celery, carrots, potatoes, garlic, bay leaf, and pepper. Simmer for 2 hours. Remove meats from pot and chop, then return meat to soup. Add parsley and salt to taste. Serves 8 to 12.

This is a popular dish served regularly in the U.S. Senate Cafeteria.

Mrs. John M. (Anna Kohrs) Boardman
Helena, Montana

SPICED GOOSEBERRIES

6 qts. gooseberries	1 tbsp. cinnamon
9 lbs. sugar	1 tbsp. cloves
1 pint vinegar	1 tbsp. allspice

Put berries into kettle with 1 cup water and half the sugar. Boil about 1½ hours. When nearly done, add remainder of sugar. Remove from fire and add vinegar and spices.

Background: During almost half a century of active life in the Northwest, John M. Boardman rose from modest circumstances to a position of wide influence in the state of Montana, and acquired a reputation which extended beyond its boarders. He leaves a distinguished record as a business man and state legislator. Like many young men of the period, however, he was attracted by the possibilities of adventure and fortune in the West and in July, 1876, he arrrived at Fort Benton, in Montana to settle. He worked as a cowboy for a time and then became associated with Conrad Kohrs, the Montana cattle king. In 1900, he was appointed manager of the Pioneer Cattle Company. During Theodore Roosevelt's administration there was a senatorial investigation into the causes of the bloody conflicts between the cattlemen and sheepmen of the West. Mr. Boardman was asked to testify. He was elected a member of the First Montana State Legislature, which convened on November 23, 1891, at the Church of Deer Lodge, he married Anna Kohrs, daughter of Conrad Kohrs, his associate in ranching and business.

Patrick Beres
Alpine, Texas

PACKER'S CHOWDER

3 or 4 potatoes, cubed	½ c. canned milk
1 onion, cubed	3 tsp. whole allspice
2 trout, boned and cut up	Butter
Flour	

Boil potatoes and onions in small amount of salted water until almost done. Put fish on top of potatoes. Dot with butter. Add milk and allspice and finish cooking (about 15 minutes). Thicken with flour and water.

Background: I've used this recipe while cooking on roundup crews, hunting camps, and running packstrings.

Vaughn Kygar
Hewins, Kansas

⌒
ΗΚ

SQUIRREL SOUP

2 squirrels (duck or	1 tsp. salt
prairie chicken is also good)	1-10 oz. can tomato soup
6 c. water	1-16 oz. can tomatoes, mashed
3 tbsp. chicken bouillon	½ Bermuda onion, chopped
1 doz. peppercorns	⅓ c. parsley flakes
¼ tsp. thyme	½ c. butter or margarine
1 c. barley	

Cook first 6 ingredients together until meat is tender enough to pull off bone easily but not until it falls off. Remove meat and strain broth. Cut meat into small pieces or grind coarsely. Add to broth the tomato soup and mashed tomatoes with juice, the onion, parsley flakes and butter. Bring to boil. Add barley and simmer over low heat until tneder. Add meat to pot and simmer 10 minutes. Serves eight.

Background: Game has been harvested in season for three generations on this ranch. We manage our range land to provide water, food and shelter for a bountiful wildlife population just as carefully as we manage for a productive cow herd.

John & Denzil Mills
Charleville, Australia

HARTY BEEF & VEGETABLE BROTH

1½ lb. shinbone and knuckle cracked	2 onions sliced
2 lb. round or bladebone steak	½ c. diced celery
cut into 1 inch cubes	3 sprig parsley
2 oz. butter	3 c. coarsely diced swede turnip
6 pts. water	4 carrots sliced
5 tsp. salt	2 whole cloves
1 tsp. tabasco sauce	2 c. coarsely cut cabbage
1 bay leaf	2 large tomatoes, peeled and diced

Brown bones and steak in butter in heavy saucepan, cover with water. Add 3 teaspoons of salt, tabasco, by leaf, onions, celery, parsley, 1 cup of turnips, 1 sliced carrot and cloves. Add remaining 2 teaspoons salt, 2 cups turnip, 3 carrots, cabbage and tomatoes. Cover, bring to the boil and simmer for 30 minutes until vegetables are tender. Serves 8-10.

Ray Hall
Manassas, Virginia

WYOMING TROUT CHOWDER

4 10- to 12-in. trout	2 c. milk
4 medium sized potatoes	2 tbsp. flour
2 medium sized carrots	1 tbsp. butter
2 stalks celery	Salt and pepper to taste

Dice potatoes, carrots and celery into ⅜ to ½ inch chunks. Cover with water and boil until completely fork tender. Drain off water and set aside.

Clean and skin trout and boil for five minutes. Drain off water and allow to cool until fish can be handled. Remove all bones and flake flesh into small chunks. Add fish meat to vegetables. Add milk and flour and bring to slow boil, stirring regularly. Add butter and salt and pepper to taste. Cook until desired thickness is reached.

Serve with crackers to 4 to 6 hungry campers. This makes an excellent appetizer or meal in fishing or hunting camps, or anytime the larder is low.

Background: This recipe was passed to me in 1960 by an old gentleman who, for many years, had been the chief cook at the U.S. Weather Bureau Station in Point Barrow, Alaska. I have used it many times in the past 25 years in fishing and hunting camps, cow camps and back-country pack trips.

Nebraska Pioneer Cookbook
Nebraska

CREAM POTATO SOUP

4 large potatoes, sliced	1½ qts. milk
1 tbsp. butter	1 c. (small) whipped cream
Salt and pepper to taste	

Cook potatoes with as little water as possible. When thoroughly done add butter, salt and pepper and mash very fine. Add milk and stir thoroughly. Allow to come slowly to a boil. Pour into the soup tureen, add whipped cream and serve immediately.

SRM   SOCIETY FOR RANGE MANAGEMENT

John & Denzil Mills
Charleville, Australia

SPAGHETTI SOUP

1 kangaroo tail	1 tin tomato soup
2 onions	1½ cups spaghetti

Salt and pepper to taste

Cooking time: 20 minutes. Boil Kangaroo tail or joints until tender, with chopped onions. When cooked add tomato soup and spaghetti, simmer until tender, about 20 minutes. Add salt and pepper.

CHILI

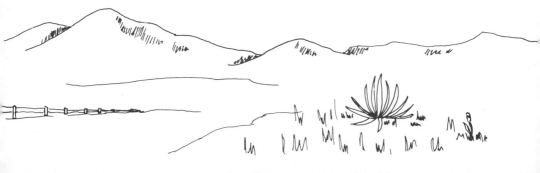

Facts

Range management is ecologically managing range and rangeland to provide habitat and forage for cattle, sheep, horses and numerous kinds of wildlife, while protecting and ensuring the flow of other goods and services obtainable from rangelands.

Generally, "good range management" means to take half and leave half. This helps insure food, fiber and other resources for the present and the future.

Over nine million big game animals graze the rangelands of the United States alone.

CHILI

Arlene Supola
Fairfax, Virginia

GREEN CHILI

1 pork roast	Cumin
(trimmed and cut in small pieces)	6 10-oz. cans tomatoes & green chili
1 onion chopped	1 can chopped HOT green
2 cloves garlic	chili peppers

Brown pork in oil, add and brown onion and garlic. Make a smooth paste and add to meat. Add tomatoes and green chili, hot pepper and two or three cans of water, add salt, pepper and garlic salt and a little cumin. Simmer most of day — thicken as needed.

The Four Sixes Ranch
Guthrie, Texas

6666

TEXAS RED CHILI

⅛ lb. suet, finely chopped	½ to 1 tbsp. cayenne
3 lbs. round steak, coarsely cubed	2 large cloves garlic, minced
6 tbsp. chili powder	1 tbsp. Tabasco, if you dare
1 tbsp. ground oregano	1½ quarts water
1 tbsp. crushed cumin seed	½ c. white cornmeal or
1 tbsp. salt	3 tbsp. masa harina

In Dutch oven, fry suet until crisp; add steak cubes and brown. Add seasonings and water; heat to boil. Reduce heat, cover and simmer 1½ hours. Skim off fat. Stir in cornmeal and simmer, uncovered, for 30 minutes. Stir occasionally. Serve with pinto beans or cornbread. Serves 8 to 10.

Background: "Chili pangs" strike a man when the skies get gray and the wind turns cold. And a bowl of Texas Red is the only cure. The "Original Texas Red" chili dates back to the 1800's when it was served by vendors on the streets of San Antonio.

Congressman Mike Synar
The Hayhook Ranch
Muskogee, Oklahoma

2

SYNAR CHILI

Cooking oil
2 heaping c. frozen chopped onions
2 heaping c. frozen bell peppers
3-4 celery stalks, finely chopped
8 lbs. lean, coarsely ground beef
¼ lb. beef fat
1 8-oz. can tomato paste
2 14½-oz. cans stewed tomatoes
Garlic salt to taste

2 #2-cans tomato sauce
3-4 large garlic cloves, finely chopped
2 bottles Gebhardt's Eagle Brand
chili powder (3-oz. each), or to taste
3 tbsp. salt or to taste
Sprinkling of oregano
1 c. chili salsa, hot or med. hot
1 med. green hot chili pepper
Coarsely ground pepper to taste

Rub a 10-quart pot with a little cooking oil. Add onions, peppers and celery, cook gently, stirring often, for about 10 minutes. Increase heat and add the meat, stirring until the redness is gone. Splash in a generous amount (about 1¼ cups) Worcestershire sauce at the end. Add the remaining ingredients and simmer uncovered for at least 2½ hours, preferably 3½. Stir from time to time so it doesn't stick to bottom. Add water, 1 cup at start and 1 cup after the first 30 minutes, and maybe one cup before serving. Serves 12 to 16 chili lovers.

Background: This recipe was developed by Joe Synar, Hayhook Ranch. It was entered in the Oklahoma State Chili Cookoff in 1977 and won the State Championship.

Catherine M. Jameson
Fort Collins, Colorado

MALE CHAUVINIST CHILI

6 slices bacon	1 tsp. chili powder
10 oz. hamburger	½ tsp. salt
10 oz. hot Italian sausage,	1 15-oz. can kidney beans
cut into 1-inch slices	1 15-oz. can pinto beans
1 large Spanish onion, chunks	½ jalapeno chili pepper, diced
1 bell pepper, cut in pieces	½ c. Worcestershire sauce
2 cloves garlic, minced	1 tsp. celery seeds
1 c. dark red wine	1½ tsp. black pepper
1 tsp. hot dry mustard	6 c. Italian tomatoes (pearshaped)

Brown bacon in chili pot (preferably 4½ quart iron Dutch oven). Drain, crumble bacon and set aside. Pour bacon fat from pot, leaving only a film. Brown sausage and set aside with bacon. Pour sausage fat from pot, again leaving only a film. Fry hamburger, drain and set aside with other meats. Pour excess fat from pot. Cook onion, pepper, garlic and chili pepper over low heat 2 to 3 minutes. Stir in wine and Worcestershire sauce, simmer uncovered about 10 minutes. Stir in mustard, celery seeds, chili powder, salt and pepper. Simmer 10 more minutes. Mash tomatoes and add with liquid and the meats to the onion mixture. Heat to boiling, reduce heat and simmer, covered ½-hour, stirring occasionally. Reduce heat, cover and simmer 1 hour, stirring occasionally. This recipe is best made a day ahead and reheated as the flavors will meld to their spice best.

Vicky & Dan Kipp
The Butler Ranch
Aundale, Colorado

POLE LINE CHILI

2 lbs. ranch beef	1¼ tsp. dried oregano
8-oz. can tomato sauce	Scant ½ tsp. paprika
12-oz. beer	1½ tsp. ground cumin
¼ c. red chili	1¼ tsp. salt
2 med. cloves garlic, chopped	Pinch cayenne pepper
1 onion, chopped	¾ lb. Jack cheese, grated

1 can chili beans

Brown meat. Add tomato sauce, beer, ground chili, garlic, onion, oregano, paprika, 1 tsp. cumin & salt. Stir to blend. Bring to boil; lower heat and simmer 1 hour, uncovered, stirring occasionally. Taste — adjust seasonings and add cayenne and beans, simmer uncovered another hour. Stir in cheese, remaining cumin. Simmer ½ hour, watching that cheese doesn't stick.

Background: Pole Line is an old line camp on this historic ranch Primitive as it is, we gather there with friends and family to cut our Christmas trees. It is a wonderful recipe that expands to 30 people. Children enjoy it and it cooks up well on a wood burning stove.

Dick Hart
Cheyenne, Wyoming

PORK AND RED CHILI

3 lbs. lean boneless pork	½ c. whipping cream
2 tbsp. salad oil	2 onions, chopped
2 cloves garlic, minced	2 tbsp. chili powder
1 tsp. ground cumin	1½ tsp. oregano
1¼ c. water	1 tsp. sugar
1½ tsp. salt	3 tbsp. tomato paste

Trim fat and cut meat into 1 inch cubes. Brown in oil, remove. Add onion, garlic, chili powder, cumin and oregano; cook until onion is limp. Stir in water, sugar, salt and tomato paste, return pork and simmer covered about 1 hour. Skim off fat, add cream, bring to boil stirring constantly. Serve in warm flour tortillas, garnish with avocado, tomato and/or sour cream. Serves 6

Background: Pigs, according to Celtic mythology, were a gift from the King of Faery, although the Welsh and Irish disagree as to which was the original recipient. In any case, the Spanish brought pigs to Mexico, and the natives developed mouth-watering combinations of pork with local ingredients. This recipe is so good it converted a would-be vegetarian friend, who hadn't eaten pork for 4 years, into a temporary carnivore!

Doug and Virginia Sellars
Society for Range Management
Washington, D.C.

TEXAS-STYLE CHILI

2½ lbs. beef round steak, cubed	1 tsp. sugar
1 clove garlic, minced	1 to 2 tsp. cumin seed, crushed
3 tbsp. cooking oil	½ tsp. salt
1 10½-oz. can condensed beef broth	2 bay leaves
1½ c. water	1 4-oz. can green chili peppers,
2 tsp. dried oregano, crushed	seeded and mashed
2 tbsp. cornmeal	

In large skillet, brown the beef cubes and garlic in hot oil; drain off excess fat. Add beef broth, water, oregano, sugar, cumin, salt, and bay leaves. Reduce heat and simmer til the meat is tender, about 1½ hours. Stir in the chili peppers and the cornmeal. Simmer 30 minutes, stirring occasionally. Remove bay leaves. Serve over corn bread, if desired. Serves 4 to 6.

STEWS

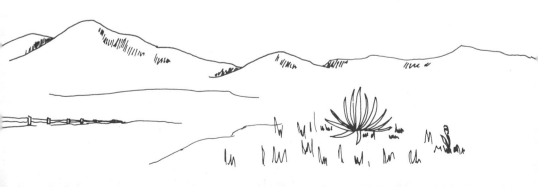

The daily strategy of a typical spring round-up focused on a moving chuck wagon from which the men fanned out in the morning and to which they circled back with the cattle for sorting and branding each afternoon.

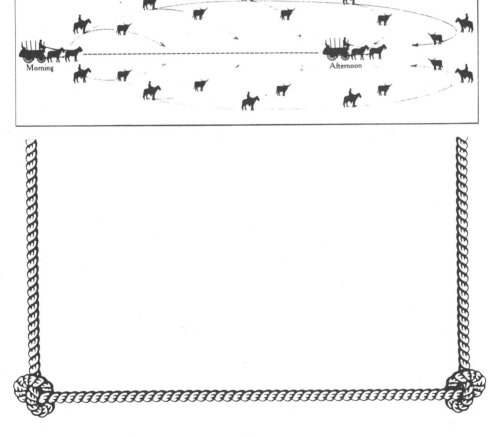

W.T. Waggoner Estate
Waggoner Ranch
Electra, Texas

BILL'S COOKHOUSE STEW

10 lbs. floured stew meat
1 bunch celery
10 medium potatoes in chunks
3-4 c. cut green beans
2 cans stewed tomatoes

2 large onions, medium chopped
2 lbs. carrots, cut in ½ rounds
3-4 c. whole kernel corn
4 cans sliced mushrooms
1 medium bell pepper, chopped

Brown meat in small amount of oil. Add onion and celery and saute. Cover meat with water and season with salt, pepper and garlic salt. Simmer until meat is getting tender, 1½ hours, approximately. Add carrots and continue simmering 30 minutes. Add remaining ingredients and bring to boil. Reduce heat and simmer until meat and vegetables are all tender. Stir occasionally while cooking and keep ingredients covered with liquid. Total cooking time approximately 3 hours.

Background: The 510,000 acre Wagonner Ranch, now the W. T. Wagonner Estate, was started in 1849 and is now the largest ranch in Texas under one fence. Started in Hopkins County, the Waggoner operation was moved to Decatur, then to Wichita Falls and finally to Beaver Creek near Electra, Texas. The ranch farms 26,000 acres and raises some of the country's finest cattle and horses. It was the home of Poco Bueno, a world-famous quarter horse.

Family of the late Rep. Don. L. Short
Beach, North Dakota

COW CAMP MULLIGAN STEW

4 or 5 lbs. shoulder beef, cut
4 onions
4 carrots
1 pkg. vegetable soup mix

½ cabbage head
5 potatoes
1 rutabaga
Salt and pepper to taste

Place meat in large kettle, cover with water and boil until meat is tender. Cut meat into serving pieces and siphon or spoon off all fat from meat broth. Place vegetables and meat back into kettle and cook until the vegetables are tender Serves 8 to 10. Serve with buttered toast.

Background: Wonderful after a long day of feeding cattle in below zero weather. Suggested dessert if you have room — rice with raisins.

George Chavez for Kay Graber
Broken Bow, Nebraska

SON-OF-A-BITCH STEW
(Nebraska style)

One young calf

½ the heart	All the butchers steak
½ the spleen	(the strips of lean meat on the inner
¼ the liver	side of the ribs), or an equal
All the tongue	amount of tenderloin
All the sweetbreads	2 c. of melted leaf fat
Marrow gut (about 3 feet)	One set of brains

After the calf was killed and while the meat was still warm, the heart, liver, tongue, marrow gut, some pieces of tenderloin or butcher's steak, sweetbreads and the brains were taken to be prepared. The cook cut the fat into small chunks, put them into the pot. While this fat was being melted he cut the heart into small cubes, adding it first because it was tougher. The tongue was also skinned and cubed, then added, thus giving the two toughest ingredients longer cooking time. While these were cooking, the cook cut the tenderloin, sweetbreads and liver into similar pieces, using the liver sparingly so as not to make the stew bitter. To all this was added the marrow gut after being cut into rings, or inch long pieces. Cover all this with lukewarm water, adding more and more from time to time. The ingredients were added slowly, a handful at a time, the whole being slowly stirred after each addition. During this time the brains were cleaned of blood and membranes, then cooked separately, some cooks adding a little flour to make them thicker. When they become beady they were added to the stew, this being the last ingredient added except salt and pepper to taste, or a little onion if desired.

Background: Beef was the cowboy's meat, and he ate every part of the animal that could be made edible. "Son-of-a-bitch stew", roundup fare par excellence, gave "cookie" a chance to express his culinary creativity. The one ingredient which gave this stew its bad name among the uninitiated was the word "marrow guts." This is no "gut" at all, but the long tube connecting the two stomachs of young cud-chewing animals. It is good only when the calf is still nursing, being then tender and full of substance which resembles marrow. Hence the name. Through this, the partically disgested milk passes. This is why calves not completely weaned are selected for this stew. The marrowlike substance is left in when cooking this stew and is what gives it its delightful flavor.

There are at least a dozen recipes for this dish. Each is a little bit different. Where one uses the kidneys, another does not. Some use the spleen, others leave it out. Some call for onions; others a dash of chili pepper.

Doug Sellars
Fairfax, Virginia

SON-OF-A-BITCH-STEW
(Trail Drive Style)

1 lb. lean beef	*1 set brains*
Half a calf heart	*1 set marrow gut*
1½ lb. calf liver	*Salt, pepper*
1 set sweetbreads	*Louisiana hot sauce*

Kill of a young steer. Cut up beef, liver and heart into 1-inch cubes; slice the marrow gut into small rings. Place in a Dutch oven or deep casserole. Cover meat with water and simmer for 2 to 3 hours. Add salt, pepper and hot sauce to taste. Take sweetbreads and brains and cut into small pieces. Add to stew. Simmer another hour, never boiling.

Jeffrey W.Bailey
Prairie Ridge Ranch
Cheyenne, Wyoming

`·J·`

WYOMING SON-OF-A-GUN STEW

From a freshly-killed beef take the following: liver, heart, brains, sweetbreads, kidneys and marrow-gut. Wash them very good. Cut into pieces suitable for stew. Put them into a Dutch oven with a small piece (one-inch square) of suet tallow. Cover with water. Season with salt, pepper and chili powder. Boil until meat is tender. Add a handful of flour (adding warm water, if necessary). Stir until mixture cooks for half and hour. Serve.

Background: Son-of-a-gun stew was a favorite concoction of the Wyoming cowboy.

SRM **SOCIETY FOR RANGE MANAGEMENT**

The Four Sixes Ranch
Guthrie, Texas

6666

SON OF SON-OF-A-GUN STEW

¼ lb. salt pork, cut into slivers
1 lb. beef, cut in cubes
1 veal heart, about ¾ lb.
1 large carrot, thinly sliced
2 medium onions, thinly sliced
2 tbsps. flour
¼ tsp. black pepper

1 tsp. salt
1½ c. tomato juice
1½ c. beef broth or 2 bullion cubes
dissolved in 1½ c. hot water
2 cloves garlic, minced
1 bay leaf
1 pair veal sweetbreads, about 1 lb.

1 veal brain, about ½ lb.

In Dutch oven, lightly brown salt pork; remove and set aside. Heat fat until hot; add beef, brown quickly. Wash heart, remove membrane and excess fat; cube and add to beef. Add carrot, onion; sprinkle with mixture of flour, salt and pepper. Toss with meat and vegetables, letting flour brown lightly. Pour over tomato juice and beef broth; add garlic, bay leaf. Cover, bring to boil. Reduce heat. Simmer 2 hrs. Simmer sweetbreads in boiling salted water 35 min.; drain and slip off thin membrane under water. Remove connecting tissue; cube. Soak brains in salted water 15 mins. Check beef in oven, skim excess fat. If sauce is thin, turn up heat, cook rapidly a few min. Reduce heat; add sweetbreads, brains. Heat thoroughly. Serve over rice or noodles. Serves 6.

Background: When a wagon cook yells "Grab a plate an' growl," it's time for Son-of-a-Gun Stew. A meal that's been called as many names as the ingredients that go into it. Common practice was for "Cookie" to call on the nearest cowhand—count off all the things he'd put in his stew—and then ask that cowhand to taste it. Well, it just so happens that one mouthful of Son-of-a-Gun Stew brought out all the honesty in a man. And the truth didn't always set too well with the cook! So, we've taken a few liberties with the original recipe and made it a whole lot easier to swallow.!

Jim Riggs
Crossed J Ranch
Cochise County, Arizona

COWBOY OVEN STEW

3 lbs. roast or stew meat	1 can cream of mushroom soup
1 pkg. dry onion soup mix	1 soup can water

Put meat in roasting pan or casserole. Sprinkle soup mix over meat. Pour mushroom soup over meat and add water. Cover tightly and bake at 350° for 3 hours. When done, the meat is simmering in a gravy. Makes 6-8 servings. This recipe can be used in a dutch oven or crock pot also.

Background: The Riggs ranchers' wives are modest about their outfits but there are few items of interest. The Jim Riggs ranch in southeast Arizona is part of the Riggs clan holdings. In fact, there are so many of them there is a Riggsville. The Riggs family members are long-time active members of the SRM.

Historic Traildrive Recipe

COWPUNCHER STEW

1½ lbs. beef stew meat,	1 tsp. Worcestershire sauce
cut in 1-inch cubes	½ tsp. dired oregano, crushed
2 tbsp. all-purpose flour	⅛ tsp. cayenne
1 tsp. salt	1½ c. water
2 tbsp. shortening	4 carrots, cut in ½-inch slices
1½ c. strong coffee	2 small onions, quartered
2 tbsp. molasses	3 medium potatoes, peeled and cut up
1 clove garlic, minced	½ c. cold water
1 tsp. salt	3 tbsp. all-purpose flour

Coat beef cubes with a mixture of 2 tablespoons flour and 1 tsp. salt. In Dutch oven brown meat on all sides in hot shortening. Stir in the coffee, molasses, garlic, 1 tsp. salt, Worcestershire, oregano, and cayenne. Cover; simmer over low heat till meat is almost tender, about 1½ hours. Add the 1½ cups water, carrot slices, onion quarters, and potato pieces. Simmer, covered, till vegetables are tender, about 30 minutes. Blend ¼ cup cold water into the 3 tbsp. flour; add to stew mixture. Cook and stir till mixture is thickened and bubbly. Serve in bowls. Makes 6 to 8 servings.

Historic Pioneer Recipe

BURGOO

*1-3 lb. ready-to-cook broiler-fryer
chicken, cut up
2 tbsp. beef shank cross cuts
12 c. water
1 tbsp. salt
¼ tsp. pepper
6 slices bacon
2 28-oz. cans tomatoes
1 c. cubed peeled potatoes
2 c. coarsely chopped carrots
1 c. chopped onion*

*1 c. chopped celery
1 c. chopped green pepper
2 tbsp. packed dark brown sugar
¼ tsp. crushed dried red pepper
4 whole cloves
1 bay leaf
1 clove garlic, minced
4 ears corn
2-16 oz. cans butter beans
1-10 oz. package frozen cut okra
⅔ c. all purpose flour*

½ c. snipped parsley

In 10-quart Dutch oven combine chicken, beef cross cuts, water, salt, and pepper. Cover; cook till meat is tender, about 1 hour. Remove chicken and beef from broth, reserving broth. Remove chicken and beef from bones; discard skin and bones. Cube beef and chicken. Set aside. Cook bacon till crisp; drain, reserving drippings. Crumble bacon; set aside. To reserved broth in Dutch oven add cubed beef, undrained tomatoes, potatoes, carrots, onion, celery, green pepper, sugar, red pepper, cloves, bay leaf, and garlic. Cover; simmer 1 hour, stirring often. Remove cloves and bay leaf. With knife, make cuts down center of corn kernels on each row; scrape cob. Add corn, cubed chicken, undrained beans, and okra to Dutch oven; simmer 20 minutes. Blend flour and reserved bacon drippings; stir into soup. Cook and stir til soup thickens. Salt to taste. Garnish with parsley and bacon. Serves 20.

Background: Politicians have always resorted to all sorts of way of getting votes. One of the more colorful was the political barbecue where voters were swayed more by what they ate and drank than by rhetoric. These vote-getting rallies were at their greatest during the 1840 presidential campaign of William Henry Harrison. The featured dish was often Burgoo, a hearty concoction, which took all night to prepare. As if to prove that the food was more important than the speeches, the rally itself was often called a burgoo.

Ann Gates
Corvallis, Oregon

SLUM GUM

1 lb. hamburger	¼ can whole kernel corn, drained
1 medium onion, chopped	1 small can mushrooms
1 can spaghetti with tomato sauce	½ small can tomato sauce
1 can kidney beans	Chopped olives, if desired

Brown onion, add hamburger and fry until pink is gone. Add rest of ingredients. Season with ½ cup catsup, chili powder to taste, and Worcestershire Sauce. Simmer 30 minutes. Makes a very large recipe.

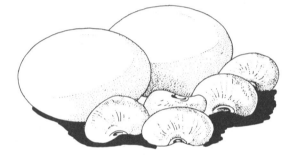

Herbert Allard
Allard Ranch
Savage, Montana

S⊥-

ROUNDUP STEW

1½ lbs. hamburger	6 potatoes cut in chunks
1 large onion, chopped	1 can tomato soup
½ c. celery, chopped	1 can cream of mushroom soup
1 c. sliced carrots	Water as desired

Brown hamburger, onion and celery in fry pan and season to taste. Boil potatoes and carrots together slightly. Drain and add seasoned hamburger mixture and the soups. Add water as desired from potatoes and carrots. Put in casserole or small roaster and bake about 45 minutes at 350°. Serves about 6 cowboys. This stew may be baked at a lower temperature and left for several hours, if necessary without being ruined.

Background: This stew was used many times on the Allard Ranch at roundup time when all hands, including the cook, had to help ride.

Ray Margo
Solicited from New Mexico Cowbelles
Albuquerque, New Mexico

GREEN CHILI STEW

1 round steak, cubed	*Small can of tomatoes*
4 cans of whole green chili	*2 qt. water*
2 medium potatoes, diced	*Salt and pepper to taste*

Cut round steak in cubes and roll in flour. Brown in bacon drippings in cooker. Add water, salt and pepper, tomatoes, potatoes, and green chili. Simmer for 4 hours. This will serve 6 people. Serve with sopapillas and honey, or flour tortillas.

Mrs. Helen A. Jensen Bradford
Circle Bar One Ranches
Rio Blanco County, Muher, Colorado

SHEEPHERDER STEW

2 to 3 lbs. of lean lamb or beef (cubed)	*6 carrots*
4 med. potatoes halved	*3 parsnips*
4 onions	*½ to ⅓ c. barley*
Garlic salt, pepper, rosemary to season	

In a large heavy iron dutch oven, flour, season and brown cubes of meat. Drain off surplus fat. Cover with stock or water and cook slowly until nearly done. Add the barley and stir very often or it will burn or stick. Simmer for one hour, then add other vegetables and cook very slowly for about three more hours keeping plenty of moisture in it.

Background: This ranch, owned by my late husband and myself for over 60 years, was headquarters for our other ranches. This stew was one of our favorites for trailing to winter ranges or the high country. This brand is listed in the Centennial Brand Book of Colorado Cattlemen's Association, and is one of the oldest brands in the State of Colorado. I am the great granddaughter of Lucien Seldon Smith, and I am a life member of SRM.

87

Belinda Style
Tuba City, Arizona

MUTTON STEW
(Navajo)

2 lbs. mutton
6 c. water
3 medium potatoes, peeled and
cut into small pieces
1 onion, cut into small pieces

1 stalk celery, without leaves,
cut into small pieces
3 roasted green chilies, peeled, seeded
and chopped
Carrots, peas, squash, tomatoes and
Corn can also be used in this stew

Put all the ingredients in a heavy pot and bring to a boil. Then simmer for 1½ hours until done. Add salt to taste after cooking is finished.

Background: Sheepherding is a necessity for the Navajo Indians. In the spring, the family shears the wool and takes it to the local trading post where it is sold. Stew is the standard main meat dish. Fried Bread and coffee complete the typical meal. Also the ribs of a freshly killed lamb are broiled over open coals as a change from the usual broiled meat.

Joanne Manygoats
Bar N Ranch
Gallup, New Mexico

–N

NAVAJO MUTTON STEW
(Lamb Stew)

2 lbs. of mutton, cut up
1 x 1-inch, along with stew bone
4 sticks of carrots (lg. size) cut up
about 1-inch in chunk size

1 stalk of celery, cut up 1-inch in size
3 med. potatoes cut up 1-inch in size
1 small cabbage cut up in lg. strips
½ tsp. of garlic salt
A dash of black pepper

3 quarts of water in large (4 qts.) stewpot. Place mutton and vegetable in stewpot and bring to med-high boil for 1½ to 2 hours. In about 1½ hours add the garlic salt and black pepper (optional: add small can of tomato sauce - 4 oz.). Serve with Fry Bread or tortilla. Serves 4-5 people.

Background: This recipe originated from the traditional mutton stew of the older Navajo generation. Mutton is one of the staple meat groups of the Navajo. They raise sheep for food as well as economic and religious purposes of the Navajo culture. The vegetables are added for variety in taste and appetizing appeal.

Tom & Shirley Cook
Cook Ranch
Fernley, Nevada

LAMB HATERS STEW

*2 lbs. fat-free lamb cut in
bite size pieces
1 chopped yellow onion
½-1 c. white wine*

*3-4 chopped garlic cloves
1 can mushroom soup
1 pt. sour cream*

Brown and cook meat for 20-30 minutes. Add onion and garlic at middle of cooking period with enough cooking oil to keep them from burning. Add soup, sour cream and wine when meat is fairly done. Simmer 10-15 minutes. Serve over noodles or boiled potatoes or by itself.

Background: I call this stew lamb haters stew because that is what Shirley cooked for visitors who express a dislike for lamb. Without being told what they were eating, they never failed to take a second helping. For a number of years we had a family get-together which also included close friends and neighbors. Shirley was a Pyramid Lake Paiute Indian, so many Indian people throughout the state of Nevada attended. We would have as many as 150 "guests" at our gatherings. Lamb, beef, and pork, all home-raised, was served along with salads and desserts. After eating, we had Indian dancing, handgames, and Indian gambling games.

Maurice and Barbara Bidart
Leonard Creek Ranch
Nevada

MB

BACCALA
(Codfish Stew)

2 lbs. cod fish	1 small can tomato sauce
3 tbsp. oil	¼ c. celery
1 diced onion	4 medium potatoes in chunks
1 diced garlic clove	1 bay leaf
1 diced bell pepper	1 c. water
1 tbsp. diced parsley	Salt and pepper to taste
1 tbsp. basil	

If dried, salted codfish is used, it must be soaked in cold water, changing water frequenty. Boil cod til tender, then flake meat off bones. Saute in oil the onion, pepper, garlic, parsley and celery. Then add potatoes, tomato sauce, bay leaf and simmer until potatoes are tender. Then add cooked cod. I add a little table wine and a shake of catsup to the sauce.

Background: We served this dish at the ranch on Fridays when fresh fish wasn't available.

Mrs. Harlan De Garmo
Elmwood, Nebraska

GRAVE-YARD STEW

2 c. milk	Cinnamon
½ c. sugar	Butter
Salt	

Heat in pan. Pour over toast. Must be served in a tin pie pan.

Background: Supper was fun when we had grave-yard stew. Is almost as good as bread, milk and brown sugar.

Sue Field
Botswana, Africa

DIKGOBE

½ c. butter beans (brown beans   ¼ tsp. pepper
   can also be used)   1 c. samp (maize meal)
   ½ tsp. salt   3 c. water
            1 tsp. beef fat (not oil)

Wash the beans and soak overnight. Wash the samp and cover with water and soak overnight. Strain and wash the beans and samp. Boil 1 cup water in a large pan and add the beans and samp. Boil. Add water when necessary and cook until tender. When really tender, add the fat, salt and pepper and allow the mixture to simmer for another half hour. Serve hot with a good beef stew.

Background: This sort of porridge is eaten all over Africa. It is called "ugari" in Kenya and Tanzania. Always eaten with stew, it is served up at the communal table and people take a little in their fingers and dip it into the stew and eat. Remember that African herdsmen do not have knives and forks or tables and chairs, so they sit on the ground in circle around the food. Before they eat the youngest boy takes a pot of water around to each person to wash his hands.

June Southwood:
Dubbo, Australia

BRUSHMEN'S BREAKFAST

2 c. self-raising flour   Bacon
   Pinch of salt   Any leftover cold meat or vegetable
   1 egg   Eggs
   Milk   Oil for cooking

Place flour, salt and egg into a bowl. Mix well while slowly adding milk until smooth batter results. Chop up all left over meat and vegetables until very fine, mix into batter. Spoon mixture one at time into heated oil in camp oven. Turn when sides are golden brown. Serve with Bacon and eggs.

Background: A quick meal, using leftovers from previous evening meal. Filling and tasty.

Recipe Notes

CASSEROLES

The Indispensable Art of Roping

From the earliest moment in the morning—when he went to the remuda to catch out his day's mount by slipping a rope around its neck—the cowboy was rarely out of reach of his lariat. Snugly coiled, it hung from his saddle whenever he mounted up. On the trail he had it ready to drop over the horns of a rebellious herd quitter or to pull out a bogged cow or wagon. And the knot end was a convenient whip for a balky horse or steer. At roundup time he used the rope to catch calves or stray cattle for the branding iron. Sometimes he even made his rope function as a crude adding machine, totaling up the newly branded animals by shifting a coil of the lariat from one hand to the other for every hundred head.

A lariat was not just any piece of rope. It was made of carefully braided rawhide or twisted grass and had to be stiff enough so that when a cowhand paid out a broad loop and then sent it flying toward its target the loop stayed flat and open. Moreover, the lariat had to be strong enough to take the wrenching shock of a roped 1,200-pound steer yanking it as taut as any blue-water fishing line. A lariat could be dangerous, too, in inexperienced hands. One Texas greenhorn who got tangled up in loose coils found himself lashed to the side of his pony upside down, a target for the horns of the steer he had just roped.

Most cowboys spent a fair portion of their leisure time practicing with the rope, refining their skill and fooling around with fancy casts. But woe to the cowboy who got too enamored of his lariat and busted cattle unnecessarily or used the working day as an occasion to try out his trick roping, for he risked being fired. For practical purposes a cowboy had to know only two catches plus one potentially lethal variation. With these basic catches, and a smart, willing cow pony, he became the master of the Western plain and of its four-legged creatures.

CASSEROLES

Mrs. Earl Pelton
Bone Springs Ranch
Halliday, North Dakota

BEEF & POTATO ROLL

1-½ lbs. lean ground beef
1 c. soft bread crumbs
1-½ tbsp. instant minced onion
½ c. dry white wine
1-½ tsp. salt
1 egg, beaten
¼ tsp. Italian herb seasoning

¼ tsp. pepper
1 pkg. (12 oz.) frozen hashed brown
potatoes, thawed
⅓ c. grated parmesan cheese
¼ c. chopped parsley
1 tsp. onion powder
tomato sauce (see directions below)

Preheat oven to 375°. Mix crumbs, onion, wine, salt, egg, herb seasoning and pepper, let stand a few minutes to moisten bread crumbs. Add meat, and mix with a fork until well-blended. Shape into a flat 10" square on a sheet of waxed paper. Mix potatoes with cheese, parsley, and onion powder. Arrange in an even layer over meat, leaving 1" uncovered on two opposite sides. Roll up starting with one side where meat is not covered with potatoes, using paper to lift meat. Place seam side down in shallow, lightly greased roasting pan. Bake in moderately hot oven about 35 minutes. Spoon tomato sauce over meat, and bake 5 to 10 minutes longer. Remove to serving platter, slice and serve. This is an easy one dish meal, and my family always enjoys it.

Background: My husband Earl and I moved to our present home 26 years ago. The Ranch name is used because of the spring that is in our pasture. In homestead days all of the springs in the area had names. This spring still waters our cattle herd, as it did when Earl's grandfather homesteaded here. The Campstool brand has also been in the family for four generations and is used only by our families as we have every location available.

96

Mrs. Steve Symms
Boise, Idaho

APPLE ONION CASSEROLE

3 large mild onions, sliced
½ c. brown sugar, or less
salt & freshly ground black pepper

¼ c. butter
6 tart apples, peeled & sliced
buttered bread crumbs

Lightly grease casserole. Arrange layer onions in bottom; sprinkle with half of brown sugar. Season and dot with half the butter. Add half of the apples in a layer; top with remaining sugar. Season and dot with remaining butter. Top with bread crumbs and bake at 300° for 1-½ to 2 hours. 6 servings.

Marie Rumburg
Springfield, Virginia

BAKED GRITS CASSEROLE

1 c. uncooked grits
cube margarine
2 pkgs. Jalapanio cheese

1 small can diced green chiles
2 garlic cloves, mashed
2 beaten eggs

Cook grits. Mix all ingredients together and bake at 350° for 1 hour. Cover for the first ½ hour, uncover for the 2nd ½ hour.

Mrs. Lester (Joan) Hallman
Long Valley, New Jersey

BREAKFAST CASSEROLE
(Pennsylvania Dutch "Cowboy")

6 eggs
2 c. milk
1 tsp. salt
1 tsp. dry mustard

2 slices white bread, cubed
1 lb. sausage, browned
1 c. cheddar cheese, grated
(mild or sharp)

Beat eggs, add milk, salt and mustard, mixing well. Grease bottom of a 9 x 13" baking dish. Place in layer of bread cubes, the sausage, then cheese. Pour egg ture over the top. Refrigerate overnight. Bake at 350° for 45 minutes. Let stand about 5 minutes before cutting. Serves 6. (For 8 people, use 3 slices of bread and 8 eggs.

Miss Vickie Hansen
Roughrider Polled Herefords Ranch
Ludden, North Dakota

CHEEZY BEEF TWIZZLER

2 lbs. ground beef
½ c. diced celery
½ c. diced green pepper
¼ c. diced onion
1 can (10-½ oz.) cream of
mushroom soup
½ c. water

2 c. Bisquick
10 oz. shredded mild cheddar cheese
5 stuffed green olives (sliced if desired)
1 egg, beaten
1 tbsp. water
½ can (5-½ oz.) cream of
mushroom soup

¼ c. milk

Lightly brown ground beef in large frying pan. Add celery, green pepper and onion; cook until beef is thoroughly browned and vegetables are tender. Pour off drippings. Stir in 1 can mushroom soup into beef mixture. Add ½ c. water to biscuit mix, stirring to form soft dough, then beat 20 strokes. Place dough on floured surface and roll into a 14 x 11" rectangle. Place on lightly greased baking sheet. Spoon beef mixture lengthwise down center of rectangle. Sprinkle with 5 oz. of shredded cheese and sprinkle with olive slices, if desired. Make cuts, 2" long, at 1" intervals on long sides of rectangle; fold sides over filling and pinch to seal along top. Mix egg and 1 tbsp. water; brush over dough. Bake in hot oven (425°) for 15 to 20 minutes or until lightly brown. Combine ½ can cream of mushroom soup, milk and remaining cheese; cook over medium heat, stirring occasionally, until hot. Serve over slices of "twizzler". Serves 8.

Background: This recipe was an original and won the North Dakota Beef Cookoff Contest in 1980.

Irene L. Dawson
Oak Coulee Ranch
17 mi. N.E. of Flasher, North Dakota

STEW BEEF CASSEROLE

2 or 3 lbs. stew meat, cut into cubes

ADD:

1 pkg. onion soup mix   *1 can mushroom soup*
2 tbsp. lemon juice on meat

Mix all above items in casserole. Cover and bake for 3 to 3-½ hours at 275°. Add package frozen mixed vegetables, ½ to ¾ hour before end of cooking time. Number of servings seems to depend on how hungry everyone is.

Background: My husband, Lyle L. Dawson Sr., born in Iowa, came to North Dakota with his parents in 1903, when he was 3 years old. The family lived in a sod house for 6 years, built by Simon Friesz who sold it to Mr. Dawson. In 1909 they built the 5 bedroom house in which I live. Angus Cattle were raised by Lyle and his father, John Dawson. Lyle died in June 1982. We celebrated our 50th anniversary in 1981 in Flasher. We have 4 children, 9 grandchildren, and 1 great grandchild.

Pat Seeley
Seeley Ranch
Halsey, Nebraska

BRANDING CASSEROLE

3 lbs. hamburger   *2 cans cream of chicken soup*
onion (diced)   *2 cans cream of cheese soup*
1 c. water   *2 cans cream of mushroom soup*
3 c. rice   *Grated sharp cheese*
Salt & pepper to taste

Brown hamburger and onion in large skillet. Cook rice in 3 cups of water until tender. Mix together rice, hamburger, onion and soups in large casserole dish. Sprinkle grated cheese over top. Bake one hour at 350°. Serves 25 people.

Background: This recipe is very easy and will serve a large group. The Seeley Ranch is located near Halsey, Nebraska and is a 4 generation Sandhills Ranch.

Mrs. Melvin (Violet) Utt
Riverside, Washington

MEAL-IN-A-FRYPAN

1 lb. ground beef	*2 (1 lb.) cans pork and beans*
2 tbsp. shortening	*1 tsp. salt*
2 tbsp. chopped onion	*¼ tsp. pepper*
1 (1 lb.) can whole tomatoes	*1 tsp. prepared mustard*

Brown beef in hot shortening in electric skillet, set at 380°. Stir in onion, tomatoes, beans and seasonings. Cover, reduce heat to 300°; simmer for 30 minutes, stirring occasionally to prevent scorching. Makes 6 servings.

Mrs. C. H. Wasser
Fort Collins, Colorado

LAYERED MEXICAN DIP

2 tbsp. butter or margarine	*1 can (no. 303) cream corn)*
½ c. chopped celery	*2 large eggs, beaten*
¼ c. chopped onion	*1 tsp. salt*
¼ c. chopped green pepper	*¼ tsp. pepper*
¼ c. chopped pimiento	*¼ tsp. dry mustard*
¼ c. chopped ripe olives	*½ tsp. chili powder*
½ c. grated parmesan cheese	

Saute celery, onion and green pepper in butter until onion and green pepper is transparent. Add remaining ingredients except cheese, mixing well. Sprinkle cheese on top. Bake, covered at 350° for 45 minutes. Makes 4 servings.

Background: I grew up in Southern Colorado among the mining camps and cattle ranching and their corn casserole was served at church and other gatherings in the community.

Bayne Grubb
Chambers, Nebraska

GI

GARBAGE CAN DINNER
(For a Very Large Crowd)

Layer 1—scraped carrots (whole)
Layer 2—unpeeled potatoes (whole)
Layer 3—onions (whole)

Layer 4—corn on the cob
Layer 5—cabbage wedges
*Layer 6—sliced and tied ham and/or
polish sausages*

In a new garbage can (30 gal.) or large restaurant cooking container: Place 2 inches of corn husks in bottom, add a grate. Then add at least 2 inches of boiling water. Place layers of vegetables and meat according to above sequence. Place on outdoor fire or grill and steam for 1-2 hours.

Background: This recipe was given to us from our friend, Dr. Helen Heitgard of Armidale, University, N.S. Wales, Australia.

Claire Ewing
SN Ranch
Claresholm, Alberta, Canada

SN SPECIAL

1-½ lb. lean ground beef
1-½ onions, chopped
1 tbsp. salad oil, or more
1 can (15 oz.) kidney beans, undrained
*1 can (16.oz.) solid pack tomatoes,
well drained*

3 oz. bottled taco sauce
3 tbsp. chile powder
1 can (4-½ oz.) sliced olives, drained
1 pkg. (4 oz.) shredded cheddar cheese
1 med. pkg. corn chips
shredded lettuce

2 c. commerical sour cream

In a large frying pan brown beef and onions in oil. Drain well. Add beans, tomato, taco sauce, chile powder, olives. Stir and simmer for 15 minutes uncovered. In the bottom of a 3 qt. casserole, put half meat mixture, sprinkle with half the cheese. Cover with corn chips. Repeat. If baking later, omit top layer of chips till before baking. Bake at 350°, covered, for 45 minutes. Don't forget the layer of chips. Let stand 5 minutes out of oven. Top with layer of lettuce and sour cream.

Background: This recipe has been in my "Favorite Recipe" book for years and seems to be a favorite of everyone who eats it! We had it often at the ranch for company or just every day.

Madeline Scholz
Tonasket, Washington

T

GROUND BEEF AND ZUCCHINI CASSEROLE

1-½ lbs. ground beef
1 medium zucchini, or more if needed
to cover ground beef
1 can mushroom soup

½ soup can water
1 small onion, chopped
1-½ c. grated cheese
salt & pepper to taste

Lightly brown ground beef and onion. Drain off fat. Layer beef and zucchini in a 12x7x2-inch dish. Cut zucchini in ¼" slices to cover the beef mixture. Pour mushroom soup and water over the layers. Top with grated cheese. Bake in 350° oven until zucchini is tender and cheese is melted.

Background: My father Dan Graham came here from Ontario, Canada in 1888 and homesteaded where we now live. Through the years he expanded the ranch until 1930. He then retired and my husband Bill Scholz and I continued to operate the ranch. We, too, expanded the operation. Our son Gerald worked with his Dad until 1976 when Bill passed away.

Gerald and I continue to operate the ranch, his son Gerald makes the 4th generation to be operating the ranch in 95 years.

The brand is one my father constructed from a wrench that was used to remove wagon wheels. It also served another purpose. It was used as a bolt (clevis pin) to fasten double trees on a wagon tongue.

Mrs. Sue Field
Kenya, Africa

MEALIE PIE

5 or 6 mealies (corn on the cob)
1 heaping tbsp. flour
1 pint milk

1 tbsp. butter
2 eggs
salt & pepper to taste

Cut the grains off the cob and put through the mincer. Mix flour and butter in a saucepan over a low heat.to a smooth paste and gradually add the milk and bring it to a boil. Remove from the heat and add the eggs (well-beaten), add the mealies, salt and pepper and pour into a baking dish and bake in the oven for ½ hour at 350°. Serve with stew. Serves 6.

Mrs. Gale Wolters
Springfield, Virginia

RICE-A-RONI CASSEROLE

1 Box Rice-A-Roni Mix	*4 green onions*
(Fried Rice with Almonds)	*1 can sliced water chestnuts*
1 4 oz. can mushrooms	*8 oz. frozen mixed vegetables*

Prepare Rice-A-Roni mix as directed. Cook frozen mixed vegetables and set aside. When Rice-A-Roni mix is nearly cooked, add rest of ingredients, cook a minute or two and serve. Any chopped meat may be added.

Myrtle Hendee
Bethesda, Maryland

TEXAS HASH

1 c. chopped onions	*1 c. cooked rice*
1 lb. ground meat (beef)	*1 tsp. chili powder*
1 #2 can tomatoes	*Salt & Pepper to taste*
1 c. green peppers, chopped	*1 c. celery, chopped*
½ c. tomato soup	*Cheese & crumbs topping*

Brown onions in bacon fat, and add meat. Cook until pink is gone. In the meantime, simmer tomatoes, pepper and celery until celery and pepper are tender. Combine meat, onions, rice, vegetables, chili powder, salt and pepper. Bake in shallow casserole, 350° for one hour.

TEXAS HASH FOR 100

8½ lbs. ground beef	*3½ chopped onions*
10 # 2 cans tomatoes	*5 chopped green peppers*
1 large bunch of celery	*20 c. cooked rice*
10 tsp. chili powder	*Salt & pepper to taste*

Brown onions in bacon fat; add meat and cook until pink is gone. Simmer tomatoes, rice, pepper, celery and chili powder until celery and pepper are tender. Add meat and onions. Season and bake at 350° for one hour.

District 2 Cowbelles
North Dakota

BEEF AND BROCCOLI BAKE

2 lbs. ground beef	1 8 oz. can tomato sauce
2 med. onions, chopped	1 6 oz. can tomato paste
1 clove garlic, minced	½ c. sour cream
1 10 oz. pkg. frozen broccoli	1 8 oz. pkg. spiral macaroni
1 1.5 oz pkg. spaghetti sauce mix	4 oz. grated American cheese
½ c. soft bread crumbs	¼ c. salad oil
2 eggs, beaten	½ tsp. salt
1 3 oz. can mushrooms & juice	¼ tsp. pepper

Brown beef, onion and garlic. Prepare broccoli and save liquid. Add spaghetti mix to meat, plus tomato sauce, paste, mushrooms and liquid from broccoli. Simmer. Cook and drain macaroni. Beat eggs, bread, cheese, broccoli and oil—stir into macaroni and spread in 9x13 inch pan. Put sour cream over top. Top with meat sauce and some Parmesan cheese. Bake 30 minutes at 350°. Serves 12 to 15.

Background: This recipe was originated by our district Cowbelles for the 1981 Pastaville.

District 2 CowBelles

BEEF KLUSKI

2 lbs. ground beef	1 c. American Cheddar cheese
1 tsp. salt	¼ tsp. cumin (spice)
½ tsp. pepper	¼ tsp. basil
1 8-oz. pkg. Kluski noodles	1 tbsp. green pepper
1 10-oz. pkg. frozen broccoli	4-oz. can mushrooms
1 3-oz. can French fried onions	1 10-oz. cream of chicken soup
1 c. Cottage cheese	

Brown and drain beef and spices. Cook and drain noodles. Cook broccoli and reserve liquid. Mix all remaining ingredients together. Put into a greased 9x13 inch baking dish. Sprinkle grated cheese over top. Bake at 350° for 30 minutes. Serves 12 to 15.

Background: This recipe was developed to use at Pastaville USA in 1982. It tied for first place in a recipe contest using Beef and Pasta.

Virginia Jackson
Harrison, Montana

♡

HOT SPAGHETTI

⅜ cup onion or
2 tbsp. dried minced onion
2¼ c. uncooked macaroni

4 slices bacon, cut up
Black pepper
1 15-oz. can tomato sauce

In medium or large sauce pan, fry bacon and onion until crisp. If using dried minced onion, add after bacon is crisp or it will burn. Drain most of the fat off, add tomato sauce and at least 1 tsp. black pepper; add more pepper for hotter flavor. Simmer 10-15 minutes. Cook macaroni in salted water, drain and add sauce to it. Instead of bacon, side pork or even hamburger can be used. If you like lots of pepper, tastes great with cold beer!

Kay Hussa
Hussa Ranch
Cedarville, California

38

AUNT MAY'S LASAGNA

1 c. ripe olives
1 lb. ground lean beef
¼ c. olive oil
1 c. chopped onion
2 cloves garlic, minced
1 #2½ can tomatoes
2 6-oz. cans tomato paste

1 tsp. dried basil
½ tsp. dried oregano
¼ tsp. black pepper
½ bay leaf
1 8-oz. pkg. lasagna
½ lb. Mozzarella cheese
½ c. grated Parmesan cheese

2 tsp. salt

Cut olives in large pieces and set aside. Brown beef in hot olive oil. Add onion and garlic; cook until transparent. Add tomatoes, tomato paste, salt, basil, oregano, pepper and bay leaf. Cover and simmer 1 hour, or until sauce is thickened. Stir in olives. Meanwhile cook the lasagna in boiling salted water,m about 20 minutes. Drain. Slice Mozzarella cheese. In a shallow baking dish, about 7x12x2 inches, spread about ¼ sauce. Cover with a layer of lasagna, arranging strips lengthwise of the dish. Add layer of Mozzarella cheese, using about ⅓ of the cheese, then layer of Parmesan cheese. Repeat layers ending with sauce and cheeses. Bake ½ hour at about 350°. Serves 8-10 people. This sauce freezes well, as does the whole casserole. This is a terrific dish to have on hand when unexpected company drops in.

Ann Gates
Corvallis, Oregon

DREAMY CASSEROLE DELIGHT

1 7-oz pkg. spaghetti	COMBINE:
1 tbsp. butter	½ lb. cottage cheese
1½ lb. ground beef	1 8-oz. pkg. cream cheese, softened
Salt & pepper to taste	¼ c. sour cream
1 8-oz. cans tomato sauce	⅓ c. chopped scallions (green onions)
	1 tbsp. minced green pepper

Cook spaghetti, pour melted butter over spaghetti. Brown meat, add tomato sauce, salt and pepper. Spread ½ spaghetti in 8 cup casserole. Add cheese combination on top. Add remainder of spaghetti ending with the remaining meat on top. Bake 45 minutes at 350°.

Mrs. Don (Diane) Fancher
Pilot Wheel Ranch
Tonasket, Washington

BAKED LASAGNA

¼ c. olive oil	½ soup can of water
1 small onion, chopped	3 tbsp. grated Cheddar cheese
½ tsp. minced garlic	2 lbs. hamburger
⅓ tsp. basil leaves	Salt & pepper
1 tbsp. dried parsley	1 pkg. lasagna noodles, cooked
1 pt. canned tomatoes	Approx. ¾ each of Swiss and
1 can tomato soup	Cheddar cheese, grated

Lightly saute onions in olive oil. Add hamburger, salt & pepper and cook until brown, drain off excess fat. Add tomatoes, soup, water, 3 tablespoons grated cheese, spices, and small can of mushrooms if desired. Mix well and simmer for ½ hour. Cook noodles while sauce is simmering. When noodles are tender and sauce is cooked, layer noodles, sauce, and cheeses, alternately, in a large flat baking dish. Bake at 350° for ½ to ¾ hour, or until lasagna is bubbling and cheeses are melted.

Background: The Pilot Wheel Ranch has been in the Fancher family through four generations. The Ranch, at present is located southeast of Tonasket, Washington in the Aeneas Valley. Robert M. Fancher homesteaded in 1910, near Tonasket, moving the ranch headquarters, in 1912 to the Antonine Creek area.

Edi Ann Otto
Otto Ranch
near Osnabrock, North Dakota

PIZZA HOT DISH

1½ lb. ground beef	2 c. macaroni
1 cans tomato soup	8 oz. Mozzarella cheese
	6 oz. American or Cheddar cheese

Brown and drain beef. Add soup and American or Cheddar cheese. Turn heat to medium and melt cheese in mixture. Boil and drain macaroni. Add to hamburger mixture. Pour into a square baking dish and top with Mozzarella cheese. Bake ½ hour at 350°. Let stand 5 minutes before serving.

Myrtle Hendee
Bethesda, Maryland

SLUM GULLION

2 lbs. lean ground beef	1 can (8½ oz.) green peas or
1 large onion, thinly sliced	frozen peas
1 can (15 oz.) spaghetti sauce	Garlic salt and pepper to taste
1 can (2½ lbs.) tomatoes	2 large potatoes, peeled and sliced
paprika to taste	2 tbsp. butter

Line bottom of casserole with ground beef. Add onion, spaghetti, tomatoes and peas in layers, seasoning each with garlic salt and pepper. Cover with potato slices. Shake on paprika to taste and dot with butter. Cover casserole and bake in oven at 325° for 1½ hours. Remove cover for final 15 minutes to brown top of potatoes.

John and Denzil Mills
Charleville, Queensland, Australia

AUSTRALIAN MEAT PIE

PIE BASE:
1 c. plain flour
½ tsp. salt
⅓ c. water
30 g (1 oz.) beef dripping

PIE TOP:
375 g (12 oz) packaged puff pastry
1 egg yolk
1 tsp. water

FILLING:
500 g (1 lb.) minced steak
2 beef stock cubes
Salt & pepper
1½ c water
½ tsp. nutmeg
2 tbsp. plain flour
1½ c. water, extra
3 tsp. soy sauce

BASE: Sift flour and salt into basin. Place water and dripping on stove until melted. Remove from heat. Make a well in centre of dry ingredients, add hot liquid, stir until combined. Turn out on lightly-floured surface, knead lightly. Roll out pastry to line 20 cm (8 in.) pie plate. Fill centre with cold meat filling.

FILLING: Place meat in pan, stir over low heat unti it is well browned. Drain off any surplus fat. Add crumbled stock cubes, water, salt, pepper and nutmeg, stir until boiling, reduce heat, cover, simmer gently 30 minutes; remove from heat. Add flour to extra water, stir until flour mixture is smooth. Add flour mixture to meat, stir until it boils and thickens. Add soy sauce; remove from heat, allow to become cold.

PIE TOP: Roll out puff pastry on lightly-floured board, brush edges of pie with combined egg yolk and wter, place puff pastry over top of pie, press edges together firmly, trim and flake. Brush top of pie with combined egg-yolk and water, make 2 slits in top. Bake in hot oven 10 minutes or until golden brown, reduce heat to moderate, cook further 15 to 20 minutes.

Clermont Branch

Mrs. Ed (Carol) Harrell
Harrell Ranch
Armstrong County, Texas

BEEF NOODLE CASSEROLE

8 oz. fine noodles	1 can cream of mushroom soup
3 tbsp. butter	1¼ c. milk
1 c. chopped onion	¼ c. soy sauce
2 lbs. ground beef	8 oz. sharp cheddar cheese, shredded
1 4-oz. can mushrooms	1 5 oz. can Chow Mein noodles
¼ lb. salted mixed nuts	

Cook noodles according to package directions. Drain and set aside. Cook onions in butter until tender. Crumble ground beef and cook until lightly brown; drain off excess grease. Mix onions, beef, mushrooms, soup, milk and soy sauce. Gently stir in cooked noodles. Pour mixture in 9x13 inch baking dish. Top with shredded cheese. Heat in 350° oven for 15 minutes until cheese melts. Top with chow mein noodles and salted nuts. Return to oven for another 10 minutes until noodles and nuts are lightly toasted. Serves 8-12.

Background: The site of Charles Goodnight's "Old Home Ranch" in the Palo Duro Canyon is on our ranch. Established in 1876, this was the first permanent white settlement in the Panhandle of Texas. Today we use the Palo Duro Canyon as winter range for our cattle. It is also home to auodad sheep, imported from Africa, and native deer, turkey and quail.

V. Heinemann
Australia

TASTY RISSOLES

1 lb. mince	2 tbsp. Worchestershire sauce
1 large onion	2 tbsp. tomato sauce
1 medium carrot	1 egg, beaten

Dice onions, grate carrot, bind all together, add salt and pepper to taste. Form into balls and roll in plain flour, then beaten egg and milk mixed and lastly breadcrumbs. Deep fry.

Historic Range Recipe

BASQUE SHEPHERD'S PIE

4 slices bacon	¾ tsp. salt
3 med. potatoes	⅛ tsp. dried thyme, crushed
2 tbsp. sliced green onions, with tops	Dash pepper
1 tbsp. finely snipped parsley	4 eggs
2 tbsp. milk	

In 8-inch skillet cook bacon till crisp; drain, reserving 2 tablespoons of the drippings. Crumble bacon and set aside. In same skillet combine reserved drippings, peeled, thinly sliced potatoes, onion, parsley, salt, thyme, and pepper. Cover tightly; cook over low heat till potatoes are barely tender, 20 to 25 minutes, stirring carefully once or twice. In small bowl beat together eggs and milk; pour over potato mixture. Cover and continue cooking over very low heat till egg is set in center, 8 to 10 minutes. With a wide spatula, loosen sides and bottom and slide potatoes out onto serving plate. (Or, serve from skillet.) Sprinkle crumbled bacon atop. Serve at once. Makes 4 servings.

Mrs. Bob (Nancy) Barnes
Ellis-Barnes Livestock Ranch
Tonasket, Washington

PIZZA CASSEROLE

1½ lbs. hamburger	1 tsp. salt
1 med. onion, chopped	1 15½-oz. jar pizza sauce
¼ c. chopped green pepper (opt.)	1 pkg. pepperoni slices
2 c. noodles	1 16-oz. pkg Mozzarella cheese, grated

Brown hamburger, onion and add green pepper. Season with salt and pepper. Boil noodles with 1 tsp. salt. Mix hamburger, noodles and pizza sauce. Layer in casserole: 1st layer—hamburger/noodle mixture; 2nd layer—pepperoni slices; 3rd layer—cheese. Heat thru til hot and bubbly. Serves 6.

Background: We are partners in the Ellis-Barnes Livestock Company with Bob's parents, aunt, uncle and cousin. The Lazy Spade brand is our own, not the ranch's. The ranch was originally started by William A. Barnes in 1924. We are the third generation to be involved in the ranch. The main ranch headquarters is located in the Whitestone Creek and Whisky Creek areas northwest of Tonasket, Washington.

Diane Palmer
Offham Station,
Charleville, Australia

OFFHAM MULLIGAN MEAT DISH

1 packet noodles	*minced mutton or beef*
2 large white onions	*5 cloves garlic*
¼ tsp. cayenne pepper	*1 tin tomato soup*
2 tins anchovies	*¾ lb. grated cheese*
Salt	*1 tin champignons*

Parsley

Fry chopped onion and garlic in oil, add minced meat, browning well. Then add anchovies, champignons, pepper, salt, parsley, and tomato soup. Finally, add most of the grated cheese, leaving enough to sprinkle over the top of the completed dish. Add noodles which have been cooked in salted water until tender, then drained. Mix into meat well, sprinkle with remaining cheese. Place in 350° oven for 30 minutes.

RONALD REAGAN'S FAVORITE
MACARONI AND CHEESE

½ lb. macaroni	*1 tsp.dry mustard*
1 tsp. butter	*3 c. grated cheese, sharp*
1 egg, beaten	*1 c. milk*
1 tsp. salt	

Boil macaroni in water until tender and drain thoroughly. Stir in butter and egg. Mix mustard and salt with 1 tablespoon hot water and add to milk. Add cheese leaving enough to sprinkle on top. Pour into buttered casserole, add milk, sprinkle with cheese. Bake at 350° for about 45 minutes or until custard is set and top is crusty.

Jerry and Libby Toman
TT Ranch
Little Fort, British Columbia

DUMPLINGS & SWEET AND SOUR CABBAGE
(Served with Pork Roast)

DUMPLINGS:

3 c. flour
1 c. Semolina or Cream of wheat
1 tsp. baking powder
1 c. milk

2 tbsp. butter
1 tsp. salt
2 eggs, separated
2 c. fried bread cubes

SWEET & SOUR CABBAGE

1 cabbage, shredded med. to fine
¼ c. lemon juice or wine vinegar

1 large onion, chopped
¼ c. sugar

2 tbsp. caraway seed

DUMPLINGS: Sift dry ingredients. Heat milk to melt butter in it. Cool, add egg yolks. Add to dry mixture to form stiff dough. Add bread cubes and whipped egg white. Form into two large dumplings (log shaped) and let rest one hour. Boil in salted water for about 20 minutes, until toothpick inserted comes out clean. Slice and serve with gravy from your pork roast.

CABBAGE: Fry onion in some bacon fat until transparent. Add cabbage and cover with a lid, stirring frequently until tender. Add lemon juice and sugar to taste (amounts vary according to size of cabbage) and caraway seed and simmer for one hour. This is better made one day before.

Background: Jerry is originally from Czechoslovakia and this is virtually the Czech National Dish. It is traditionally accompanied by lots of cold beer!

BARBECUE SAUCE

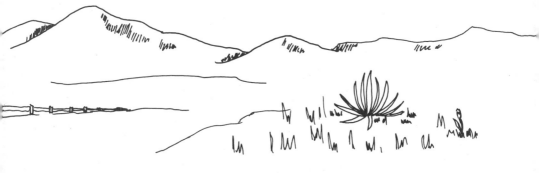

THE BASIC CATCHES
FOR BRINGING IN BEEF

The most common ways of roping was head and heel catches. For a calf, one was enough, but with a steer, cowboys may team up and use both. Here the lead cowboy makes an overhand toss for the horns.

Pulling the loop tight around the steers horns, the lead cowboy reins in his pony. Another cowhand then rides up behind to make a heel catch, using a sidearm cast to slip the rope under the animal's hind leg.

The second cowboy secures the heel catch by pulling his rope up and back to take up the slack and draw the loop tight. Often, depending on the speed of this maneuver, the heel catch may snare only one of the steer's legs.

While the lead roper rides ahead slowly the second cowboy stops his pony so that the steer is stretched out and topples over. If only one leg has been caught, a cowboy on foot must throw the steer to the ground.

Once the steer is down, other hands can move in to brand it. The riders can even dismount and do the work themselves, leaving their ropes tied to saddle horns while the ponies lean back to hold them taut.

SRM SOCIETY FOR RANGE MANAGEMENT

The Four Sixes Ranch
Guthrie, Texas

6666

LONE STAR STEAK SAUCE

½ c. butter
2 tbsp. worcestershire sauce
¾ tsp. black pepper
2 drops Tabasco

⅓ c. lemon juice
1 small clove garlic, minced
½ tsp. dry mustard
Salt to taste

Combine all ingredients; heat until butter melts. Broiler pan juices may be added. Serve with Salt Steak.

Background: Some Texans claim this steak sauce is good enough to bring out the flavor in any meat — even wild coyote.

Virginia L. Jackson
Harrison, Montana

ALL PURPOSE BARBECUE SAUCE

¼ c. salad oil
2 tbsp. soy sauce

¼ c. bourbon, sherry or wine
1 tsp. garlic powder

Freshly ground black pepper

Combine ingredients and pour over meat. Marinate in refrigerator. Also use to baste meat as you cook it. Good on red meat, fish or chicken.

Myrtle Hendee
Bethesda, Maryland

BARBECUE SAUCE

¾ c. chopped onion
¾ c. tomato catsup
⅓ c. lemon juice
3 tbsp. worcestershire sauce
2 tsp. salt

½ c. salad oil
¾ c. water
3 tbsp. sugar
2 tbsp. prepared mustard
½ tsp. pepper

Cook onion until soft in oil. Add remaining ingredients. Simmer 15 min. Good for steak, chicken or other barbecue favorites

Sam H. Coleman
Fredericksburg, Texas

BARBECUE SAUCE — TEXAS

Juice from 12 lemons
1 c. catsup
¼ c. worcestershire sauce
¼ c. chili sauce
1 tbsp. black pepper
Optional: ¼ c. brown sugar
and onion juice

½ c. salt
2 or 3 tbsp. prepared mustard or
2 tbsp. dry mustard
1 tsp. chili powder
1 lb. margarine, salad oil, or butter
1 lb suet fat
(or 2 lb. margarine, salad oil, or butter)

Combine ingredients and allow to simmer until thoroughly blended. If desired, chill sauce until grease has solidified, then stir so as to distribute bits of grease throughout sauce. This permits sauce to be used as a spread on meat while barbecuing. It can be used in oven on meats, however it is best to apply sauce toward end of cooking to avoid scorching from the tomato ingredients. It is also a good condiment for frijoles and other foods. It has long refrigerator life. Will serve 20 lbs. ribs or 40 lbs. steak.

Background: This recipe was used by the Texas A&M Range Club at their first annual outdoor club activity in 1948. The recipe was given to the club by Omer E. Sperry, SRM Charter member and charter range professor at TAMU.

Dick Rhea

PIT BARBECUE SPICE MIXTURE

1 pkg. (7½ lbs.) Morton's Sugar Cure
2 oz. garlic powder
4 oz. black pepper

8 oz. chili powder
4 oz. onion powder

Rub into meat surface, removing excess. Wrap in butcher paper (not plastic coated), cheese cloth or foil. Re-wrap in burlap, tie with wire, make sure burlap covering is at least two layers thick over entire package. Soak packages in water, put in pit.

H.F. Heady
Berkley, California

BARBECUE SAUCE — CALIFORNIA

¼ lb. butter
⅓ c. catsup
Dash tabasco
½ tsp. garlic powder
1 tsp. horseradish

½ c. worcestershire sauce
Dash Liquid Smoke
Juice of 2 lemons
1 tsp. salt
½ tsp. mustard

Mix all together and bring to a boil. Brush on any barbecuing meat. Left over keeps in refrigerator.

Mrs. Joe Rogers
Caddo, Texas

HART'S BARBECUE SAUCE

1 gal. apple vinegar
8 oz. bottle french dressing
6 lemons
1 tbsp. black pepper

2 lb. light brown sugar
10 oz. worcestershire sauce
3 tbsp. salt
1 stick margarine

Mix ingredients together and stir over medium heat until desired thickness is attained.

Guy Goen & Sons
Goen Ranch
Dickens County, Texas

GOEN RANCH BARBECUE SAUCE

1 gal. worcestershire sauce
1 gal. catsup
½ pint vinegar
1 box corn starch
3 c. paprika
6 6-oz. cans coca-cola
¾ c. chili powder

1 gal. mustard
1 gal. barbecue sauce (prepared)
½ pint lemon juice
3 c. ground cumino
½ gal syrup
8 c. sugar
½ c. black pepper

Mix together and put it on thick. Better than this, pour sauce in pan, add meat and let sit for a while.

Background: I invented this sauce myself and have fed thousands of people with it, and it has really gone over great. Don't be afraid to try it. Be sure you get enough on your meat!

The Four Sixes Ranch
Guthrie, Texas

6666

BLACK NIGHT BARBECUE SAUCE

1½ c. worcestershire sauce
1 c. catsup
¼ c. lemon juice
1 tbsp salt

1 c strong black coffee
½ c. butter
2 tbsp. sugar
2 tsp. cayenne pepper

Combine ingredients. Simmer 30 min. over low heat, stirring occasionally. Serve with beef or ribs.

Recipe Notes

BARBECUE MEATS

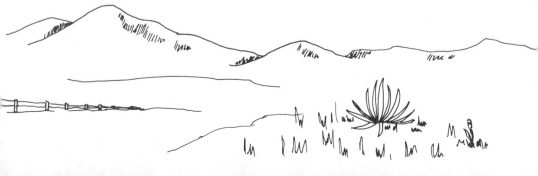

THE ANATOMY OF THE
CHUCK WAGON

The mother ship for trail drives was a broad-beamed, sturdily built vehicle that carried virtually everything 10 men might need on a prairie voyage lasting as long as five months. Credit for the ultimate design of the wagon belongs to cattle baron Charles Goodnight, who in 1866 rebuilt for his trail crew a surplus Army wagon, picked primarily for its extra-durable iron axles. To the basic wagon bed, where bulk goods such as foodstuffs and bedrolls were to be stored, Goodnight added three already customary traildrive appendages: on one side a water barrel big enough to hold two days' supply of water; on the other a heavy tool box; and on top bentwood bows to accommodate a canvas covering for protection against sun and rain.

But the innovation that made the Goodnight wagon unique at the time, and a useful prototype for all self-respecting wagons that followed, was the design and installation of a chuck box. Perched at the rear of the wagon, facing aft, it had a hinged lid that let down onto a swinging leg to form a worktable (*side view, below*). Like a Victorian desk, the box was honeycombed with drawers and cubbyholes (*rear view*). Here — and in the boot beneath — the cook stored his utensils and whatever food he might need during the day. A typical arrangement is shown on these pages, with the most convenient of the niches occupied by the coffeepot and the whiskey bottle, the latter being in the cook's sole charge as medicine (to which cooks were known to be especially partial). Above them is the so-called "possible drawer," a combination first-aid kit and catchall, containing everything from calomel to sewing needles. The design of Goodnight's wagon proved so practical that cattle outfits all over the West imitated it, using redesigned farm wagons and Army vehicles. Inevitably the idea went commercial and became a standard item produced by major wagon builders, including the famous Studebaker Company, which sold chuck wagons for $75 to $100.

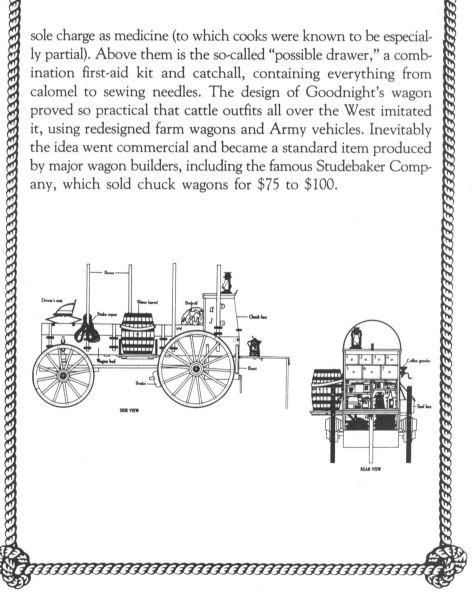

SIDE VIEW

REAR VIEW

H. Dee Galt
Vancouver, Washington

BARBECUE — DAKOTA STYLE

Any barbecue sauce preferred by chef
Garlic cloves (buds) 3 or 4 per roast   *Black pepper*
Roast beef or brisket   *Ham or turkey is good, as well*

Dig a pit about 4 x 6 x 4 feet deep. Fill hole with dried hardwood and allow to burn down to coals. Immediately follow with a second filling and allow to burn down to coals a second time. After meat is prepared as follows and wrapped, it is placed on top of the coals and the pit is filled with soil.

The size of roast is usually about 10–12 lbs. A person could cook as many as six roasts of this size in the pit described. Sprinkle meat with pepper. Cover generously with barbecue sauce. Make a small cut in meat and stick in several garlic cloves as preferred. Wrap meat in butcher paper. Then wrap in a piece of burlap.

Background: This method of cooking is known over the west. Mr. Walter Nevans, Bismark, N.D. has prepared many barbecues this way. He cooks annually for members of the Bismark 200 as well as for other groups. At the Bismark Bicentenniel Celebration several thousand people were served this barbecue. Mr. Nevans owns and operates a western wear store near the SCS state office in Bismarck, across the street from the American Legion.

Bettejoe R. Pendleton
R Bar Ranch
Caddo, Texas

Janet Holcombe
Holcombe Ranch
Bowring, Oklahoma

Sue Shiflet
Springfield, Virginia

Dora Kittredge
Prescott, Arizona

BRISKET A LA TEXAS

5-6 lb. beef brisket
Celery salt
Garlic salt
½ bottle Worchestershire sauce

Salt & pepper
Onion salt
½ bottle Liquid Smoke
Barbeque Sauce

Season brisket with salt & pepper, celery salt, onion salt, and garlic salt. Place in glass baking dish and soak with ½ bottle each — Liquid Smoke and Worchestershire sauce. Seal with foil (Liquid Smoke may cause metallic taste if foil touches meat). Bake covered at 275° for 5 or 6 hours. The last hour put 6 oz. of barbecue sauce over meat, cover and return to oven for 1 more hour. Cool, slice and reheat in foil. (Slices best when cool.)

Diane Fancher
Pilot Wheel Ranch
Tonasket, Washington

OVEN BAR-B-QUE BEEF AND BEANS
Washington Style

2 lbs. hamburger
1 can pork and bead (31 oz. size)
1 can kidney beans (15 oz.)
1 c. brown sugar

Salt & pepper
1 can garbanzo beans (15 oz.)
1 med. onion, sliced
½ c. hickory smoke flavor bar-b-q sauce

Heat oven to 350°. Brown hamburger, adding salt & pepper to taste. Mix hamburger, beans, sliced onions, brown sugar and bar-b-q sauce in large casserole dish or baking dish. Bake at 350° for 1 to 1½ hours, until onions are tender.

Alice L. Eider
North Dakota

NO-FRY BARBEQUE BEEF MEAT BALLS

3 lbs. lean ground beef
10 strips beef bacon
12 soda crackers, crushed
2 slices bread, torn into crumbs
½ c. onion, finely chopped
2 eggs, slightly beaten
½ c. milk
1 tbsp. soy sauce

1 tsp. salt
½ tsp. pepper
4-oz. can mushrooms, drained & chopped
2½-oz. Cheddar or American cheese
2 cans tomato soup
2½ c. brown sugar
¾ c. white vinegar
2 tsp. dry mustard

Cut cheese into ¼ in. cubes. Place ground beef in large bowl. Fry beef bacon until crisp; drain. Place in blender and blend until finely chopped. Add bacon, crackers, bread crumbs, onion, eggs, milk, soy sauce, salt and pepper to ground beef; mix well. Using portion of mixture about the size of large walnut, flatten in hand and top with a cheese cube: shape into a ball around cheese. Place balls in single layer in 13x9 inch baking dish. Bake at 350° for 15 minutes. Pour off drippings. Meanwhile, combine tomato soup, brown sugar, vinegar, dry mustard and soy sauce in mixing bowl. Pour sauce over meat balls. Cover with foil, leaving vent for steam to escape, and continue baking 30 min., uncovering during last 15 to 20 min. To serve as hors d'oeuvres, place in chafing dish and garnish with parsley. To serve as main dish place meat balls on bed of rice and garnish with parsley or orange slices. Yield: about 60 meat balls, or 8 to 10 servings.

Marvel Quilliam
Y Lazy T Ranch
Kildeer, North Dakota

Y-1

BARBECUE BEEF AND BEANS - North Dakota Style

1 lb. ground beef
1 tall can B&M baked beans
1 tsp. prepared mustard
1 tsp. salt

1 medium onion, diced
1 large can tomatoes, drained
⅔ cup brown sugar

Brown beef in frying pan and drain off fat. Mix all ingredients together and bake for 2 hours in a medium oven. Serves 15 to 20 people. Good for branders or a bunch of hungry people.

Background: Marvel lived on the Y-1 Ranch for 30 years and is now retired and lives in Killdeer, North Dakota.

BBQ MEATBALLS

1 can evaporated milk
2 lb. hamburger
2 eggs
2 c. quick oatmeal
1 c. onion, minced
½ tsp. pepper

Sauce:
2 c. catsup
1½ c. brown sugar
2 tbsp. Liquid Smoke
2 tsp. salt

Mix and make 72 walnut sized balls (any larger and sauce won't cook through). Place in flat pan in single layer. Mix sauce over low heat and pour over meatballs. Bake at 350° for one hour. These freeze well before or after baking.

Helen Brooks
51 Ranch, Bloody Basin
Yavapa County, Arizona

BAR-B-QUED ROUND STEAK

1 round steak
2 c. water
1 tbsp. Worcestershire sauce
1 tbsp. wine vinegar
Diced chili peppers, if desired

1 can tomato sauce or whole tomatoes
½ tsp. mustard
¼ c. molasses
Chopped onion
Salt & pepper to taste

Brown steak and add above ingredients. Simmer 1 hour.

Background: The recipe came from Blue River Cowbelles, Mrs. Bill (Elaine) Marsk, Blue Az. in approximately 1955. Original recipe was for barbequed ribs, but we prefer it with steak.

Mrs. John F. Hughes
Hughes Ranch

BAR-B-QUE FLANK STEAK

2 flank steaks (not scored or tenderized)
2 tbsp. dry sherry
2 tbsp. worcestershire sauce
1 tsp. salt

2 tsp. monosodium glutamate
1 tbsp. sugar
1 tbsp. honey

Prick steaks with fork on both sides. Marinate all day, turning often. Cook over charcoal 3 to 4 minutes on one side and 2 minutes on second side. Slice thinly at an angle. Serves 4 to 6.

Background: Men are crazy about this recipe. In fact, it is the favorite of my son, husband, and two son-in-laws. Very unusual flavor.

Hawley & Barbara Jernigan
Seven Jay Ranch
Mullin, Texas

J

PAPA'S BARBECUE GOAT (OR BARBADO), TEXAS STYLE

20 lbs goat or barbado	Barbecue Sauce
1 c. salt	2 c. sugar (to taste)
1 dry jalapeno (ground)	1 c. prepared mustard
1 tbsp. black peper	½ c. apple cider vinegar
1 tsp. cumin (approx.)	1 tsp. salt
	1 tsp. black pepper

Mix salt, jalapeno, black pepper and cumin. Sprinkle meat generously. Cook slowly on grill 2 hours (or less depending on cut of meat). Be sure meat is well above fire (at least 20 to 24 inches). Meat may be brushed with cooking oil occasionally to prevent dryness. While meat cooks prepare sauce.

At least 30 min. before removing from fire; brush meat with sauce so it will "set". Continue cooking and turn the meat often, brushing on sauce at every turn.

Background: This was originated by Malcolm Jernigan, Sr. a rancher from the "Hill Country" of central Texas, which is a major sheep and goat producing area, famous for barbecue goat, barbado and lamb. Mr. Jernigan was called "Papa" as is Hawley, therefore the name of the recipe.

Willis & Betty Orr
Lakeside, Nebraska

⅃ち

BAR-B-CUE BEEF RIBS

3 lbs. of meaty short ribs	2 large onions, chopped
1 tsp. salt	1 c. catsup
1 tbsp. worcestershire sauce	1 tsp. dry mustard
1 c. water	½ c. chopped celery

Combine ingredients to make sauce. A dash of tabasco sauce may be added if desired. Season ribs with salt & pepper. Place flat in greased 9x13 inch pan and spoon on sauce. Bake at 300° for about 2 hours.

Background: The L-lazy-S brand has been in use by the Orr Ranch for well over 60 years. For the past 15 years we have owned this brand on the whole animal (both sides and in all positions).

Mrs. Neil Hamilton
Dickinson, North Dakota

BARBEQUED POT ROAST

3–4 lb. beef arm or blade pot roast	3 tbsp. lard or drippings
¼ tsp. pepper	1 tsp. salt
½ c. catsup	½ c. water
1 tbsp. vinegar	1 tbsp. brown sugar
2 tbsp. lemon juice	1 tbsp. worcestershire cause
½ tsp. salt	1 med. onion, sliced

Brown pot roast in lard or drippings. Season with pepper and 1 tsp. salt. Mix remaining ingredients and add to meat. Cover tightly and cook slowly 3½ to 4 hours or until tender. Thicken liquid or gravy. 6 to 8 servings.

Background: This recipe has been in the family for many years and is great to serve for any occasion. The contributor owns a grain farm at Cortenay, North Dakota and is a member of The North Dakota Cowbelles and National North Dakota Beef Assoc., and is their Cook-Off Chairperson.

Mrs. Richard M. Tokach
Tokach Angus Ranch
St. Anthony, North Dakota

BEEF BARBECUE SANDWICH

1 c. chopped onion	2 tbsp. butter
4 lbs. hamburger	1 32 oz. bottle catsup
1 c. water	½ c. celery or green pepper
¼ c. lemon juice	1 tbsp. worcestershire sauce
1 tbsp. salt	2 tsp. vinegar
1 tsp. flavor enhancer	½ tsp. dry mustard

Saute onion in butter. Add hamburger and brown slightly. Drain off fat. Add remaining ingredients and simmer for thirty minutes. This will easily serve fifty people on a ranch size hamburger bun. It can be made up, kept in the refrigerator or frozen. Easily reheated in a microwave oven.

Background: This recipe was used to feed a large group of 4–H members when I came to this farm as a young bride. Now, my children are nearly through their years in 4–H and FFA and I still use it for Homemakers or large gatherings. It was given to me by my Mother-In-Law who was a 4–H Leader for 32 years.

SRM **SOCIETY FOR RANGE MANAGEMENT**

Barbara Michieli

BARBECUE RIBS

4 lbs. spareribs, cut into serving size pieces
1 c. brown sugar   ½ c. chili sauce
¼ c. catsup   ¼ c. dark rum
¼ c. soy sauce   ¼ c. worcestershire sauce
1 tsp. dry mustard   2 cloves garlic, crushed
                  Dash of pepper

Wrap ribs in double thickness of foil and bake for 1½ hours at 350°. Unwrap and drain drippings. Combine ingredients and pour over ribs. Marinate at room temperature for 1 hour. Bake at 350° 30 min. basting with sauce, or grill 30 min., 4 inches above coals turning and basting.

RECIPE FOR HAPPINESS

2 heaping cups of patience
2 handfuls of generosity
1 heart full of love
Dash of laughter
1 head full of understanding

Sprinkle generously with kindness. Add plenty of faith. Mix well. Spread over a period of a lifetime and serve everybody you meet.

The Four Sixes Ranch
Guthrie, Texas

6666

7-RIB CUT

Select a standing rib roast, well marbled with fat. Allow at least ½ lb. per person. Trim off excess fat. Spit the roast on diagonal for best balance; insert meat thermometer. Cook roast to 125° on thermometer. Remember meat will cook as long as 20 min. after removal from fire or oven. Let meat rest before carving so juices can settle. If you prefer it more well done, cook longer but give the temperature 15°–20° to rise while waiting to be carved.

"Barbecue these ribs on a windy day and half the next county will be standing in line."

Dennis Swisher
Jordan Valley, Oregon

PIT BARBECUE FOR 500 TO 600 PERSONS

The Pit: With backhoe dig pit 6 ft. deep and 12 ft. long. One cattle truck load of mountain mahogany, oak or any of the harder woods. Must be dry. Feed the load of wood into the pit in three hours. Allow 2½ hours to burn down to coals. This makes about two and one half feet of coals.

The Meat: Use 400 lbs. of roasts, rolled chuck or rump. Each should weigh about 15 lbs. Place 2 or 3 cloves of garlic in each roast, or put three peeled onions in each bundle. Cover meat with mixture of barbecue sauce and sugar cure. Wrap two roasts in cheese cloth. Use the tubular type used to wrap deer after it has been skinned. Wrap this in aluminum foil. Wrap in wet burlap. Tie with iron wire, making a loop on top of bundle to hook into in lowering and raising beef from the pit. Place a little sand with shovel under each bundle, on the coals. Be quick placing beef on coals and covering it up. Across top of pit place steel fence posts every two feet. Cover this with steel sheeting. Cover airtight with dirt. Cook 17 to 18 hours. The pit, meat and sauce may be added to or cut down to fit any occasion.

The Sauce:

6 gals. tomato sauce	*1 qt. molasses*
20 lbs. onions, ground fine	*2 tbsp. dry mustard*
1 bottle worcestershire sauce	*Cumin*
Vinegar and brown sugar until you get a sweet and sour taste	

Start with 10 c. of brown sugar. Then add vinegar slowly. Simmer eight hours. You have lots of time to get the sweet and sour just right. Make barely warm with a little red pepper. Absolutely do not make hot or you will not be able to enjoy the wonderful flavor of the beef.

RED MEATS

Cattleman's Prayer

Now O Lord, please lend thine ear,
The prayer of the Cattleman to hear;
No doubt many prayers to thee seem strange,
But won't you bless our cattle range?

Bless the round-up year by year
And don't forget the growing steer;
Water the land with brooks and rills
For my cattle that roam a thousand hills.

Now, O Lord, won't you be good,
And give our livestock plenty of food;
And to avert a winter's woe
Give Italian skies and little snow.

Prairie fires won't you please stop,
Let thunder roll and water drop;
It frightens me to smell the smoke,
Unless it's stopped, I'll go dead broke.

As you, O Lord, my herds behold—
Which represents a sack of gold—
I think at least five cents per pound
Should be the price of beef the year round.

One thing more and then I'm through,
Instead of one calf, give my cows two.
I may pray different than others, but then,
Still I've had my say, and now, Amen!

Author—unknown, circa 1890

The Elements of a Catch Rope

For ordinary roundup work like calf catching most American cowboys used a grass rope averaging 40 feet in length. At the head of the lariat was an eyelet called a honda, through which the main line of the rope slid to form a loop usually four feet or more in diameter. To toss the lariat, a cowboy grasped both the main line and the loop in his throwing hand, with the honda about a quarter of the way down the loop for balance. In his other hand he held the coiled remainder of the rope, letting out extra line with his thunb and index finger. The last two fingers of the same hand held the reins in order to guide the cow pony through the quick stops and turns of the roping sequence.

Two Kinds of Ropes and Hondas

The lariat introduced by the vaqueros was made of braided rawhide and was so easy to throw that the average length for one was 60 feet. But it was expensive and a little delicate, and most Americans turned to tough grass. The grass rope was also more practical in that it could easily be knotted to form the honda, while rawhide usually had to be spliced around a piece of cowhorn.

From those days when a cowboy first rode across Texas soil, he developed a strong, almost vehement, dislike for milk and cream, especially in his coffee. He didn't mind herding cattle, but he'd be damned if he would drink their milk. He didn't mind his breath smelling of whiskey and tobacco, but he certainly didn't want it smelling like that of a young calf.

In time, canned milk made its way to the plains. Women were delighted. Cowmen did not even like to talk about it. Charlie Russell once pulled a can of Eagle Brand from a cook's shelf and said, "I think it came from that bird. It's a cinch it never flowed from any animal with horns."

Carnation milk even advertised in stock newspapers that it would give a prize for the best jingle written praising the product. One ranching wife eagerly sat down and wrote:

> Carnation milk, best in the lan',
> Comes to the table in a little red can.

She gave it to a cowboy to mail, then waited with excitement to hear from the company. She heard. By letter they told her they could not use her poem because it was not fit to print.

The wife was at first angered, then bewildered, then confused. She called the cowhand and demanded an explanation. Had he altered her letter?

The cowboy grinned a shy, slow grin, then reddened under her boiling gaze. "Well, Ma'm," he said, "I read your poem an' figgered it was too short. I wanted to see y'u win that prize, so I figgered I could add a verse and make it better."

"Then what in creation did you write?"

"Oh, I jes' gave it a little more punch by makin' it read:

> Carnation milk, best in the lan',
> Comes to the table in a little red can.
> No teats to pull, no hay to pitch,
> Jes, punch a hole in the sonofabitch."

BEEF

Vicky & Dan Kipp
Fort Union Ranch
Watrous, New Mexico

ROUND-UP BEEF

10 lbs. round, cut into strips	1¼ c. brown sugar
1 c. flour	1¼ c. red wine vinegar
cooking oil to brown	5 tbsp. Worcestershire sauce
5 c. water	5 chopped onions
3 c. catsup	Salt & pepper

Dredge strips of beef in flour, salt & pepper, brown in oil. Combine water, catsup, brown sugar, vinegar, worcestershire and onion. Stir well, heat and pour over beef. Bring to boil, reduce heat and cook covered until beef is tender—about 2 hours. Stir occasionally. Serves 20-25 and freezes well.

Background: This makes a terrific round-up dinner as it is hearty and holds well. We serve it with baked apples, slaw, hot rolls and brownies, but is also wonderful over noodles or rice.

Ann Gates
Corvallis, Oregon

JIFFY HAMBURGER STROGANOFF

1 lb. chuck beef, ground	1 4-oz. can sliced mushrooms, drained
½ c. onion, coarsely grated	1 can cream of mushroom soup
1 small garlic clove, minced	¼ c. shredded Cheddar cheese
Salt & pepper to taste	

Break meat into bite sized chunks in large skillet. Add onion, garlic, mushroom soup, cheese, salt and pepper. Mix well and cover skillet. Cook on low heat in electric fry pan for 25 minutes. At end of cooking period stir in the following: *1 cup sour cream and 2 tbsp. Worcestershire sauce.*

John & Denzil Mills
Charleville, Australia

GYMKHANA HAMBURGERS

1 kg./2 lbs. minced meat	1 onion, chopped finely
2 eggs	1 capsicum, chopped finely
1 chilli, chopped finely	

Mix the eggs with the minced meat to bind them. Add the onion, capsicum and chilli. Mould meat into balls, so you can press them into patties. When you place them on a grill plate have about ½" thick by 3" in diameter. Keep turning until cooked, about 30 minutes. Nice for a barbecue.

Joy Woodbury
W9 Ranch
McLeod, North Dakota

W9

HAMBURGER TURN-OVERS

1 lb. ground beef	1 pkg. onion soup mix, dry
1 c. cheddar cheese, grated	1 pkg. crescent rolls (8)

Mix 3 ingredients. Place spoonfulls of mixture on Pillsbury Crescent rolls and seal each one. Place on cookie sheet and bake at 350° approx. 20 minutes. Makes excellent "finger food" for a teen party.

Mary Shoop
Fort Collins, Colorado

KRAUT BURGERS
(Bierochen)

1 lb. ground beef (crumbled)	1 basic bread dough recipe or
1 onion (chopped fine)	2 loaves of frozen dough
3 tbsp. shortening	1 small head of cabbage (shredded)
salt & pepper to taste	

Melt shortening in skillet. Add beef, cabbage and onion. Cook until cabbage is nearly done. Do not brown. Drain, salt and pepper to taste. Roll bread dough which has risen once to ¼" thick. Cut in 5 or 6" squares. Place 2 or 3 heaping tbsp. of mixture on each square, bring corners together and pinch sides shut. Let rise 20 minutes. Bake at 375° for about 20 minutes or until brown. Brush tops with melted butter.

Alice L. Eider
North Dakota

RANCH BURGERS

2 lbs. ground beef chuck	½ tsp. pepper
dough*	1 jar (8 oz.) cheese spread with
1 large onion, chopped	jalapeno peppers
1 tbsp. chili powder	2 cans chili beans, drained
1-½ tsp salt	¼ c. margarine, softened

Prepare dough. Brown ground beef and onion in large frying pan; pour off drippings. Add chili powder, salt and pepper; mix well. Add cheese spread; stir in chili beans and cook slowly 10 to 15 minutes. When dough has risen, divide into four portions. Roll each portion into 10 x 14" rectangle, ¼" thick. Cut into 6 squares. Place approximately ¼ to ⅓ c. meat mixture on each square. Pull up opposite corners and pinch together at center top. Place pinched side down on baking sheet. Bake in hot oven (400°) for 12 to 15 minutes or until golden brown. Brush with margarine. Yield: 24 burgers. Note: Burgers may be frozen and reheated.

DOUGH:

2 pkgs. yeast	¼ c. shortening
⅔ c. warm water	2 tsp. salt
⅔ c. warm milk	2 eggs
¼ c. sugar	4-½ to 5 c. flour

Dissolve yeast in water in large mixer bowl. Add milk, sugar, salt, shortening, egg and 1-½ c. flour. Blend together at low speed on electric mixer 30 seconds. Beat 2 minutes at medium speed, scraping bowl occasionally. Stir in enough remaining flour to make dough easy to handle. Turn dough onto lightly floured surface; knead until smooth and elastic, about 5 minutes. Place in greased bowl, turn greased side up. Cover, let rise in warm place until double, about 1 to 1-½ hours.

Jeffrey W. Bailey
Prairie Ridge Ranch
Cheyenne, Wyoming

'J'

ROCKY MOUNTAIN OYSTERS

Select only small ones and cook them whole. Soak in salt water, roll in corn meal, fine cracker crumbs or flour; season with salt and pepper. Fry in quite a bit of shortening until brown and cooked through. When done, they pop open.

ROCKY MOUNTAIN OYSTERS

12 med. or 24 small mountain oysters	*3 c. crushed cracker crumbs*
6 eggs	*oil for frying*

If using medium sized oysters, cut into smaller pieces. Beat eggs until just blended. Dip in eggs and roll in cracker crumbs. Saute on high heat till browned. Place on cookie sheet and season with salt and pepper. Bake in 350° oven for 20 minutes.

Background: As soon as the last calf was branded on branding day, several of the men cleaned the oysters and rushed them to the house to soak in cold water. Several hours later the ranch wife brought out the platter of fried mountain oysters, along with the other food and fed the branding crew consisting of friends and neighbors. Just being able to feast on this delicacy made the work of the day seem worthwhile.

Mrs. Gale (Justine) Wolters

BAKED ROUND STEAK

1 lg. piece of aluminum foil	*1 pkg. dried onion soup mix*
1 2" thick round steak of beef	*1 can cream of mushroom soup*

On foil, place steak. Cover with onion soup mix and mushroom soup. Seal foil. Bake at 300° for 2 or 3 hours. Open foil, cut and serve meat with the gravy which has formed on the meat.

Mrs. Robert L. Storch

BEEF EATERS STEAK

1-½ to 2 lbs. round steak	*1 pkg. Lipton dry onion soup mix*
	1 can Golden Mushroom soup

Place large piece of foil in pan. Lay ½ of steak on foil. Spread all of golden mushroom soup on steak; sprinkle pkg. of onion soup mix on top; place other half of steak on top of mixture. Wrap tightly with foil Scrape as much sauce as possible off steak to make gravy. If more is needed add 1 more can of mushroom soup and heat.

Margaret Brock Hanson
Brock Live Stock Company
Kaycee, Wyoming

FRIED MOUNTAIN OYSTERS

mountain oysters	*flour*
salt & pepper	*bacon grease*

Shuck fresh oysters, taking off all extraneous membrane leaving only the oyster, like a gland. Before cooking, cut the gland part-way through. The outer membrane shrinks and the oyster will open up as it cooks. Season, dredge with flour, and fry in grease as you would chicken.

Background: A. L. and Julia Ann Brock homesteaded in Johnson County in 1884. Their great, great grandchildren live on this same ranch they started in 1890. The Hole in the Wall outlaws and their adversaries used their home as they chased each other around during the range war years.

Shelly (Jackson) Van Haur
Van Haur Polled Herefords
Hilger, Montana

MONTANA BEEF PASTIES
(Butte Pasties)

1 double recipe for pie dough	*1 c. leftover gravy*
1 lb. diced, cooked roast beef (3-4 c.)	*1 tsp. salt*
½ lb. diced, cooked	*¼ tsp. pepper*
(boiled or baked) potatoes	*1 minced garlic clove or*
1 lge. onion, diced	*½ tsp. dried garlic*
3 diced carrots	*2 tbsp. parsley flakes*

Mix all ingredients in a large bowl except pie dough. Roll pie dough into 1/8" thick, 8" round circles. Place ¾ or 1 c. of meat mixture on half of dough circle, bring other half over and seal edges. Put small slit in top of each pastie. Cook at 400° for 1 hour. Serve with gravy or catsup.

Background: The old Welch miners were known for their lunch of pasties they took down in the mines of Butte, Montana. Later these pasties took on a variety of different ingredients and styles according to the nationality of the miner's wife who made them, and later the ranch wives.

June Southwood
Dubbo, N.S.W. Australia

AUSSIE STYLE HOT POT

1 kg. beef (steak)	1 tbsp. plain flour
4 potatoes	1 tsp. mustard
2 onions (medium)	1 tsp. plum jam
4 tomatoes (skinned)	½ c. tomato paste

salt & pepper to taste

BATTER:

2 c. self-rising flour	milk
1 egg	salt to taste

Place layers of meat, sliced onion, tomato and potato in the camp oven, repeat until required quantity is reached. Mix together flour, mustard, plum jam, tomato paste, salt and pepper with a little water to make a paste. Pour over meat and vegetables. Simmer for 2 hours or until meat is tender. Mix batter by adding beaten egg, salt and a little milk to flour until a thickish paste is obtained. Pour over top of meat. Place lid on camp oven, cover with hot coals and leave for further 15-20 minutes. Batter should be golden brown.

Background: Welcomed by most, especially in cold weather, after a long day's droving. Lamb or kangaroo can also be used in this dish.

Mrs. Violet Utt
Utt Ranch
Riverside, Washington

UTT RANCH STROGANOFF

½ c. minced onion	2 tbsp. salt
1 clove garlic, minced	1 8-oz. can mushrooms
¼ c. butter	1 can cream of chicken soup
1 lb. ground beef	¼ tsp. pepper
2 tbsp. flour	1 c. sour cream

Parsley

Saute onion and garlic in butter over medium heat. Stir in meat and brown. Stir in flour, salt, pepper and mushrooms. Cook 5 minutes; stir in cream of chicken soup. Simmer uncovered for 10 minutes. Stir in sour cream. Heat through. Serve over rice or noodles. Garnish with parsley.

Haeberle Ranch
Conconally, Nebraska

CHINESE BEEF

1 lb. round steak, cut into thin strips
oil
1 clove garlic, chopped fine
1 small onion, chopped
1 c. beef boullion

1 tsp. soy sauce
1 can or 1 pkg. frozen thinly sliced
green beans
½ tsp. cornstarch
2 tbsp. water

salt to taste

Brown steak strips in oil. Add garlic and onion. Saute 5 minutes. Add boullion and soy sauce. Cook until steak is almost tender. Add green beans and cook till beans are tender. Blend cornstarch with water, add to steak mixture.

Background: John Haeberle bought the home ranch on Johnson Creek in 1939. Richard worked the ranch after graduation in 1942. They started out with 60 head and gradually expanded the herd and acquired some adjoining property. John passed away in 1967 and Rod Haeberle joined Richard, his father in 1975.

Mrs. Earl Stoltenow
Wahpeton, North Dakota

ROUND STEAK STROGANOFF

3 lbs. round steak
¼ c. butter or margarine
1 large onion
¼ c. sifted flour

1 can consomme, undiluted
1 can tomato soup, undiluted
1 3-oz. can mushrooms
½ c. sour cream

Salt & pepper to taste

Cut steak into strips ½-inch thick by 2-inches long, remove skin and fat. Heat in large frying pan with butter and thinly sliced onion; cook several minutes. Sprinkle flour over top of steak until blended; add consomme, tomato soup and stir until sauce is thickened. Add whole or sliced mushrooms (optional), salt and pepper, cover and cook over low heat 1 to 1-½ hours or until meat is tender. Just before serving, slowly add ½ cup sour cream. This serves 6 to 8 people. Serve with rice, hot buttered noodles or mashed potatoes.

Background: This recipe has been handed down at least two generations. It was originally made with real sour cream, but commercial sour cream works equally as well.

Mrs. Suzanne Field
Trinidad

WELSH FAGGOTS

1-½ lbs. ox liver	8 oz. breadcrumbs
½ lb. minced meat	3 oz. beef suet
2 tsp. sage	2 large onions, finely chopped
2 tsp. salt & pepper	1 egg

Mince the ox liver and beef suet. Mix all ingredients well and leave to rest for 5 minutes. Make into small balls the size of snooker balls and put into a baking dish. Bake in the oven in a little water covered for 10 minutes and then take the cover off and cook another 15 minutes till they look nice and brown. Serve with green peas and mashed potatoes. Serves 6-8 people.

Background: The Welsh are mainly connected to the coal mines and never had enough money to buy expensive meat, so they often buy the cheaper cuts of meat and make it stretch to feed the whole family by mixing it with a little amount of good lean meat and a lot of herbs.

Mrs. Vern (Marjorie) Jacobson
Jacobson Ranch
Bowman, North Dakota

PIZZABURGERS

2 lbs. hamburger	sm. jar of stuffed green olives, chopped
2 small cans tomato sauce	1 lb. cubed Mozzarella cheese
salt, pepper & oregano to taste	

Brown hamburger; add tomato sauce and seasonings. Simmer until thick. Cool. Add olives and cheese. Spread in hamburger buns. Wrap in foil or saran wrap. Refrigerate until ready to eat. Reheat in microwave or oven. Makes 14 to 16 buns.

Background: It's a favorite recipe at the Jacobson Ranch when youngsters eat at different times and especially if they fix for themselves.

Vic & Betty Barnes
Ellis-Barnes Livestock Company
Tonasket, Washington

EB

POLYNESIAN SHORT RIBS

3-4 lbs. beef short ribs or boneless pieces	½ c. sugar
2 tbsp. salad oil	1 c. water
4 tbsp. flour	¼ c. soy sauce
	⅔ c. vinegar

Cut short ribs in one rib pieces, trim off fat and parboil about 30 minutes. Drain. Heat oil in fry pan. Mix flour with sugar. Roll ribs in mixture and brown slowly on all sides. Add 1 medium, chopped onion. Mix soy sauce, water and vinegar. Pour over browned meat. Cover and simmer very slowly about 2 hours or till meat is tender and juice is thickened.

Background: The E B brand was first used in 1916 on Shorthorn and on Hereford cattle by a partnership of Charles Embody and Willfrid A. Barnes. The ranch was located at Blue Lake near the mouth of Sinlahekin creek, eleven miles south of Loomis, Washington. The ranch was sold to the Whitestone Irrigation District in 1921 when the Blue Lake Dam was built. In 1924 W. A. Barnes became associated with George Ellis and formed the Ellis-Barnes Livestock Co. and moved to the present location seven miles northwest of Tonasket. In the late forties W. A. and sons Vic and Bill bought out the Ellis estate. Now in the Eighties, Vic and Bill have taken in their sons Jim and Bob for a third generation ownership of mostly Hereford cattle.

Tom & Shirley Cook
Fernley, Nevada

DUTCH OVEN ROAST

Any cut. One of my favorites is chuck or brisket.

Thaw out roast, insert slivers of garlic. Put shortening or oil in dutch oven, and get sizzling hot over charcoals, open fire, or on stove. Brown roast on all sides to deep crusty brown. Then add an inch or so of water, put on lid and let cook over a medium heat for about 1-½ hours depending on size.

Later add carrots, onions, green peppers, celery. 20 minutes later add potatoes, salt and pepper. Bring roast from bottom of oven and place over vegetables, cooking until potatoes easily accept a fork, about 30-40 minutes after they were put in oven. Roast in foil. Stuff again with slivers of garlic, a couple handfulls of cut onions, salt and pepper. Wrap in foil with all your closures on top of roast. Set on charcoal grill and cook for 2-½ to 3 hours. If foil starts to leak, wrap again over old foil. Keep a fairly hot fire.

Mrs. Dale (Kathy) Duchow
Tonasket, Washington

OPEN FACE HAMBURGERS

8 slices bread	*3 tbsp. onion soup mix*
1 lb. hamburger	*8 slices cheese*
½ c. catsup	*salt & pepper to taste*

Toast bread on 1 side under broiler. Mix meat, catsup, and seasoning together. Divide evenly on untoasted side of bread. Broil until nearly done. Top with cheese slices, broil until melted.

Background: Julias August Duchow was a German Lutheran minister at Havillah, Washington from 1910 to 1915. At that time he felt that the ministry couldn't support his family of 12 children, so he looked for good farmland in Havillah. He farmed until 1938 when his son Carl and his wife bought the land and raised their 6 children there. Upon retiring in 1975 their son Dale and his wife Kathy bought the place. They live there now with their 3 boys. The brand is still carried from the pioneer grandfather who began it all.

Four Sixes Ranch
Texas

6666

DUTCH OVEN POT ROAST

Beef takes on a whole new flavor when it sets in a Dutch oven next to potatoes, carrots and onions.

1 5-lb. round bone pot roast	*8 carrots, pared & cut in 2" pieces*
2 tsp. salt	*6 potatoes, peeled & quartered*
2 tbsp. shortening	*2 onions, sliced*
½ c. barbecue sauce	*1 10-oz. pkg. frozen okra or*
½ c. apple cider	*½-lb. fresh okra*

Rub meat with salt. Melt shortening in Dutch oven; add meat and cook over medium heat, turning once. Reduce heat; pour over barbeque sauce and cider. Cover and simmer on top of range or in 325° 3 to 4 hours. Add carrots, potatoes, and onion 1-½ hours before end of cooking time. Add okra 15 minutes before end of cooking time. Serves 6-8.

SRM **SOCIETY FOR RANGE MANAGEMENT**

Mrs. Earl Pelton
Bone Springs Ranch
Halliday, North Dakota

ᴛᴛ

ORIENTAL POT ROAST

4 lbs. beef rump or top round roast	8 small onions, peeled
1 to 2 tsp. salt	½ c. water
½ tsp. ground ginger	2 tbsp. soy sauce
1 med. onion, sliced	2 tbsp. flour
¼ c. water	1 med. green pepper, diced
3 stalks celery, sliced	hot, cooked rice

fresh parsley

Trim excess fat from roast; cut fat into small pieces. Cook fat slowly in Dutch oven until about 1 tbsp. drippings have melted; remove remaining fat pieces and discard. Meanwhile, rub salt thoroughly into roast. Brown meat slowly in drippings on all sides to a rich brown color (should take about 25 minutes). Slip rack under meat, sprinkle with ginger. Cover with onion slices. Add ¼ c. water, cover tightly and cook over very low heat for 2 hours. Add celery and small onions; continue cooking, covered, 25 minutes or until meat and vegetables are tender. Remove meat and vegetables to platter; cover to keep warm. Skim off excess fat from cooking liquid. Combine ½ c. water, soy sauce and flour in jar; shake to make smooth paste. Stir into cooking liquid in Dutch oven. Add green pepper. Cook, stirring until smooth and thickened. If necessary, add more water to make 1-½ c. gravy. Carve roast and serve slices with gravy and rice. Garnish with fresh parsley. Makes 8 servings.

Carolyn Frisk (Howard)
H-F Ranch
McLeod, North Dakota

HF

ROAST BEEF SANDWICHES

5-6 lb. roast	3-4 c. water
3-4 beef boullion cubes	1 pkg. dry onion soup mix

Roast the 5-6 lb. roast at 275° uncovered for 1 hour. Add the next 3 ingredients and cook at 275° for 3-4 hours. Remove from oven and take out bone and fat. Spread apart and cook one hour more, uncovered, at 325°. Serve on buns and use juice for dripping. This recipe freezes well. Makes a large amount.

Background: The Frisks raise Simmental cattle and are active in the Simmental Breeders' Association. Howard is a director and their daughter Lori was North Dakota Simmental Queen for 1982-83.

148

Ralph Bick
BIX Ranch, Ltd.
British Columbia, Canada

B
I
X

DEVIL'S STEAK

2-3 lbs. round steak, ¾" thick
2 tbsp. dry mustard
1-½ tsp. salt
¼ tsp. pepper

2 tbsp. cooking oil, or as needed
1 10-oz. can mushrooms, bits & pieces
1 tbsp. Worcestershire sauce
½ c. dry wine

Cut meat into small pieces. Trim all membrane and fat from pieces. Pound each piece until ¼" thick or less. Mix mustard and spices and dredge meat on both sides in mixture. Have large frying pan medium hot with oil. Fry a few pieces at a time 1 to 1-½ minutes on each side, until golden brown. Keep warm. Drain mushrooms, set aside. Add mushroom liquid and Worcestershire sauce to pan. Simmer and scrape off pan drippings. Add mushrooms and wine to liquid, heat, may thicken with flour or corn starch if desired, and serve over meat. Makes 8 to 10 small servings. Meat may be pounded ahead of time if desired. Refrigerate in single layers or dry slightly before dredging as it browns more quickly.

Background: Since this rancher's wife has an allergy to wheat, dredging with dry mustard was an alternative to flour which turned out to please all members of the family. The present owners of BIX Ranch are transplanted Montanaians, bringing the name and brand with them in 1967. The original settlers came in 1918 from Holland via Saskatewan. Mr. Scheepbauwer walked into the area from the nearest railroad, 80 miles, walked the surrounding area and filed his homestead. They raised a family of 9 children, most of whom still live in the general area. They built a log home and outbuildings and made miles of log snake fence, Rustle split rail, and a stake and rider type made from smaller poles; some are still in use after 40 years.

Margaret Pegler
Trinidad

WAKEFIELD STEAK

1 dessertspoon Worcestershire sauce
1 dessertspoon anchovy sauce
Salt & pepper to taste

1 dessertspoon tomato sauce
1 tbsp. sugar
Steak

Mix the sauces and add sugar and salt and papper. In this mixture soak the quantity of steak required, turning several times for 3 hours. Add warm water until covered and cook in oven slowly for 2½ to 3 hours. Thicken gravy slightly if required. (Sliced leg of mutton can be used instead of steak).

The Four Sixes Ranch
Guthrie, Texas

6666

CHICKEN-FRIED STEAK

Just about everyone knows what frying does for the taste of chicken. Out West they like their steaks done the same way.

Cut 2 lbs. of ½-in. thick roundsteak into 6 pieces. Remove excess fat. Mix ⅓ c. flour, 1-½ tsp. salt, ½ tsp. pepper; sprinkle over meat, pounding into both sides.

Fry out fat cut from steak, adding enough shortening for ½ cup. Fry steak 5 minutes each side. Serves 6.

Ivan Thornton

ROLLED BEEFSTEAK

4 slices ¾" thick round steak	⅔ c. chopped, cooked/smoked
salt & pepper to taste	meat or ham
¼ lb. sliced bacon	1 tbsp. flour
2 pickles, chopped (dill)	3 tbsp. lard (or margarine)
	1 med onion (chopped)

2 c. water

Pound meat, slash borders. Sprinkle with salt and pepper. Cover each steak with sliced bacon. Mix pickles and ham; spread over bacon. Roll meat, fasten with skewers or toothpicks. Dust with flour. Brown well in lard or margarine. Remove meat, add onion to pan-fry until yellow. Return meat to pan, add 1 c. of water, cover and simmer until tender (about 1 hour), adding more water as it evaporates. Remove skewers or toothpicks before serving. Serves 4.

The Four Sixes Ranch
Guthrie, Texas

6666

SALT STEAK

Grill a steak in a cake of salt—crack off the coat—then lay some crisp bread on your plate to soak up all the juice.

Select 2-3" thick, boneless sirloin steak. Remove excess fat; skewer. Rub both sides with 2 cut cloves garlic, sprinkle with pepper. Mix 4 c. coarse salt with enough water to make thick paste. Press half salt mixture on top of steak. To charcoal broil: place salt-side down over hot coals 12-15 minutes. Cover other side with salt, turn and repeat. To broil in oven: broil salt-side up close to heat for 15 minutes; remove salt. Turn steak, cover other side with salt and repeat. To serve; remove salt crust from steak, place on warm deep platter. Pour steak sauce on platter, then slice. Serve with crisp bread slices.

Jeanne Edwards
Saval Ranch
North Fork, Nevada

∧L

COOKHOUSE STEAK
(Cut Down to Family Size)

1 lb. round steak	*½ c. tomatoes*
salt & pepper	*½ clove garlic*
flour	*1 stalk celery, diced*
shortening	*1 small onion, diced*
1-½ c. water	*1 small carrot, grated*

1 tsp. vinegar

Salt and pepper steak and wrap in flour. Brown in small amount of grease in frying pan. Place in heavy pan with tight fitting lid. Set aside. To grease left in frying pan, add enough to make 2 tbsp. Stir in 1 tsp. of flour and stir until smooth. Add water, stir until boiling. Add rest of ingredients and bring to a boil again. Pour over steak, bring to a boil, turn to simmer. Cover tightly and cook 2 hours. Good with rice or noodles.

Background: A cookhouse favorite with the Saval hands . . . brought to the ranch by a retired railroad chef.

Watt R. Matthews
Lambshead Ranch
15 miles N.W. of Albany, Texas

∫ʋ

RANCH STYLE CHICKEN FRIED STEAK AND GRAVY

STEAK:		GRAVY:
4 lbs. round steak		*4 tbsp. fat*
1 c. milk & flour		*4 tbsp. flour*
salt & pepper	*1 qt. milk*	

Tenderize round steak. Dip in milk and then flour; salt and pepper to taste. Fry in deep fat at approximately 375° until golden brown. After steak is done, pour off fat leaving about 4 tbsp. in pan. Add 4 tbsp. flour. Stir until smooth. Add the quart of milk. Stir and cook until thickened for steak gravy. Serves 8.

Background: Provided by John White, cook on the Lambshead Ranch for over 20 years. He usually feeds 10-20 people for lunch each day who might be visiting or working on the 42,377 acre ranch.

Jack Absalom
Australia

SEASONED POCKET STEAK

1 lump of meat 1 to 1-½ kgs./2-3 lbs., either kangaroo, beef or mutton

SEASONING:

¼ loaf bread	*1 tomato, finely chopped*
1 onion, finely chopped	*1 egg*
1 slice bacon, finely chopped	*salt & pepper to taste*

Take a knife and poke into meat forming a pocket. Now make seasoning, cut crust from bread and crumb. Mix this together with the onion, bacon and tomato. When all mixed add the egg and salt and pepper. Mix well. Stuff this into the pocket of meat. Close up with skewer or sew up. Place in camp oven and bake for 3 hours. Remember if the meat you are using is kangaroo you must baste it every now and then because it has no fat.

Tom J. Bradley
Phoenix, Arizona

MARIACHI BEEFBALLS & RICE

2 lbs. ground beef	2 c. sliced onion
1 egg, slightly beaten	1 clove garlic, crushed
1 c. crushed corn chips	1 tsp. chili powder
½ c. milk	¼ tsp. powdered cumin
2 tsp. salt	4 oz. green chiles, drained
2½ tbsp. flour	1 lb 3 oz. tomatoes, undrained
2 tbsp. butter	½ c. sliced ripe olives

In a large bowl, lightly toss beef with egg, corn chips, milk and 1 tsp. salt. Refrigerate 1 hr. covered. Shape into 15 meatballs (2 tbsp. each); roll into 2 tbsp. flour. In hot butter in large heavy skillet, saute meatballs until brown. Remove. Using same skillet, saute onion & garlic, about 5 min. Remove from heat. combine chili powder, cumin, remaining salt & flour. Stir into skillet with green chiles & tomatoes, add olives. Cover, simmer 30 min. Add meat, simmmer 20 min.; uncover 10 min. Serves 6. Excellent over Mexican Rice. Combine 1 pt. sour cream, 4 oz. chopped green chile and ¼ tsp salt. In 13x9 inch pan, layer this alternately with 3 c. cooked rice. and strips of Monterey Jack cheese (¼ lb.) ending with rice. Bake 25 min. at 350°. Sprinkle with ¼ c. grated Parmesan, top with meatballs; bake 5 min. more.

Ed & Martie Hoyt
Greybull Valley Ranch
Basin, Wyoming

RANCH ROUND STEAK

3 lbs. beef round steak, ½" thick,	1-½ tsp. salt
cut in serving-size pieces	1/8 tsp. pepper
¼ c. flour	¼ c. shortening
2 tsp. dry mustard	½ c. water
1 tbsp. Worcestershire sauce	

Trim excess fat from meat; slash edges to prevent curling. Combine flour, dry mustard, salt and pepper; use to coat meat. Reserve remaining flour mixture. In skillet, brown meat, half at a time, on both sides in hot shortening. Push meat to one side; stir in reserved flour mixture. Combine water and Worcestershire sauce; stir into skillet mixture. Cook and stir until thickened and bubbly; reduce heat. Cover and simmer for 1 to 1-¼ hours or until meat is tender. Remove meat to platter. Skim excess fat from gravy. Drizzle gravy over meat. Makes 8 servings.

Background: This brand was used by Ed's father, E. Roland Hoyt, in Colorado at his Green Valley Ranch east of Denver.

Mrs. Rueben Knutson
Dunn Center, North Dakota

DRIED BEEF

100 lbs. of beef	5 lbs. non-iodized salt
3 lbs. sugar	2 oz. salt peter (2 tbsp. — 1 oz.)

Use the hind quarter of beef. Strip the beef along the membrane. The pieces will vary in size. Place a heavy string in the end of each piece so it can be hung up. Mix the salt, sugar and salt peter together. Divide into thirds. Use ⅓ of the mixture and rub into the individual pieces, covering all surfaces. Pack into a crock jar as tightly as possible. Let stand for three days, then rub again with ⅓ of the mixture. Let stand three more days, then rub again with the last ⅓ of the mixture. Let stand three more days. Hang up the pieces for one day (place newspapers under them to catch the drippings). Hang the pices in a smoker, smoke for 4 hours at 125°. Hang to dry until the pieces are firm when squeezed hard. Slice very thin with an electric slicer. The smaller pieces will dry more quickly, so you will not be able to slice it all at once.

Clementina Reihl
Raleigh, North Dakota

MEAT BALLS GOURMET

1½ c. ground beef	1½ tbsp. instant minced onions
1½ tsp. salt	⅛ tsp. ground black pepper
⅛ tsp. garlic powder	¼ c. fine dry bread crumbs
½ c. grated sharp cheddar cheese	1 tsp. ground ginger
	Tomato sauce

Combine beef, onion, salt, pepper, garlic powder and bread crumbs. Divide into 8 equal portions. Mix cheese with ginger and shape into 8 balls of equal size. Wrap a portion of meat around each cheese ball, keeping the cheese in the center. Brown on all sides over medium heat in a baking pan, pour tomato sauce over all. Bake 30 to 40 min. at 350°.

James Newland
Greenwood Ranches
Bell Fourche, South Dakota

W
+

FRIZZLED BEEF

¼ c. butter	¼ c. flour
2 c. milk	1 3-oz. pack dried beef, cut in thin strips

Cook beef in butter til it frizzles in the skillet. In a pan melt butter and add flour and blend. Add milk and stir until smooth and thickened. Serve the beef separately with the sauce or mix together. If too salty, boil meat first. 4-5 servings.

Bob Papworth

HAMBURGER SALAMI

5 lb. lean hamburger	5 tsp. Tender Quik salt
2½ tsp. mustard seed	2½ tsp. coarse ground pepper
2½ tsp. garlic salt	2 tsp. Hickory Smoke salt
	Optional: 2 tsp. chili peppers

Mix well, cover and refrigerate overnight. Mix again on 2nd and 3rd day. On fourth day form 5 equal rolls. Place on rack over pan in oven 140-150°. Place on bottom rack in oven for 8 hours, turning every 2 hours. Refrigerate to store.

Alice L. Eider
North Dakota

ROAST BEEF PARTY LOGS

2 lbs. boneless beef chuck roast, cubed
2 c. water
½ tsp. pepper
⅔ c. mayonnaise
¼ c. sweet pickle relish
2 8-oz. pkg. cream cheese
1 c. shredded cheddar cheese
2 tbsp. chopped green pepper
¼ c. paprika

2 tbsp. cooking oil
1½ tsp. salt
¼ tsp. ground allspice
½ c. chopped celery
1 tbsp. steak sauce
2 4-oz. pkg. whipped cream
  cheese with chives
1 tbsp. chopped pimento
2 c. chopped pecans

Brown beef in oil in heavy 4 to 5 qt. pan or dutch oven. Add water, salt, pepper and allspice. Bring to a boil; reduce heat to med. low. Cover and cook for approximately 1½ hours or until tender (If desired a pressure pan may be used; reduce water to 1 cup and cook according to manufacturer's directions.) Remove beef from cooking liquid; cool. Grind beef. Combine beef, mayonnaise, celery, relish and steak sauce; mix well. Divide into 12 portions; shape each portion into a "log" approximatley 5 in. long. Press mixture firmly to hold shape. Refrigerate while preparing cream cheese mixture. Combine cream cheese, whipped cream cheese, cheddar cheese, green pepper and pimento; mix well. Spread cheese mixture over each log, covering well. Sprinkle with paprika and roll in nuts. Chill until firm enough to slice. (In freezer, allow approximately 15 min. or 45 to 60 min. in refrigerator.) Slice logs as needed, cutting each into approximately 12 slices. Garnish with cherry tomatoes, green onions and parsley. Serve with assorted crackers and horseradish mustard, if desired. Yield: approximately 144 appetizers. Note: logs freeze well so can be made well in advance.

Background: Alice Eider was the North Dakota Beef Cook-Off winner in 1982.

Wilma Newman
Montana

5̄P

HOME MADE SALAMI

2 lbs. extra lean ground beef
1 tbsp. liquid smoke
½ tsp. garlic salt
½ tsp. onion salt

1 c. water
2 tbsp. curing salt
½ tsp. pepper

Mix together and let stand at least 12 hours. Shape into 6–8 inch long rolls. Wrap in aluminum foil. Leave ends open, place on cookie sheet. Bake 1½ hours at 350°. Grease will run out ends of foil. It may smoke.

Lorraine Loh
JL Bar Ranch
Manning, North Dakota

MEAT LOAF

2 lbs. hamburger	2 eggs
1½ tsp. salt	½ tsp. black pepper
½ tsp. red pepper — cayenne	⅔ c. cream or carnation milk
1 medium onion, chopped fine	

Mix well. Form a loaf, add points of butter on top — pour about 1½ inch cold water around loaf. (Use a roaster or kettle that will hold this meat loaf so there is room for basting and a cover.) Baste water in bottom of pan over the meat. Baste often. Bake about 1½ hours at 350°. When nearly finished remove cover and let brown — baste while browning.

Background: I received this recipe from an aunt while attending grade school. It is a tasty meat loaf as the red pepper can be varied — remember it is a hot seasoning. This is a simple recipe for beginners and one the family will enjoy.

Dalice Wolters
Portis, Kansas

TOP STOVE MEAT LOAF

1 can tomato soup	1½ lbs. ground beef
½ c. fine bread crumbs	1 egg
½ c. finely chopped onion	1 tsp. salt, dash pepper
¼ c. water	½ to 1 tsp. horseradish
1 tbsp. shortening	

Mix thoroughly ½ can soup with all ingredients save the shortening. Shape firmly into two loaves. In skillet, brown on both sides in shortening. Cover; cook over low heat for 25 minutes. Spoon off fat. Top with remaining soup, water and horseradish. Cook uncovered 10 minutes.

Oven Method: Place loaves in shallow baking pan. Bake at 350° for 40 minutes. Top with remaining soup (omit water and horseradish). Bake 5 minutes more or until done.

SRM SOCIETY FOR RANGE MANAGEMENT

Fred G. Bank
Circle L-M Ranch
San Jose, California

CIRCLE L-M BURGERS

2 lbs. lean ground beef	1 med. red onion
½ tsp. garlic salt	⅛ tsp. pepper
English muffins	Red tomato salsa

Start oakwood fire. (*Q. douglas* preferred). Peel and finely chop onion. Mix onion, pepper and garlic salt into ground beef. Form ground beef mixture into ½-lb. burgers (size may very depending upon how hungry the hands look). Grill burgers over coals. Serve immediately between toasted English muffins with plenty of salsa. Great with canned peaches and reheated scalloped potatoes.

Background: The Circle L-M Burger is a renowned culinary delight that originated in the annual rangelands of Central California. Invented in 1962 by Eugenial "Burger Chef" McClay, it has become a standard noontime fare beloved by the hungry dry-grass cowhands, squirrel hunters, ditch diggers, and fence menders at the Circle L-M

Susie Body
Body Ranch
Casper Wyoming

GRAUTBURGERS

1 large head of cabbage	1 pkg. yeast
2 lbs. hamburger	¼ c. warm water
Salt & pepper to taste	½ c. sugar
½ c. shortening	1½ c. boiling water
2 eggs, beaten	6-7 c. flour

Cut cabbage fairly fine. Add hamburger and a little water. Cover and cook until done. Set aside. Dissolve yeast, 1 tsp. suger in ¼ c. warm water. Dissolve sugar, salt & shortening in boiling water. Cool. Add yeast and eggs. Stir in flour. Knead and let raise. Roll dough fairly thin, cut in 4x8 inch pieces. Place ½ heaping cup meat mixture in center, fold edges and seal. Let raise. Bake 350° until golden and bread is done. Makes about 15.

Background: This recipe is our family's traditional Christmas Eve dinner.

Joy Wilson
Wilson Ranch
Riverside, Washington

FINGERSTEAK

1 lb. round steak	*Meat tenderizer*
1 egg, beaten	*Flour*
Seasoning salt	*Oil*

Cut steak into 1 in. strips, 4 inches long. Sprinkle with meat tenderizer and beat with hammer or knife. Heat oil to 375°. Dip steak in egg then flour, fry until done and season with seasoning salt. Great to pick up and eat. Terrific on picnics.

Background: In 1889 Henry Hedrick Wilson set out from Tennessee. After 13 years of trying to settle down he ended up homesteading in a beautiful valley southeast of Tonasket, Washington. Now his great-grandson lives and ranches in the same valley. Houses have changed, boundaries have changed, people have changed; but there are still Wilsons farming and running cattle and 5th generation Wilsons playing in the dirt.

Bill & Betty Barnes
Ellis-Barnes Ranch
Tonasket, Washington

BEEF BREAKFAST SAUSAGE

2 lbs. ground beef	*¼ c. water*
2 tbsp. parsley flakes	*1 tsp. brown sugar*
2 tsp. salt	*½ tsp. rubbed sage*
½ tsp. crumbled leaf oregano	
¼ tsp. pepper	

Mix water, parsley flakes and brown sugar and let stand several minutes. Add to ground beef and the remaining ingredients. Mix well, shape into patties. Cook slowly until browned on both sides, turning occasionally. Don't overcook!

Background: The brand was first registered by John J. Buckland about 1910. He had moved to Anglin, along Bonaparte Creek and taken up a homestead in 1902. He continued to use this brand after he moved to Spectacle Lake, in 1939. After his death in 1954, his daughter and husband, Bill and Betty Barnes, registered the brand in their names, and at the present time it is still registered to them.

STOCKMAN'S BRINE

4 gallons water
Salt
2 dessertspoons salt & pepper

1 potato
½ lb. brown or white sugar or
½ tin treacle

This is used for pickling mutton, beef or pork. Place water in a large pot. Add potato to the water. Add salt until the potato floats, stirring as you go. Remove the potato. Add the sugar or treacle and salt and pepper. This mixture will keep for months in a cool place.

Wanda Lewis
Lewis Ranch
Park River, North Dakota

D

BEEF IN THE UNDERGROUND OVEN

10 lb. boneless beef roast
1 clove garlic, minced
1 tsp. salt
½ tsp. celery salt
2 tbsp. vinegar
3 tbsp. worcestershire sauce

1 onion, chopped
2 tbsp. butter
⅛ tsp. pepper
1½ tsp. dry mustard
4 tbsp. lemon juice
1 c. catsup

1 c. water

Sauce: Saute onion and garlic in butter. Blend in dry ingredients, then add remainder and simmer for 15 minutes. Dig a 33–gallon oil barrel into the ground (upright). Burn wood in barrel for 2 hours until the coals are red hot. About 15 inches above the coals, place a round grill. Wrap the beef in cheesecloth and soak it in the barbeque sauce. Wrap in foil. Tie it up with wire, making handles. Place on top of grill. Put lid on barrel and seal completely with dirt. If any smoke escapes add more dirt. The meat will cook in 2 hours whether you are cooking 10 or 30 lbs. It will be very tender and especially delicious.

Background: The Lewis ranch was homesteaded in 1884 by Larry's grandfather. Red Angus cattle are raised there and the Lewis's are active in various ranching organizations. Larry Lewis uses this recipe to cook for groups of two or three hundred people. He was cooking on one of these occasions when his first son was born.

Jack Absalom
Australia

DOGS IN BLANKETS

Slices of cold cooked meat   Oil for frying
2 c. self-rising flour   Pinch salt
1 egg   Milk

Place flour, egg and salt in a bowl. Mix well, slowly adding a little milk until batter is smooth. Have the oil hot in the camp oven. Dip half inch slices of cold
meat into the batter and drop them into the hot oil. When cooked and brown
take out and place on a piece of paper. Now ready to serve.

Background: This is a wonderful, quick meal in the bush. Any cold meat may
be used or even a tin of luncheon meat or bully beef. They always taste good.

Doug Henriques
Falls Church, Virginia

CAMARGUE HAMBURGERS

1½ lb. ground lean beef   ½ lb. Gorgonzola or blue cheese, crumbled
Salt & pepper to taste   2 tbsp. cognac
2 tbsp. butter   2 c. sliced mushrooms
½ tsp. garlic, finely minced   2 tbsp. chopped parsley

Blend ground beef with cheese; salt and pepper to taste. Shape into 4 patties,
½ in. thick. Heat black iron skillet. do not add fat, but heat skillet until almost
smoking. Add patties and cook 3 to 4 min. per side. Add cognac and ignite. Cook
until flame dies. Transfer to warm platter.
   In separate skillet, heat butter, mushrooms and garlic. Cook for 2 minutes, tossing and stirring. Spoon mushrooms over patties and sprinkle with parsley.

Marjorie Wolters
Portis, Kansas

FAVORITE MEATBALLS

2 lb. hamburger   *1 onion chopped*
1 cup uncooked rice   *Salt and pepper to taste*

Mix all ingredients together and shape into balls the size of walnuts. Now pour over this mixture: 1 can of tomato soup diluted with 1 can water. Bake covered for 1½ hours in 350° oven.

MOCK CHICKEN-FRIED STEAK

1 c. crumbled saltine crackers   *1 beaten egg*
¼ c. milk   *1 tsp. chili powder*
¼ tsp. salt   *1 lb. ground beef*
¼ tsp. Worcestershire sauce to taste

Combine ingredients, using ½ of cracker crumbs. Add ground beef. Mix well. shape into 6 patties ½ in. thick. Coat in remaining cracker crumbs. Cook in hot oil (2 tbsp.) on med. high heat for 3 min.

Phyllis Simpson
Alton, Kansas

SALISBURY STEAK

2 lb. ground beef   *2 tsp. worcestershire sauce*
1 tsp. salt   *1 tsp. dry mustard*
¼ c. minced onion   *¼ tsp. pepper*
4 tbsp. chopped parsley   *slices of bacon*

Mix ground beef, seasonings, onion and parsley. Shape into 6 large patties. Wrap bacon slices around the outside edge of the patties and secure well with toothpicks. Broil 3 inches from heat. Brown well on one side, about 8 minutes. Turn and brown on the other side. Naturally, broiling time will depend on the size and thickness of the patties.

Joy Woodbury
W9 Ranch
McLeod, North Dakota

W9

CROCK POT MEATBALLS

2 lbs. ground beef	1 pkg. dry onion soup mix
1 c. crushed corn flakes	1 egg
¼ c. milk	1 can golden mushroom soup
1 can cream of mushroom soup	Pepper to taste
	1 can water

Mix beef, onion soup mix, corn flakes, egg and milk together. Form into small balls and brown in oven on cookie sheet. Remove from oven and put in crockpot. Add soups, water and pepper; stir gently. Cook 1 hour on low. Serves 6–8; with mashed potatoes, noodles or rice.

Cheri Reiswig (Mrs. Kim)
Bismark, North Dakota

PEPPER STEAK

2 lbs. round steak, cut into	¼ tsp. pepper
small bite-size cubes	2 boullion cubes (beef)
4 tbsp. cooking oil	1 clove minced garlic
2 tbsp. flour	1 c. finely chopped onion
2-½ c. water	4 lge. peppers cut into rings
1 c. catsup	1 4-oz. can mushrooms (drained)
6 tbsp. soy sauce	2 med. onions, cut into rings

Brown beef in cooking oil, remove. Blend flour into the oil from which the beef was removed. Add catsup, water, soy sauce, pepper, boullion cube, minced garlic and chopped onion. Bring to boil, lower heat to simmer for twenty minutes. Drop beef into sauce and cook until tender (2 to 2-½ hours). (This much can be done two or three days before serving and stored in the refrigerator). Fifteen minutes before serving add mushrooms, peppers and onion rings. Cook until crispy tender. Serve with fluffy rice.

Background: This recipe placed second in the North Dakota Beef Cook-off.

SRM **SOCIETY FOR RANGE MANAGEMENT**

GOAT

Rosemary Boykin
Gaborone, South Africa
Washington, D.C.

GOAT MASALA

1 leg (haunch of goat
2 #303 cans of green peas
2 #303 cans of chopped tomatoes
1-2 c. fresh mushrooms,
    sliced or whole

1 large green sweet pepper
8 large onions
2 c. red or white wine
    (or vinegar)
3 tbsp. masala curry or
your favorite curry blend

Cut goat into strips and boil with the bones for 1 hour in 1 quart water and wine or vinegar. If the goat has been hung for 3 days or so, drain off liquid and flush with fresh water after cooking. At this stage, peel meat from the bone and continue cooking, adding 2 teaspoons salt, the sliced onions, tomatoes, juices from the peas, mushrooms and the curry. Cook for 3 more hours to reduce liquid. Add peas, mushrooms and diced green peppers and simmer for another half hour.

Background: This is an ideal dish for bush cooking in a 3-legged black cast iron pot. It is a favorite of Kalahari cowboys. One-dish meals such as this are the mainstay at the cattle posts in Botswana. Calvin C. Boykin, Jr., my husband, is working on a USAAID/PASA project in the ministry of Agriculture in Botswana.

LAMB

DEVILED LAMB CHOPS

4 chump or leg chops
1½ oz. butter
1 c. diced celery
1 diced onion
2 tomatoes

1 beef cube
5 oz. vinegar
5 oz. water
1 tsp. dry mustard
Salt & pepper

Cut chops in halves. Melt butter in pan and brown quickly. Add chopped vegetables and saute 2 to 3 minutes. Add beef cube crumbled in water with vinegar and seasonings. Cover and simmer 1½ hours or until tender. Thicken gravy if necessary with cornflour.

John & Denzil Mills
Charleville, Queensland, Australia

"CHEEPIE CHOPS"

1½ lb. mutton chops
(or diced shoulder)
2 tbsp. flour
1 tbsp. sugar
Salt & pepper
¼ tsp. curry

¼ tsp. mustard
¼ tsp. ginger
¼ tsp. mixed spice
2 tbsp. tomato sauce
2 tbsp. vinegar
1 large c. stock

Combine the dry ingredients. Mix with the liquids. Pour over the chops and cook for 2 hours or more in a slow oven.

Susanne Stirton.

CHOPS WITH ORANGE

2 lbs. lamb chops*
2 level tbsp. cornflour
1 level tsp. salt
¼ level tsp. pepper
¼ level tsp. nutmeg

1 level tsp. cinnamon
2 med. white onions
1 c. orange juice
2 tsp. vinegar
2 large potatoes sliced

*end of neck or chump is best

Shorten bones if necessary on best end neck chops. If chump, trim away skin and any excess fat. Toss chops in paper bag with cornflour, salt, peper, nutmeg and cinnamon. Heat pan, just enough oil to grease it. Add chops. Cook quickly until lightly browned on both sides. Remove peel and slice onions and add to pan. Cook until lightly browned. Remove. Add orange juice and vinegar to pan, heat until all brownings are removed. Fill a casserole dish with layers of chops, onions and potatoes, finishing with potatoes on top. Spoon orange juice over all. Sprinkle with little salt and pepper. Cover with lid and bake in moderate slow oven until chops are cooked—about 1 hours. Skim top free of fat.

Linda Rutledge

SRM SOCIETY FOR RANGE MANAGEMENT

Josephine Carricaburu Jauregui
Carricaburu & Jauregui Livestock Co.
Wyoming

"BILOTSKIA-APHEZ ILHARRA" - EKIN
(Roast Leg of Lamb with Lima Beans)

6-7 lb. leg of lamb	2 med. sized green peppers
4-5 cloves of garlic	Salt & pepper
3 or 4 (#303) cans large lima beans	1 (#303) can small whole onions (optional)

Rub entire leg of lamb with garlic, then make small slits in several places in the leg and insert the garlic. Salt lightly. Put roast in pan skin side down in preheated oven of 400°. Turn to the other side when browned, skin side up, salt lightly and put lid on pan. Turn oven down to 300° and continue roasting for approximately 3 to 3½ hours. About 45 mins. before meat is done, wash, seed and quarter green peppers and put them around the roast. When roast is done, spoon off excess fat and add large lima beans to the rest of the drippings along with the green peppers. Salt and pepper to taste. Simmer a few minutes an add small onions. Slice roast and arrange on serving platter. Serve beans as a side dish. Serves 8 to 10.

Background: "Bilotskia eta Aphez Ilharra" or in the English translation, "Lamb with Lima Beans" is a traditional Basque dish. In Esjkual-Harria (the Basque Country) it has always been a dish fit to serve the move revered, that being the town Priest. Therefore, a Basque family serves this dish proudly. I am a second generation Basque whose family hails from the small mountain village of Banca, France.

LAMB AND EGG BAKE

2 c. diced cooked lamb	3 small onions
1 c. cooked peas	2 c. milk
3 hard-boiled eggs	1 tbsp. plain flour
Good pinch of nutmeg, salt and pepper to taste	

Peel and slice the onions, add to the milk and bring to a boil, simmer till onions are cooked. Thicken with the flour which has been mixed to a paste with a little extra milk. Add seasonings and remove from the heat. Place alternate layers of meat, peas and sliced egg in a pie-dish, pour over the onion sauce, dot with butter and bake in a moderate over 20-30 minutes.

The Cook Terachie

LAMB CHOPS ITALIAN

8 lamb chump chops
1 tbsp. oil
15-oz. can tomato soup
½ c. milk
1 green pepper

2 cloves garlic
7-oz. can champignons
2 tsp. Worchestershire sauce
2 tsp. soya sauce
1 tsp. basil

Pepper

Heat oil in pan. Cook chops on both sides until golden brown. In a bowl mix undiluted soup, milk, sliced pepper, crushed garlic, drained champignons, sauce, soya sauce, basil and pepper. Place chops in an oven-proof dish, pour sauce over. Bake uncovered in moderate oven, for 30 minutes, or until chops are tender. Serves 4.   *Robin Johnson*

NAVARIN OF LAMB

2 lbs. boneless lamb (from shoulder)
2 tbsp. butter or oil
1 med. onion, chopped
1 clove garlic, crushed
2 tbsp. flour
2 tbsp. tomato paste
1 c. stock (beef cube and water)
1 c. fresh shelled peas

½ tsp. sugar
1½ tsp. salt
¼ tsp. pepper
Bouquet garni
6-8 small onions
1 turnip sliced
12 small whole potatoes

Trim excess fat from lamb and cut into cubes. heat butter or oil in a heavy pan and brown meat on all sides. Transfer meat to a casserole as it browns. Add onion and garlic to pan and saute over lower heat until onion is soft. Stir in flour and cook until lightly coloured. Add stock, stirring sauce constantly until it thickens and bubbles. Stir in tomato paste, sugar, salt and pepper and pour over lamb. Add bouquet garni. Cover and cook in a 325° oven for 1 hour. Remove bouquet garni and discard. Add onions, turnip, potatoes and peas to casserole, cover and cook for a further hour or until meat is tender. Sprinkle with chopped parsley if desired before serving from casserole. Accompany with fresh, crusty bread. Serves 4-6. *Note:* If using mutton, cook for 1¾ hours before adding main vegetables.

John and Denzil Mills
Charleville, Australia

LAMB SWEET AND SOUR

1 lb. lean lamb from leg
4 tbsp. peanut oil
1 large onion, sliced
1 large green pepper, cut in strips
1 med. carrot, thinly sliced
1 clove garlic, crushed
Small pieces fresh root ginger, grated
or ¼ tsp. ground ginger
1 425g can pineapple pieces
Oil for frying noodles

Water
2 tbsp. cornflour
3 tbsp. white vinegar
2 tbsp. dry sherry
2 tsp. soy sauce
2 tsp. sugar
½ tsp. salt
2-oz. chow mein noodles,
boiled and drained

Trim fat from lamb if necessary, and cut into thin strips. Brown lamb strips quickly in 2 tbsp. hot oil in a deep frying pan. Remove lamb and set aside. Add remaining oil to pan and saute onion, green pepper, carrot, garlic and ginger for 3-4 minutes, stirring often. Remove from heat. Drain pineapple pieces and measure liquid, adding water to make 1½ cups. Add to pan with pineapple pieces. Blend cornflour with sherry, soy sauce, vinegar, sugar and salt and stir into pan contents. Return to heat and stir constantly until mixture thickens and bubbles. Return lamb to pan, cover and simmer very gently for 10 minutes. Do not boil rapidly or lamb will toughen. Serve with crisp fried noodles and/or boiled rice. Serves 6.

LAMB HOT POT

2 lbs. best neck lamb chops
2 sheep's kidneys
2 tbsp. flour
1½ tsp. salt
¼ tsp. pepper
1 large onion, sliced

1 med. carrot, sliced
½ c. chopped celery
1 c. hot stock (beef cube and water)
1 lb. potatoes, sliced
Melted butter
Finely chopped parsley

Remove skin and core from kidneys and slice. Coat lamb chops and kidney with seasoned flour. Place a layer of sliced onion in a casserole dish, top with half of meat and kidney. Place carrot and celery on meat and finish with remaining meat and kidney and last of onion slices on top. Pour over the hot stock, cover and cook in a moderate oven for 1 hour or until meat is almost tender. Place potato slices on top of meat, brush with melted butter, cover and cook for 30 minutes or until potatoes are cooked. Remove lid and leave Hot Pot in oven until potatoes brown nicely. Sprinkle with chopped parsley and serve from casserole. Serves 4-6. NOTE: If using mutton, cook for 1½-2 hours before adding potatoes.

SPECIAL POTTED LAMB

5 lbs. lambneck or shoulders	2 tbsp. chopped parsley
4 oz. onion	3 lbs. 3-oz. canned tomatoes
6 oz. flour	2 c. tomatoe puree
3 tbsp. water	Caraway seeds

Brown lamb well. Add onions and cook well, add flour and brown well. Add rest of the ingredients and finish cooking for 2 hours. Cook vegetables separately and add to the potted lamb. Let simmer for ½ hour. 25 servings.

Background: Ora got this recipe from Chef Gerard, a long-time renowned cook at the Hotel Utah. It became a favorite at the ranch as well as for those eating at the Hotel.

Ora H. Chipman
Delbert Chipman & Son, Woolgrowers
American Fork, Utah

LAMB RIBLETS, HAWAIIAN STYLE

5 lbs. lamb riblets

Salt & pepper	¾ c. catsup
½ c. canned sweetened pineapple juice	3 tbsp. honey

Place riblets in large pan, cover with water, add 1 tsp. salt, parboil 45 minutes until tender. Drain off and trim off excess fat and sprinkle lamb lightly with salt and pepper. Mix catsup, pineapple juice and honey in a saucepan and simmer about 5 min. Brush over lamb riblets and grill riblets until browned on both sides, brushing frequently with sauce. Serves 8.

Ora H. Chipman
Delbert Chipman & Son, Woolgrowers
American Fork, Utah

BAKED LAMB LOAF

2 lb. ground lamb	2 tbsp. minced onion
1 c. cracker crumbs	1 egg
2 tbsp. chopped parsley	1 c. milk

Combine all ingredients and mix thoroughly. Pack into a 5x9 inch loaf pan or a 2 quart ring mold. Bake in a slow oven, 300° for 1½ hours. 8 to 10 servings.

PARMESAN CUTLETS

8 cutlets	2 c. fresh breadcrumbs
Flour	½ c. parmesan cheese
1 egg	2 tbsp. chopped parsley
2 tbsp. milk	2 hard-boiled eggs

Combine breadcrumbs, cheese, parsley and finely-chopped egges in a bowl. Remove excess fat from the cutlets. Roll cutlets in flour, dip in egg beaten with milk then coat with the breadcrumb mixture, pressing firmly. Put cutlets in a greased baking dish and bake in a moderate oven 30-35 minutes or until cutlets are baked through and a golden brown. Serves 4.

G. Morris

SAVOURY LAMB HOT POT

3 tbsp. ghee or margarine	2 c. potato cubes
2 small onions	2 large carrots, cut in fine rounds
1 clove garlic	2 stalks celery (sliced)
Meat pieces cut into cubes	2 cans beef soup or
4 c. shredded cabbage	3 or 4 cups of stock
2 tbsp. chopped parsley	

An excellent way to use up cold left-over mutton, beef or chicken. Melt ghee, add onions and garlic. Saute until tender but not brown. Add cabbage and remaining ingredients. Then add soup or stock. Simmer until tender. Different spices of soy sauce may be used to change the flavour of this recipe as preferred by the cook.

Patrick Beres

SHEPHERD'S PIE

2-4 lbs. lamb, one-inch cubes	1 tsp. salt
2 tbsp. oil	¼ tsp. black pepper
1 cubed onion	1 can (14-oz.) beef broth
2 divided tomatoes	¼ c. sliced pimento-stuffed olives
1 large minced garlic glove	2 tbsp. lemon juice
1½ tsp. ground cumin	3 c. mashed potatoes

In a large iron skillet or Dutch oven, brown lamb (beef or pork will do in a pinch), in oil, a few at a time. As they are browned, remove from pan and set aside. When all pork is browned, saute onion and garlic in drippings until soft. Chop one tomato, add to pan with cumin, salt, pepper, broth, lemon juice, and meat cubes. Heat to bubbling, lower heat, cover, and simmer one hour or until meat is tender. Uncover and bubble rapidly for about 15 minutes or until liquid is thickened and reduced approximately to one-fourth the original amount. Add olives. Add mashed potatoes to top of skillet over meat mixture much as you would add pastry to the top of a cobbler. Bake in oven at 350° temperature until potatoes are golden brown and crispy. Serve with a vegetable and hot rolls.

Background: This is a tried and proven recipe which can easily be cooked at home in the wood cookstove or on the range in a Dutch oven.

SPARE RIBS

2 breasts of lamb or 4 lbs. pork spare ribs

SAUCE:

3-4 tbsp. vegetable oil	1 tsp. salt
1 tsp. minced garlic	1 tsp. basil or thyme
2 med. onions	4 tbsp. honey
6-oz. tin tomato puree	8 tbsp. beef stock
4 tbsp. white vinegar	8 tbsp. Worcestershire sauce
	1 tsp. dry mustard

Cut lamb into individual portions. Strip as much fat from bones as possible and bake in moderate oven in a shallow baking tin for 35-40 minutes, draining excess fat when necessary.
SAUCE: Heat oil in a 10-inch pan, and when a light haze forms about it, add garlic and finely-chopped onions and cook for 3-4 minutes without browning. Combine remaining sauce ingredients. Add to pan, mix thoroughly and simmer uncovered for 10-15 minutes. Thoroughly coat spare ribs with sauce, return to oven and baste every 10 minutes until spare ribs are brown and crispy. Serve at once.

PORK

Pete Petoskey
Lewiston, Michigan

ARABIAN PORK CHOPS
(with a Polish Flavor)

2 pork chops per guest	1 can mushroom soup per 8 chops
(unless one is a lady)	Wine, optional
1 tomato per 2 chops	Mushrooms, optional
1 onion per 2 chops	Flour
1 green pepper per 8 chops	Oil or shortening

Salt & pepper, garlic salt, flavor salt, and Worcestershire Sauce

Brown pork chops, using seasonings to taste, slice tomato and onions, dice peppers and split mushrooms. Remove pork chops and make a roux (gravy) using mushroom soup, flour, wine and maybe a little water. Remove roux and make a layer of pork chops, tomatoes, onions, green peppers and mushrooms. Then another layer, depending on number of guests. Pour roux over contents. Cover and cook for 1-1½ hours in 350° oven. When done, remove pork chops and vegetables to platter. Thicken roux if necessary with a bit more flour. Serve with mashed potatoes or noodles.

Maurice & Barbara Bidart
Leonard Creek Ranch
Nevada

MB

"CHORIZOS" (BASQUE SAUSAGE)

40 lbs. ground pork	3 qt. red pepper pulp
½ c. crushed garlic	9 oz. salt

Prepare pulp a day ahead. (We use sweet dry red peppers). Soak peppers, then scrap pulp out (do not use skins). Mix with 3 quarts water. Grind pork (using ½-inch blade) ⅔-meat, ⅓-fat. Put meat in pan, add garlic, salt and pulp. Let stand 24 hours. Then put in casings (We use lamb or pig casings.) Hang Chorizos a day or two, til dry—prick casings before hanging.

Background: This is a sausage recipe we use when we butcher the hogs. Before we put the Chorizo meat in the casings, we cook up a patty or two to see if it needs more salt.

S. O'Sullivan,
Clonmell, Clermont, Australia

SPANISH PORK CHOPS

4 pork chops	*1 green capsicum, sliced*
Seasoned flour	*8 ozs. can peeled tomatoes*
2 tbsp. oil	*2 tsp. Worcestershire sauce*
2 onions	*1 stock cube*

Roll chops in flour, fry to light brown in oil. Drain, place in shallow casserole. Fry chopped onions in oil. Add remaining ingredients, simmer 10 minutes. Pour over chops. Cover and bake in moderate oven 1 hour until tender.

Johnneta Jackson
Peter V. Jackson Ranch
Harrison, Montana

GRANDMA MCLEAN'S BAKED HAM

Cut a ½-inch slice of ham into 3 pieces, allowing 2 pieces per serving. Rub each piece with dry mustard. Layer the ham in a deep baking dish. Sprinkle each layer with a light dusting of brown sugar, tiny pinch of curry powder, and ⅓ cup of dry bread crumbs. Pour into baking dish, enough buttermilk to cover all the layers. Set in refrigerator overnight. Cook casserole very slowly, about 4 hours at 300°. Lower heat if it starts to boil over.

Background: The buttermilk acts as a tenderizer and adds extra zest. It was very plentiful on the ranch. Home-cured ham was dry and tough, sometimes too salty. This was Grandma's washday supper, because it didn't take any extra time — and the laundry got done!

Diane Palmer
Charleville, Australia

OFFHAM SWEET AND SOUR MUTTON

Cubed mutton or beef
2 large onions
1 large can pineapple pieces
5 tbsp. vinegar

1 green pepper
1 can pineapple juice
1-3 tbsp. soya sauce
Cornflour

Oil or margarine

Brown meat cubes in oil or margarine, add sliced onions, and pepper, cut into strips. When limp, add pineapple pieces, juice, vinegar, soya sauce, salt. Mix cornflour into a smooth paste and add to meat. Simmer until cooked.

Recipe Notes

FISH

CHUCK WAGON CHOW

The great era of cattle-driving across the Texas plains to Kansas railheads only lasted twenty years (approximately from 1865 to 1885), but enough folklore, books, songs, and movies have come out of it to make it seem like major American history. There are people all over the world who couldn't tell you who John Adams or Thomas Jefferson were, but who know all about Wild Bill Hickok. Millions who can't speak English know the meaning of the words cowpuncher, trail boss, and chuck wagon.

The cattle drives of the West were by no means the first in this country. As early as the 1790s, herds were driven from western New York and Pennsylvania or along the Cumberland Road to New York City, Baltimore, and Richmond, to be slaughtered for meat. And even before that, butchers used to drive cattle from farm to farm, trading beef-on-the-hoof or their services as slaughterers in return for farm produce. On one occasion, during the 1850s, some enterprising Texans drove 150 head of cattle all the way to New York. The cattle drive took two years, but the profit was substantial enough to justify the trouble.

Then in 1867, the Kansas and Pacific Railroad reached Abilene, Kansas, and cattle could be shipped to Chicago slaughterhouses, instead of driven there on the hoof. Later, as the rails moved westward, other towns in Kansas — notably Dodge City — took over from Abilene as the wild "cow towns."

Although the cowboys took their orders from the trail boss, the cook was the real keeper of the crew. Besides preparing three hot meals a day, he also served as doctor and barber. On starlit nights his last responsibility before turning in was to point the chuck wagon's tongue toward the North Star so the trail boss would have a sure compass heading the next morning.

The dining table on the range was anything the cowboy found usable. He used the ground, his lap, or his bedroll as a table. No one was allowed to use the cook's private workbench. The cowhand picked out his utensils, and then went from pot to pot helping himself to food and coffee. He took all he could eat at his first helping — just in case there wasn't enough for a second helping. Usually the cowboy was considerate of others, following a strict etiquette. When removing the lid from a pot for a helping, he was careful to place it so the lid wouldn't touch sand. Then he stood downwind so that any dust he kicked up wouldn't blow into someone's food. He never took the last pieces of food unless he was sure everyone was finished. It was against the rules to begin dishing up food until the cook called. It was also against custom to ride a horse into camp and to tie it to the chuck wagon — no one liked horse hair in the food. If a cowboy refilled his coffee cup and another hand called, "man at the pot," he was obliged to go around and fill any cups held out to him. Proper conduct around the wagon was as important to the cowboy as society etiquette was to his Eastern brother.

FISH

The Four Sixes Ranch
Guthrie, Texas

6666

BRAZOS RIVER FISH FRY

4 lbs. catfish	1 tsp. pepper
3 eggs slightly beaten	2 tsp. chili powder
2 tsp. salt	¾ c. yellow cornmeal

Clean, skin and fillet catfish. Mix eggs, salt, peper and chili powder. Dip fish in egg mixture, then in cornmeal. Pan fry in oil 1-inch deep about 8 minutes until flaky. Serves 4.

James Newland
Greenwood Ranches
Bell Fourche, South Dakota

MONA BASIN HAM-STUFFED TROUT

4 cleaned trout, 1-lb. each	½ tsp. thyme
4 thin slices smoked ham	½ tsp. basil
4 cloves finely minced garlic	½ tsp. sugar
½ c. breadcrumbs	½ c. parsley
Juice of one lemon plus a bit of grated rind	

Combine all ingredients but ham and trout. Add salt and fresh ground black pepper to taste. Stuff each trout with a slice of ham and enough of crumb mixture to fill body cavity. Close with a skewer if necessary.

Put about ¼ c. olive oil in a heavy cast iron or earthenware dish, add fish and put into oven at 350° until done, 15 or 20 minutes. While fish are in the oven, heat ¼ cup each butter and olive oil in a heavy pan on stove top. Add finely minced garlic, 1 tsp. paprika, 1 tbsp. fresh minced or ½ tsp. dried basil, and ½ cup cream sherry. Cook over a high flame stirring constantly until liquid is somewhat thickened. When the fish are done, cover with sauce and garnish with cress and twists of lemon.

SRM **SOCIETY FOR RANGE MANAGEMENT**

SALMON PIE

PIE SHELL:
6-oz. plain cracker-type biscuits
4-oz. butter   *¼ c. water*

FILLING:

1 med. onion	*10½-oz. can of chicken soup*
½ green pepper	*3 eggs*
7-8-oz. can salmon	*¼ cup milk*
2-oz. butter	*Salt & pepper*

PIE SHELL: Melt butter, add water. Crush biscuits finely, add to butter mixture. Mix thoroughly; press on base and sides of 9-inch pie plate. Refrigerate.
FILLING: Chop onion, pepper; drain salmon, reserving liquid. Heat butter in saucepan, add onion and pepper, saute until tender but not brown, add soup, stir thoroughly, remove from heat. Beat eggs and milk, add to soup mixture with salmon liquid; add salt and pepper. Place flaked salmon in base of pie shell, pour sauce over. Bake in moderate oven for 35-40 minutes or until filling is set and surface is golden brown.

Kay Graber
Nebraska Pioneer Cookbook
Nebraska

SCALLOPED OYSTERS

Scald one quart of oysters in their liquor, drain them, remove the beards, and place them in a scalloped shell that has been well buttered and sprinkled with breadcrumbs. Melt in a saucepan one large tbsp. of butter, stir in one tsp. full of flour, cook a little, add one gill of broth and enough of the oyster liquor as to make the sauce the consistency of cream, boil gently eight minutes, and add ½ tsp. of chopped parsley. Pour it over the oysters, sprinkle breadcrumbs over them, lay one or two bits of butter on top and bake ten or twelve minutes.

Historic Pioneer Trail Recipe

MORMON FISH CHOWDER

2 lbs. fresh or frozen haddock or
other fish fillets
4-oz. salt pork, diced
1 c. chopped onion
4 c. cubed, peeled potatoes
2 c. water

2 tsp. salt
¼ tsp. pepper
2 c. milk
1 13-oz. can evaporated milk
2 tbsp. all-purpose flour

Thaw frozen fish. In large saucepan cook salt pork slowly till golden brown. Drain, reserving 1 tbsp. fat in pan. set aside cooked salt pork. Add onion to pan; cook till tender but not brown. Stir in potatoes and water. Add fish fillets, salt, and pepper. Bring to boiling; cook over low heat till potatoes are tender and fish flakes easily when tested with a fork, 15 to 20 minutes. With slotted spatula, remove fish. Break fish into bite-size pieces; return to pan. Mix milk and evaporated milk. Slowly stir milk mixture into flour till smooth; add to fish mixture. Add cooked salt pork; cook over low heat till heated through (do not boil). Makes 8 servings.

June Schmautz
Fairfax, Virginia

PICKLED PICKEREL
(Northern Pike)

Pickerel (the amount depends on your fishing skill)

PICKLING LIQUID:

1 c. white vinegar
½ c. sugar
3 bay leaves
1 c. sliced onions

12 whole allspice
⅓ tsp. diced dill seed
Several whole small round peppers

Clean, skin and cut pickerel into small pieces. Salt and let stand overnight or for 2 days in refrigerator. Drain and cover with pickling liquid and let stand in refrigerator for 2 days. Liquid must cover the fish, if not double the liquid recipe. Ready to eat and tastes like herring.

H.F. Heady
Berkeley, California

SMOKED FISH

*1 heaping tsp. salt (non-iodized) for each 10-inch fish
or equivalent in slices or fillets.*

1 drop liquid smoke per tsp. salt

White pepper, dry mustard, & garlic powder to taste

Mix ingredients, rub 1 tsp. into each piece (inside out or both sides of fillets), pack pieces closely together in a non-metal container, a large flat bottom glass or enameled container works best. Refrigerate for 12 hours (longer is o.k., but fish will contain more salt). Drain and smoke (hickory or fruit wood with little bark for 12 to 24 hours. This works on any kind of fish, including Salmon. *Variations and hints:* A little white wine (½-cup or less) added on top after the pieces are packed in marinate adds a nice touch. Salt, but no liquids, in the marinate is purposeful to draw moisture out of the fish. Use new marinate for each batch of fish.

Mrs. Suzanne Field
Trinidad

SOMALI FISH

2 lbs. of sea fish	1 lb. ripe tomatoes
½ lb. onions	1 small can tomato puree
½ lb. green peppers	Dash of Tobasco sauce
4 cloves garlic	Seasoning

Peel and chop the onions and garlic. Lightly fry in oil until soft but not brown. Add the green peppers, tomatoes and tomatoe puree, 1 cup of water and the seasoning. Cook until green pepper is a little soft (5 minutes). Bone and cut the fish into ½-inch cubes and add to the pot. Cook only for 5 minutes until the fish is firm but not over-cooked. Serve with hot rice, and a green salad.

Background: This recipe originates from the south of Somalia where the natives living near the coast have copied a lot of Italian ways, therefore using tomato and tomato puree in many recipes. Only the tribes living near the coast will eat fish — none of the herdsmen living in the interior eat fish; preferring goat stew and raising their cattle especially to ship to Saudi Arabia.

POULTRY

Facts

Ranchers, and others who properly manage range for cattle, sheep, goats and horses are also supervising the care and production of many other important resources needed by the general public, i.e. clean air, clean water, wildlife, recreation, scenic views, and others.

Rangelands are also a great source of energy. Minerals like coal, uranium, bentonite, iron ore, oil and gas are mined from beneath millions of acres of rangelands.

The Trail Boss Says:

Today the range management profession is recognized throughout the world. Many colleges and universities offer both undergraduate and graduate degrees in this field. A range management education requires a broad subject matter background in the plant, animal, and soil sciences. Courses in other natural resource sciences are also essential. The range manager must be able to integrate a broad-based education with experience to develop solutions for today's complex range problems.

James Newland
Greenwood Ranches
Bell Fourche, South Dakota

W
+

HOLIDAY GOOSE

Prepare one young 8 to 12 pound goose the same way you would a turkey. Prick the fatty skin. Fill the cavities with dressing such as apple, prune or chestnut, or fill with cut onion, garlic cloves or leeks sprinkled with sage and marjoram.

Preheat oven to 450°. While waiting, rub herbs over goose: parsley, sage, rosemary and thyme. Place goose on rack in uncovered pan; allow about 25 minutes per pound. Reduce heat to 350° after goose is in the oven. Remove excess fat, keep for cooking. A half hour before done, turn goose over once to insure crisp skin. After your goose is cooked, decorate with cranberry garland.

H.F. Heady
Berkeley, California

SMOKED BREAST OF DUCK

One fifth of red wine	¼ c. salad oil
1 c. soy sauce	1 tsp. Wrights liquid smoke
½ c. Worcestershire sauce	1 tsp. finely ground black pepper
2 tsp. tabasco	2 tsp. cayenne pepper
½ c. brown sugar	3 tbsp. dry mustard
½ c. salt (non-iodized)	1 tbsp. garlic powder

Mix liquids. Mix dry ingredients and make a paste with small amounts of liquids. Mix into liquids. Marinate duck breasts in mixture in glass, pottery, enamel container (non-metal) for 24 hours, turn at least once, in refrigerator, smoke for 24 to 36 hours or until firm when cool. Smoker should operate at about 130° with a little draft. Use hickory or applewood, but bark and twigs are not good. Smoker does two things slowly—dries and cooks, but pieces should be red in middle when finished. This does 28 breast-pieces in my Little Chef smoker.

Other Hints: Save marinate for next batch but add one-half as much salt and seasonings. Vary to taste especially the salt, or even leave most of it out. A longer marinate is o.k. but it means mostly more salt in the meat. Final product must be frozen as it will mold in the refrigerator about as fast as bacon. If wood is dry it can be soaked for 24 hours to make more smoke.

Nancy Reagan
Washington, D.C.

BAJA CALIFORNIA CHICKEN

8 boned chicken breasts
Seasoning salt & pepper to taste
2 cloves garlic, crushed

4 tbsp. olive oil
4 tbsp. tarragon vinegar
⅔ c. dry sherry

Sprinkle chicken with seasoning salt and pepper. Crush garlic into oil and vinegar in a skillet. Saute chicken pieces until golden brown, turning frequently. Remove; place in a baking dish. Pour sherry over pieces and place in 350° oven for 10 minutes. Yields 8 servings.

Mrs. Suzanne Field
Trinidad

TRADITIONAL TRINIDAD CHICKEN PILAU

1 chicken
2 onions, chopped
½-lb. pumpkin
½-lb. chick peas

¼-lb. corn
¼-lb. chopped carrots
1 lb. rice
A little oil

Seasoning to taste

Cook the chopped onions in the oil until they are light brown and soft. Add pumpkin and chopped carrots and fry a little longer. Cut chicken into pieces and add to the pot. Stir. Add all the other vegetables and seasoning and water, boil for 15 minutes. Now add rice and continue to boil until rice is cooked and all the water in the pot has been absorbed.

Background: This is a traditional recipe from slave days of Trinidad when most of their food was cooked in one pot. Being a small island there is not enough room for cattle ranches as such, so chicken and fish is eaten far more than beef, which is imported.

Kay Norris
N 4 Ranch
Junction, Texas

N4

POOR MAN' DUMPLINGS

2 c. flour sifted   *1 rounded tbsp. Crisco*
½ c. hot chicken broth

Mix flour and Crisco. Make a well in the center of mixture and add broth. Mix until a stiff dough. Roll out very thin and cut in squares. Place dumplings in a pot of boiling chicken broth, a few at a time, placing lid on pot after each addition. Simmer slowly until done.

Background: This threshing recipe was my grandmother's and was always a favorite during round-up and thrashing times. Our ranch has been owned and operated by our family for 77 years. The ranch was one of the first in Kimble County to irrigate alfalfa and raise Hereford cows before the turn of the century in the years before Grandfather bought it.

Rosemary Boykin
Botswana, South Africa
Washington, D.C.

KING RANCH CHICKEN
(Casserole)

1 3-lb. chicken	1 can cream of chicken soup
1 med. onion	⅔ c. tomato & green chilies
1 rib of celery	1⅓ c. chicken broth
2½ tsp. salt	1 doz. corn tortillas
Water	2 c. grated American cheese

1 c. chopped onion

Cook until tender: chicken covered with water, onion, celery and 2 tsp. salt. Bone and cut into small pieces. Reserve 1⅓ cups chicken broth. Combine: soup, tomatoes with green chilies, broth and ½ tsp. salt in saucepan and heat. Layer chicken, tortillas (cut into ½-inch strips), cheese, onion and heated sauce in casserole. Repeat layers, ending with cheese. Bake 250° for 20 minutes, then 200° for 40 minutes. Serves 10.

Ann Gates
Corvallis, Oregon

QUICK FIX CHICKEN

1 frying chicken, cut up

⅓ c. Heinz 57 sauce	2 tbsp. lemon juice
2 tbsp. Worcestershire sauce	Paprika

Place chicken in single layer in baking pan with cover. Mix Heinz 57 sauce, Worcestershire sauce and lemon juice, and brush over chicken pieces. Sprinkle with paprika. Cover and bake at 400° until tender, approx. 40-60 minutes. Juice makes a delicious gravy. Serve with rice.

SRM **SOCIETY FOR RANGE MANAGEMENT**

Recipe Notes

WILDLIFE

The Society for Range Management is the broadest, most knowledgable organization concerned with rangelands and their renewable resource products and values. Its purposes are:

• to promote a more comprehensive understanding of rangelands and their use;

• to provide information about range management principles and practices;

• to foster a public appreciation of the economic, social, and environmental benefits to be gained from intelligent range management.

Mary Lewis
Gaithersburg, Maryland

ELK CHILI

2 lb. ground elk
1 med. onion
1 tsp. basil
½ tsp. oregano
1-2 tbsp. chili powder
2 cloves garlic, minced

1 large can tomatoes
2 8-oz. cans tomato sauce
1 tbsp. liquid smoke
1 16-oz can kidney beans
1 c. water
Salt and pepper to taste

Cook meat, until all pinkness is gone. Add remaining ingredients, simmer for 2 hours. Serves 6-8. Venison can also be substituted.

James Newland
Greenwood Ranches
Belle Fourche, South Dakota

BLACKBIRD PIE

12 blackbirds
(or any other small game birds)
1 c. diced salt pork
2 c. sliced potatoes
1 chopped onion

3 whole cloves
¼ c. minced parsley
2 tbsp. browned flour
2 tbsp. butter
pastry crust

water to cover and season

Dress and clean the birds. Split each in half. Place in stew pan with water and boil, skimming off scum. Add a sprinkling of pepper, parsley, onion and cloves, then add pork and boil until meat is tender—about an hour. During the last half hour of cooking, add potatoes.

Thicken broth with flour and boil for a few minutes. Add one tbsp. of the butter, mix and remove from fire. Grease baking dish with one tbsp. butter and put in alternative layers of birds and potatoes moistening each layer with broth. Cover with pastry crust. Slit crust in several places. Bake for 15 minutes at 425° or until browned, then bake another 15 minutes at 75°.

Historical Pioneer Recipe

BUFFALO STEAK

fat
sirloin of buffalo steak

1 tbsp. flour
1 c. milk

salt

Render some fat in a hot skillet. Add sirloin of buffalo steak and sear on both sides. At lower heat, cook as beefsteak until done. For gravy, add a tablespoon of flour to the pan drippings and cook until brown. Stirring constantly, add a cup of milk and bring to a boil. Salt to taste.

Mrs. Lyndon B. Johnson
The LBJ Ranch
Johnson City, Texas

LBJ

Greetings . . . From the deer country of Texas to the deer country of Montana.
In Texas, from November 15 on, the hills are alive with the sound of hunters.
Should you just happen to have the ingredients on hand, try our favorite recipe
for . . .

DEER MEAT SAUSAGE

GRIND:

one-half deer	*20 oz. black pepper*
one-half hog	*8 oz. red pepper*
25 oz. salt	*2 oz. sage*

Mix together for 200 pounds of sausage. Place uncut in a 400° oven in an open
pan with a small amount of water. Cook 10 minutes on one side and turn to
repeat on the other side. Slice in inch-long pieces and serve.

Jack Absalom
Australia

CASSEROLE OF ANY MEAT OR GAME IN THE BUSH

500 g. or 1 lb. meat	*½ pint stock or water*
2 slices bacon	*1 stick celery*
1 onion	*1 carrot*
2 tomatoes	*1 level tbsp. flour*
2 dessertspoons peas	*salt and pepper to taste*

Cut meat into slices or pieces and dip into the seasoned flour. Peel and slice the
vegetables. Place bacon in dish then half the vegetables, add meat and rest of
vegetables. Cook over slow fire for 2 hours.

Historical Pioneer Recipe

BUFFALO JERKY

Slice buffalo meat along the grain into strips 1/8" thick, 1/2" wide and 2 to 3"
long. Hang them on a rack in a pan and bake at 200° until dry. To prepare outside, suspend them over a fire or drape them on bushes to dry in the sun.

Kathleen Mullendore
Mullendore Cross Bell Ranch
Copan, Oklahoma

BUFFALO ROAST

20 lb. buffalo roast
4 large onions, chopped
8 tsp. salt
4 c. sour cream
4 tbsp. brown sugar
12 tbsp. bourbon
8 c. beer

8 tbsp. flour
juice of 4 lemons

2 16-oz. bottles Wishbone
Italian dressing

Marinate roast all night in the Wishbone Italian dressing. Salt roast on all sides and put in a very heavy large roaster or Dutch oven. Add onion, brown sugar, whiskey and beer. Cover and bake for 4 hours at 300°, or until tender. If pan juices begin to dry up, add more beer. Add flour to sour cream and lemon juice to drippings for gravy.

Background: For 40 years the Mullendore Cross Bell Ranch ran buffalo and at least 5,000 cattle a year. Now we raise quarter horses exclusively and have offspring from some of the greatest cutting horse sires. My husband, Gene, and I have stocked the ranch with many kinds of deer and wild birds, including 800 turkeys. All the ponds are stocked with fish and the ranch has become a wonderful wildlife refuge.

Ruth Buchanan
Thermopolis, Wyoming

COMMUNITY BUFFALO BARBEQUE
(1000 to 1500 people)

Dig pit 5 feet wide, 10 feet long and 5 feet deep. Build fire for 48 hours before placing meat in to cook.

Bone and roll into 40-lb. pieces approximately 800 pounds of buffalo meat. First wrap meat in butcher cloth (about 80 pounds each.) Add a generous amount of barbecue sauce and wrap in heavy foil. Then wrap with 1-inch chicken wire. Use strong wire to fasten each piece to a two-inch pipe, approximately five feet long. Place in pit so that there is white ash no closer than one foot from the bottom of the meat as it hangs in the pit. Cover with galvanized sheet metal and then with 2 feet of dirt on top. Let cook for 11 hours, or a little longer if well-done meat is preferred. **See Barbeque Sauce recipe, next page.**

BARBEQUE SAUCE

2 green peppers	1 gallon tomato juice
6 stalks celery	½ c. salad oil
3 large onions	½ c. vinegar
6 small jalapeno peppers (hot)	2 c. sugar
1 bottle Worchestershire Sauce	1 gallon tomato puree
1 bottle steak sauce	

Blend peppers, celery, onions and jalapenos together and cook. Then add other ingredients and simmer for one hour. Makes 3 gallons. 15 gallons are needed for one buffalo. Add some of this sauce to the meat juice when it is served. Scrap meat can be ground for buffalo burgers—delicious!

Historic Pioneer Recipe

STUFFED VENISON STEAKS

2 lbs. venison steak, ¾-in. thick	Salt
1½ c. milk	Pepper
6 slices bacon	½ c. cold water
⅓ c. sliced green onion, with tops	¼ c. all-purpose flour

Cut venison steak into six serving-size pieces. Place in a shallow pan; pour milk over meat. Cover and refrigerate overnight, turning meat several times. Drain meat; pat dry with paper toweling. Cook bacon till crips. Drain, reserving 2 tablespoons drippings. Crumble bacon and set aside. With sharp knife, carefully cut a pocket in the side of each piece of meat. Mix bacon and green onion. Stuff onion mixture into pockets in meat. In 10-inch skillet brown steaks in reserved bacon drippings. Season with salt and pepper. Add ½ cup water. Cover and simmer over low heat till tender, 45 to 60 minutes. Remove meat to platter. For gravy, measure pan juices; add enough water to make 1½ cups. Blend ½ cup cold water slowly into flour. Stir into pan juice mixture. Cook, stirring constantly, till mixture thickens and bubbles. Season to taste with salt and pepper. Makes 6 servings.

Background: Before the great surge of settlers moved in, deer, bear, and elks were abundant on the frontier. The hunter lucky enough to shoot one could feed his family for a long time. The Pioneer cook had several ways or removing the "wild game taste." One method was to soak the meat overnight in salted water. For the very tough cuts, the meat was soaked in a mixture of vinegar, water, and spices sometimes for as long as several days. Another method, which is more suited to modern tastes, is to soak the meat in milk as in this recipe.

Jeanne Edwards
Saval Ranch
North Fort, Nevada

∧L

VENISON WITH SOUR CREAM

2 lbs. venison	1 clove garlic
½ c. fat	1 c. diced carrots
1 c. diced celery	2 c. water
½ c. minced onion	1 tsp. salt
1 bay leaf	4 tbsp. flour
4 tbsp. butter	1 c. sour cream

Cut venison in pieces and melt fat in heavy frying pan. Add meat and garlic. Brown on all sides and arrange in dish. Put vegetables in remaining fat and cook for 2 minutes. Add salt, pepper and water, pour over meat. Bake in a slow oven until meat is tender. Melt butter in frying pan and stir in flour. Add water that the meat was cooked in and boil until thick. Add sour cream and more salt, if necessary. Pour over meat and vegetables.

Background: This recipe was given to me by a deer hunter that was stranded at the Saval Ranch during an unexpected snow storm.

H.R. Heady
Berkeley, California

VENISON SALAMI

4 lbs. fine ground venison	1½ tsp. garlic powder
(add 1 lb. suet when grinding)	1½ tsp. ground black pepper
¼ c. curing salt	2 tbsp. liquid smoke

Thoroughly mix ingredients, cover and chill for 24 hours. Divide into quarters, shape each quarter into 8 inch logs and roll each in a 12x10 inch nylon net. Roll tightly and tie ends. Place logs on rack on broiler pan and bake 4 hours in a 200° oven. Remove net, pat roll with paper towel to absorb extra fat. Wrap in foil and refrigerate or freeze. Slice thinly for snacks with cocktails.

Variations do well, for example, half venison and half pork, without the suet. Keep fat under 25 percent.

SMOTHERED PHEASANT

2 tbsp. all-purpose flour
½ tsp. salt
⅛ tsp. pepper
2 medium onions, sliced
2 tbsp. lard
1 1-to-3-lb. pheasant
ready-to-cook, cut up

1 c. water
¾ c. milk
2 tbsp. all-purpose flour
1 tsp. salt
Paprika
Dash pepper

In plastic bag combine 2 tablespoons flour, ½ salt, and pepper. Add pheasant pieces, a few at a time; shake to coat. In skillet brown pheasant slowly in hot lard. Arrange onions atop pheasant; add 1 cup water. Cover tightly; cook over low heat till tender, 45 to 60 minutes. Remove pheasant; measure liquid in pan. Add water, if necessary, to equal 1 cup. In screw-top jar shake milk, flour, salt and pepper till blended. Stir into pan liquid. Cook, stirring constantly, till thickened and bubbly. Cook and stir 2 to 3 minutes more. Before serving, sprinkle pheasant with paprika. Pass gravy with pheasant. Makes 2 to 4 servings.

Background: In addition to big game, there were also a great number of wild birds on the frontier. The prairie hen, duck, wild turkey, and goose were the most common. They were usually prepared by braising in a skillet as in the recipe for Smothered Pheasant. The first time Americans saw what has become a most popular game bird was when pheasants were brought from China in 1880.

J. W. Bailey
Prairie Ridge Ranch
Cheyenne, Wyoming

ROASTED RATTLESNAKE

Skin rattlesnake and cut into pieces. Place pieces on a skewer and put the skewer over glowing coals and keep it turning. When the meat quits sizzling it is done.

For a different taste treat, roll the cooked meat in a flour tortilla with refried beans and eat it like a sandwich.

Deseret Land & Livestock Corp.
Deseret Land & Livestock Ranch
Woodruff, Utah

J X

GROUND VENISON JERKY

5 lbs. venison, ground
1-½ tsp. Morton's Tenderquick salt
9 tsp. salt
2 tsp. black pepper
2 tsp. garlic powder

1 tsp. cayenne pepper
1-½ tsp. cardamon
3 tsp. Accent
1 tsp. marjoram
1 oz. (2 tbsp.) liquid smoke

1 oz. (2 tbsp.) water

Mix ground venison with spices. Roll meat between sheets of wax paper to ¼"
thickness. Flip over and replace top sheet of wax paper with fresh piece. Then
flip back over and remove other piece of wax paper and brush meat with liquid
smoke and water. Then place another fresh sheet of wax paper on this side (both
sides should have fresh wax paper.) Bake at lowest temperature of oven for 3 to
4 hours. When meat is cool and dry, cut into strips.

This recipe came from *Farm Wife* or *Farm Journal* Magazine.

Bill Mabbutt

SMOKED VENISON JERKY (DRY PREPARATION)

5 lbs. choice venison roast or venison
pieces, cut with grain of the meat
⅔ c. Morton's Tenderquick
½ c. sugar

2 tbsp. black pepper
1 tsp. garlic powder
1 tsp. cayenne pepper
1 tsp. Accent

If using venison roast, chill and slice with grain 1/8" thick. If using venison pieces,
remove all major tendons and tenderize by grasping each piece with both hands
and jerking lengthwise. Slice if necessary.

Combine Tenderquick, salts and spices in a large shaker. Sprinkle a layer of
the mixture into the bottom of a plastic or enamel container. Cover with a single
layer of venison slices. Repeat until all venison is used. Let set 2 days in a cool
place (about 40°.) Place venison slices in a single layer on racks in a smoker over
green alder, fruitwood or hickory chips. Smoke at 120-150° for 5 or 6 hours. Cool
thoroughly before refrigerating. Store in a dry place. Makes approximately 1-½
pounds.

RABBIT WITH CREAM GRAVY

1 to 1-½lb. *ready-to-cook rabbit, cut up*
¼ c. *all-purpose flour*
¾ tsp. *salt*
dash pepper
2 tbsp. *cooking oil*
1 c. *chopped onion*
½ tsp. *ground allspice*
1/8 tsp. *ground cloves*
1 *bay leaf*
¼ c. *water*
1 tbsp. *vinegar*
paprika
1 to 1-¼ c. *milk*
2 tbsp. *all-purpose flour*
1 tbsp. *plum preserves (optional)*

Coat rabbit with mixture of ¼ c. flour, salt, and pepper. In skillet brown meat slowly in hot oil, about 15 minutes. Add onion, allspice, cloves, and bay leaf. Stir in water and vinegar. Cover; simmer till meat is tender, 45 to 60 minutes. Add more water if needed. Remove rabbit to serving platter; keep warm. Sprinkle with paprika. Remove bay leaf from drippings. In screw-top jar shake ½ c. milk with 2 tbsp. flour, ½ tsp. salt, and dash pepper till blended: stir into pan drippings. Add ½ c. more milk and preserves, if desired. Cook and stir till thick and bubbly. If necessary, stir in additional milk to desired consistency. Serve gravy with rabbit. Serves 4.

Background: Cooking on the trail was often difficult, especially where fuel was scarce. Hardwood made the best fires, but in timberless country the pioneers often had to resort to hay, weeds, and sagebrush, which burned very quickly and produced a great many hot ashes. Sometimes, cow or buffalo chips were used as fuel. But the odor of such a fire was unpleasant and sometimes affected the taste of the food. In dry weather buffalo chips made a hot fire, but burned very quickly. When wet, they would hardly burn at all and had to be fanned to keep the fire going. In spite of these hardships, the pioneers on the trail managed to enjoy recipes such as Rabbit with Cream Gravy.

Peter N. Jensen
Lincoln, Nebraska

QUAIL STEW

Cut 2 quails lengthwise down the back. Place them in a pan with some butter and cook them. Have ready 2 large slices of toasted or fried bread and lay the quail upon them. Add a little water to the liquor, thicken it and pour over the birds. Squeeze a little lemon juice over them.

Background: From the Blue Ribbon Cook Book, 1907.

M. L. (Pete) Petoskey
Lewiston, Michigan

PETOSKEY RABBIT

3 rabbits (hares) cut into 5 pieces each
bag containing flour or cracker crumbs,
 salt & pepper
2 or 3 tbsp. shortening, lard, or oil
¼ c. red wine—burgundy
¼ c. water
2 cans mushroom soup

2 sliced onions
Dash of tabasco sauce
2-3 strips of bacon
Dash of Worcestershire sauce
1 tsp. salt
a little garlic (discreetly)
1-2 bay leaves

Brown rabbit in fat after flouring in bag. After browning in open pressure cooker, add all above ingredients. Put strips of bacon over top. Close pressure cooker and cook at 10 lbs. for 20-25 minutes. Cool normally for 5 minutes, then place under faucet. Remove rabbit and thicken gravy as usual, if necessary. Serve with mashed potatoes or noodles. Serves 4-6.

 Can be done in Dutch oven but takes 3-4 times as long. Makes a good supper for hunting trips.

BIRDS ROASTED IN THEIR FEATHERS (HUNTER'S STYLE)

Open the bird in the usual manner and draw. Then cover with wet clay and bury in hot coals. In 45 minutes draw from coals and peel off the clay. Feathers and skin will come at the same time. Delicious cooked in this manner.

Background: From Blue Ribbon Cook Book, 1907.

Jeanne Edwards
Saval Ranch
North Fork, Nevada

STUFFING FOR GAME

2 c. grated bread crumbs
¾ c. chopped celery leaves
3 tbsp. diced bacon
1 qt. oysters, cut in pieces
2 tsp. salt

¼ lb. mushroom caps,
 halved and sauted
1/8 tsp. paprika
1 tbsp. Worcestershire Sauce
2 tbsp. catsup

Mix ingredients by tossing lightly with a fork. Pack loosely in cavity.

AT YOUR OWN RISK!
Two Typically Australian Dishes

Recommended for serving to V.I.P. visitors

Jack Absolom
Australia

BARBECUED EMU

Take 1 young hen — stretch neck.
Remove some feathers for decoration.

Have prepared a goodly-sized hole of white ash and coals.
Place bird on same, and cover with green boughs.
Cook until feathers gone and skin golden brown.
Rub with mallee (green) roots to remove quills.

Serve to old men and dogs, then the women and kids.

DELICIOUS!

CAMEL STEW

3 medium sized camels	*1 ton salt*
500 bushels potatoes	*1 ton pepper*
200 bushels carrots	*3000 sprigs parsley*
2 small rabbits	

Cut camels into bite size pieces. This should take about two months. Cut vegetables into cubes (another two months). Place meat in pan and cover with 1000 gallons of brown gravy. Simmer for 4 weeks. Shovel in pepper and salt to taste. When meat is tender, add vegetables. Simmer slowly for 4 weeks. Garnish with parsley. Will serve 3800 people. If more are expected, add two rabbits.

Background: These two recipes were given to me by a manager of one of Kidmans Stations. He told me that the Head Office in Adelaide sent these two recipes to all his stations. P.S. I haven't tried them, as I have had trouble getting the three medium sized camels.

Jack Absolom
Australia

ABSOLOM STYLE KANGAROO LEG, SEASONED

1 kangaroo leg   1 cup dripping

STUFFING:

½ loaf bread   2 soft tomatoes
1 large onion, chopped finely   1 dessertspoon mixed herbs
2 strips bacon, chopped finely   1 egg
                salt and pepper to taste

Take the kangaroo leg and cut pockets well into the leg so as to push the stuffing in. To make the stuffing, cut the crust off the bread and crumb it. Add the bacon, onion and tomatoes. Rub well together with the breadcrumbs then add the egg, mix well, adding herbs then salt and pepper and stuff this into pocket of kangaroo leg. Bake in camp oven with the cup of dripping until well cooked—about 2½-3 hours. Remember to baste the meat all the time because it has no fat.

Background: I have served this meal to governors, millionaires, T.V. crews and hundreds of ordinary people, and I never get a complaint.

OUTBACK BRAISED KANGAROO TAIL

1 medium kangaroo tail, jointed   2 carrots, sliced longwise
2 large onions   1 can peas or pkg. Surprise peas
2 tbsp. flour or gravox   3 medium tomatoes, sliced
                salt and pepper to taste

If you have a pressure cooker put the meat in and cook until the meat starts to fall off the bone. Take out and strain off the gravy. Keep it. Place a little fat or butter in the bottom of a hot camp oven and fry the onions until nearly cooked. Strain off some of the fat but leave enough to make a nice gravy. Add either the flour or gravox to the onions to make a nice thick gravy, add the salt and pepper. Place the kangaroo tail in with the onion gravy and add the carrots, peas and the tomatoes. Tip the onion gravy all over the lot then place lit on camp oven and let simmer for 1½ hours. Serve with mashed potatoes and pieces of pumpkin.

Jack Absolom
Australia

PACKSADDLE KANGAROO BRAWN

2 medium kangaroo tails   *1 dessertspoon nutmeg*
water   *1 dessertspoon mixed spices*
salt and pepper to taste

Clean and joint tails, put them in a pot and cover them with water. Boil until meat is falling off the bone, then pick bones with tongs. Now add the nutmeg, mixed herbs, salt and pepper, stir well, breaking up all meat. This should be fairly thick, as long as it has a gravy to taste. Place mixture in pie dish or tray and let set. When ready, cut into slices and use for cold lunches or let set in small moulds.

Historic Pioneer Recipe

CORNBREAD STUFFED TROUT

3 lbs. fresh or frozen
dressed trout
Salt
1 c. coarsely crumbled dry
corn bread
1 c. soft bread crumbs
(1½ slices)
½ c. chopped celery
½ c. finely chopped onion

2 tbsp. finely chopped
green pepper
½ tsp. salt
¼ tsp. ground sage
Dash pepper
¼ c. water
3 tbsp. melted butter
or margarine

Thaw frozen fish. Sprinkle fish generously with salt. Place in a well-greased shallow baking pan. Mix crumbled corn bread, soft bread crumbs, celery, onion, green pepper, ½ teaspoon salt, sage, and pepper. Gradually add water to bread mixture, tossing to coat. Stuff fish loosely with mixture. Brush fish generously with melted butter or margarine and cover with foil. Bake at 350° till fish flakes easily when tested with a fork, 45 to 60 minutes. Remove stuffed fish to serving platter. Makes 6 servings.

Background: Families that settled near water depended on fish to supplement the meager diet until they could plant crops or a vegetable garden. Fish was prepared in the fashion learned from the Indians. It was placed on a wide strip of wood or plank which was then secured at the edge of the fire so that it angled in close to the heat.

Recipe Notes

VEGETABLES

THE HERALDRY OF
THE BRANDING IRON

Arizona cowpuncher Evans Coleman once remarked that he knew cowhands "who could neither read nor write, but who could name any brand, either letters of figures, on a cow." A brand was the key to owner ship in a business where ownership was everything. Many cattlemen, in fact, named their ranches after their brands and held the symbol in as proud esteem as did any knight his crest. Branding was an ancient practice before the first cow came to America. Certain 4,000 year-old tomb paintings show Egyptians branding their fat, spotted cattle. Hernando Cortes burned crosses on the hides of the small herd he brought with him to Mexico. The vaqueros passed the custom on to U.S. cowboys, who developed and refined their own caligraphy.

On any 19th Century ranch the greenest cowhand quickly mastered the three major elements of the branding alphabet (below). He learned to read the components of a brand in correct order: from left to right, from top to bottom, or from outside to inside (a T inside a diamond translates as Diamond T, not T Diamond). In time he could pick out any one of hundreds of markings in a milling herd; a good cowboy, said Coleman, could understand "the Constitution of the United States were it written with a branding iron on the side of a cow."

VEGETABLES

Bill Mabbutt

BASCO BEANS

8 c. cold water	3½ tbsp. salt
4 c. pinto beans	4 tbsp. chili powder
2 c. chopped celery	½ tsp. cumin seed
¼ lb. salt pork, finely diced	½ tsp. black powder
5 lb. ground beef	dash cayenne
6 med. onions, chopped	8 c. canned tomatoes, with liquid
6 green peppers, cut into strips	

Put water and beans in a 4 qt. kettle. Bring to a boil for 1 min. Turn off heat for 1 hour. Return to boiling, add celery and salt pork. Reduce heat and simmer gently until beans are tender, stirring ocassionally. If necesary, add more water to keep ½ in. above level of beans. In a large kettle or Dutch oven, brown ground beef until it looses it pinkness. Add onions, cook until softened. Add remaining ingredients, simmer 30 minutes. Combine with beans, reheat if necessary. Makes approximately 20 servings. This may be made in advance and frozen.

Tom & Shirley Cook
Fernley, Nevada

COOK RANCH BEANS

My preference is pinto beans and I rarely use any other kind. The number of eaters always determines the amount. Using one pound of beans, I do not soak over night, but bring them to a boil, hopefully with a soup bone, then allow them to cool for about one hour. Simmer for a couple of hours. During the last hour of cooking I add at least three chopped onions, a button of garlic, and about two tbsp. chili powder. (Here again to your own taste.) Ready now to go with your steak or roast, this being the basic bean recipe, which at least fills the cracks. If I have ham left-overs or ham hocks, I put them in soon after you begin to simmer the beans. For chili beans, I cook on the side a couple of pounds of hamburger along with onions, garlic, chili powder, tomatoes or tomato sauce, however fancy you want to get. If you are without refrigeration, leave out the tomatoes, as they will cause the beans to spoil sooner.

Historical Pioneer Recipe
Doug Sellars
Fairfax, Virginia

R
Y

COWBOY BEANS

2 lbs. pinto beans
2 lbs. ham hock (or salt pork)
2 onions, chopped

4 tbsp. sugar
2 green chilies (or to taste)
1 can tomato paste

Wash the beans and soak overnight. Drain, place in a Dutch oven and cover with water. Add remaining ingredients and simmer until tender. Sample the beans while cooking. Add salt to taste and water as needed.

Howard and Lorraine MacDonald
Broadacres Farm
Acme, Alberta, Cananda

B
F

BEAN POT

2 tins beans in sauce (tomato)
2 tins kidney beans
2 tins lima beans
½ c. chopped onion

½ c. catsup mixed with —
1 tsp. dry mustard
1 c. brown sugar
½ tsp. garlic powder

Mix ingredients together and simmer for 1 hour. Makes 8-10 servings. Good seved with beef, ham or chicken, a tossed salad and rolls.

Judy Boothby
Fairfax, Virginia

BARBECUED BEANS

1 lb. hamburger, browned
½ c. chopped onion, browned
½ c. catsup
½ tsp. salt

¼ tsp. pepper
2 tbsp. vinegar
1 tbsp. Worcestershire sauce
¼ tsp. tabasco sauce

Blend all ingredients together and stir into a canful (28 oz.) of baked beans. Bake in a 1½ qt. casserole 30 mins. at 350° degrees. This dish can be reheated if your cowboy comes home late from the range or the office.

The Four Sixes Ranch
Guthrie, Texas

6666

CHILI BEAN SANDWICH

1 c. chopped onion	½ tsp. cumin seed
1½ lbs. ground beef	½ tsp. salt
1 tbsp. cooking oil	½ c. American cheese, cubed
1 15-oz. can tomato sauce	1 15-oz. can pinto beans
1 c. beef bouillon	¼ tsp. pepper
2 tsp. chili powder	1 tbsp. butter

Brown onion and ground beef in oil. Drain excess fat. Stir in tomato sauce, bouillon, chili powder, cumin, salt. Simmer uncovered 1 hr., stir occasionally. Add cheese; cover and simmer 10 min., until cheese melts. Mix pinto beans and pepper; fry in butter until lightly browned. Spoon beans over fried tortillas. Top with chili mixture, lettuce, tomato and sour cream.

James Newland
Greenwood Ranches
Bell Fourche, South Dakota

W
+

BEEF, BEANS AND BEER

Cook 2 cups dried red or pinto beans until tender. Drain and put into an oven-proof dish with a tight lid.

Cut 1 pound of inexpensive beef into thin strips and saute in drippings until browned. Add this to the beans. Also add:

1 large onion cut into rings	1 bell pepper cut into strips
6 to 8 cloves of garlic, peeled	1 c. molasses
and crushed	1 tsp. mixed herbs
½ small chili pepper or	1 tbsp. chili powder
½ tsp. crushed chilies	¼ tsp. cumin seeds
2 or 3 stalks celery, diced	Salt and pepper to taste

Stir gently and add enough brown ale or steam beer to come to one thumb knuckle above the level of the beans in the pot. Cover with the lid and bak at 350° until the liquid is almost gone. You may need to remove the lid part way no allow for evaporation of some of the liquid. Serve hot with corn bread.

SRM **SOCIETY FOR RANGE MANAGEMENT**

Jean M. Frischknecht
Kay Frischnecht Ranch
Manti, Sanpete County, Utah

K

"FRISCHKNECHT BARBECUED BEANS"

1 can pork & beans	1 lb. ground meat
1 can barbeque beans	1 small onion
1 can kidney beans	1 c. chopped ham or bacon

Brown the above ingredients together. Mix all together with ⅓ cup chili sauce, ⅓ cup brown sugar and 2 tbps. mustard. Add 1 can tomato sauce. Let bake slowly for 1 hour.

Background: These are the family favorite.

The Four Sixes Ranch
Guthrie, Texas

6666

CHILI BEAN SOUP

2 lbs. lean ground beef	1 to 2 tbsps. chili powder
1 green pepper, chopped	1½ tsp. salt
1 medium onion, thinly sliced	½ tsp. ground oregano
1 clove garlic, minced	½ tsp. cumin seed
¼ c. cooking oil	3 dashes Tabasco
2 1-lb. cans tomatoes	1 c. hot water
1-15 oz. cans pinto beans	

Cook beef, green pepper, onion and garlic in oil until beef is slightly browned. Add all ingredients except beans and simmer uncovered 45 minutes. Stir in undrained pinto beans; simmer 15 minutes. For a thinner mixture, add water. Serves 8.

Mona Larson
Larson Ranches
Watrous, New Mexico

ARIZONA RANGELAND SLOW COOK BEANS

This recipe really does not have a name. Years ago my father, J. David Lee, said that when they were riding they would make their own slow cooker. Northern Arizona was pretty cool even in the summers, so they would clean about 2 cups of pinto beans and soak them overnight. In the morning they would dig a hole about a foot and half or two feet deep and put their breakfast coals in the bottom of it. (These are the coals left over after having cooked their breakfast). They would put the beans in a lard can with about a quart of water, more or less, over them. Put the lid on tight and put the can over the coals. Cover the whole thing with dirt and put another small fire on top of it and let it burn down. Cover it all with a little more dirt so that it won't spread.

When you return at night, the beans are just right. They have been slow cooked all day, and all you need is a tortilla or some baking powder biscuits mixed up in the top of the flour sack and you have the greatest meal ever.

You mix the biscuits by putting the bacon grease in the top of the sack, add the baking powder and enough milk to make what you think you will need. You mix just enough flour to make it about the right consistency and put in a greased Dutch oven. You have to be careful not to stir too deep or it will pick up too much flour, but it really works. Cooking beans like this is a little difficult with the new plastic lard cans, but if you look hard enough, you can still find the tin ones around.

The Four Sixes Ranch
Guthrie, Texas

6666

COWPOKE BEANS

1 lb. dried pinto beans
1½ c. cold water
½ lb. salt pork, cut up
1 red chili pepper
1 medium onion, chopped
½ tsp. marjoram

1 clove garlic, minced
1-6 oz. can tomato paste
1½ tbsp. chili powder
1 tsp. salt
1 tsp. cumin seed

Wash and pick over beans; put in mixing bowl. Cover beans with cold water and soak overnight. Next morning, put beans and water into Dutch oven and bring to a boil; reduce heat. Cover and simmer 1 hour. Stir in remaining ingredients; cover and simmer 3 hours or until tender. Add more water if necessary. Serves 8.

Background: "You've got to treat these little Pinto beans the same way you would a newborn colt — with a lot of love and attention." — Richard Bolt

Dave Secrist
Dinner Station Ranch
Elko County, Nevada

BAKED STEAK AND LIMA BEANS

1 lb. dry Lima beans
6 c. water
4 slices bacon
2 lbs. beef round steak
(cut in 1-inch strips)
¼ c. flour

1 18-oz. can tomato juice
1 tbsp. packed brown sugar
1½ tsp. salt
1 tsp. dry mustard
½ tsp. black pepper

Rinse beans; add 6 cups of water. Bring to a boil; simmer 5 minutes. Remove from heat; let stand, covered, 1 hour. (Or combine beans and water; soak overnight.) Do not drain. Cover, simmer 30 minutes. In Dutch oven, cook bacon till crisp. Drain, reserve drippings. Crumble bacon; set aside. Coat beef with flour. Brown beef in hot drippings, pour off excess fat. Stir in beans and onion. Combine tomato juice, brown sugar, salt, pepper and mustard, Pour over beans and beef mixture. Bake covered in 325° oven till tender. about 1½ to 2 hours. Stir in bacon or top with it and grated cheese before serving. Serves 8.

Background: The Dinner Station Ranch was at one time a dinner stop-over for freight and stage coaches between Elko and Tuscaroro, Nevada, when the gold mines operated in northern Elko County.

J.W. Bailey
Prairie Ridge Ranch
Cheyenne, Wyoming

J'

RANCHER'S POTATOES

Brown five strips of bacon. Set aside. In drippings, brown hash browns, chopped onion and chopped green pepper. Beat four eggs and add to ¼ cup milk. Beat, salt and pepper. Pour over hash browns. As the mixture sets, crumble bacon on top and then Cheddar cheese. It's ready to eat when the cheese has melted.

Joe R. Conrad
Conrad Ranch
Wray, Colorado

7/11

RANCH STYLE BAKED BEANS

1 lb. (navy) beans	*¼ c. brown sugar*
12 c. cold water	*⅓ c. molasses*
2 tsp. salt	*1 tsp. dry mustard*
½ lb. salt pork	*½ tsp. salt*
1 medium whole onion	*¼ tsp. freshly ground black pepper*
2 c. boiling water, or more if needed	

Sort and wash beans. Soak beans overnight in 6 cups cold water to which 2 tsps. salt has been added. In the morning, drain. Add about 6 cups water, bring to boil and parboil for 10 minutes. Drain and rinse well with cold water. Put piece of salt pork in bottom of a 2-quart bean pot. Add beans. Mix sugar, molasses, dry mustard, ½ tsp. salt, and pepper with 2 cups boiling water. Pour over beans. Press remaining salt pork into beans. If necessary add boiling water to make liquid come just to top of beans. Bake in 300° oven for 5 hours, adding water as necessary. Makes 1½ quarts.

Background: CSU Range Seniors visited this ranch on their spring field trip several times in the '50's. Many students of wildlife have studied Prairie Chicken here at a "booming ground" that has been given to the Nature Conservancy. The ranch is located in the sandhills of Yuma County in northeastern Colorado. It is the ranch of the late Kenneth Conrad, an ASRM director in the '50's. Many range and pasture improvement practices were started here in the late '40's and '50's, such as sage brush spraying, reseeding of farmland and "go-back" land, and rotation grazing. Performance testing and fattening of commercial cattle was also begun in 1947. The ranch is about 14,000 acres in size and is divided into about 30 pastures to provide better distribution, water, separate seeded pasture from native range, and facilitate performance testing and more efficient calving of 300 to 400 cows. This is one of the very few ranches left in N.E. Colorado on which there is NO farming or irrigation.

Donald A. Cox
Cox Hereford Ranch
Mullen, Nebraska

HERB POTATOES

8 med. potatoes, cut as French fries	*Grated American cheese*
1 c. cream	*Parsley, dry or fresh*

Slice potatoes and arrange in a 12 or 14-inch baking pan, lined with foil tucked over the top. (This way there is no pan to wash!) Pour cream over potatoes, sprinkle as much grated cheese as you like, and sprinkle parsley on top of the cheese. Bake at 400° for 35-40 minutes.

Background: Branding is a spring social event in the Sandhills of Nebraska. The number of calves branded has no direct relation to the number of people showing up. We have had people from both coasts at the same branding. The follow is a notation my wife, Donna made in 1958. 17 men, 12 women, 13 children; menu: 24 lb. beef roast, herb potatoes, baked beans, corn, with oysters, carrots and peas mixed, potato salad, sweet salad, radishes, and celery, pineapple upside down cake. Afternoon was spent visiting, playing horse-shoes and trap shooting. Ten stayed to help clean up left-overs. 318 calves branded.

L. Hanson
Sunnybrook
Hutchinson County, Freeman, South Dakota

MAILBOX GREENS

Double handful wild greens (dandelion leaves, dock, nettle, lamb's quarters, etc.)
Water, Salt
Optional ingredients: butter, bacon bits, cheese, onion, black or red pepper, etc.

Put about ½-inch water in pot. Boil with ½ tsp. salt, throw in the cut greens and boil 5-10 minutes. Drain and serve or drain and add some of the optional ingredients, allowing them to blend at a lower heat for 2-3 minutes. Serves one or two.

Background: Fresh out of vegetables? During much of the year you can find fresh greens growing around the feedlot, corral, or down by the creek. Find out which you can be sure to recognize as edible and cook 'em like spinach. Sunnybrook began as a homestead on Clay Creek in the late 1800's. The garden often couldn't keep up with the weeds, so why not boil the weeds? Most taste kinda like spinach!

Jean M. Frischknecht
Kay Frischknecht
Manti, Sanpete Co., Utah

K

SOUR CREAM POTATOES

5 - 6 medium potatoes	3 tbsp. chopped green onions
1 can cream of chicken soup	1 c. grated cheese
½ stick margarine	2 tbsp. melted butter
1 c. sour cream	3 handfuls cornflakes, crushed

Cook potatoes with skins. Cool thoroughly. Peel and grate potatoes. Combine soup and ½ stick margarine in glass bowl, and heat in microwave oven 1½ minutes or until butter melts. Combine soup mixture with onions and sour cream and grated potatoes. Place in a 10-inch ceramic dish, top with grated cheese and buttered cornflakes. Bake in microwave oven 7-8 minutes or until hot.

Mrs. D.B. Harris
Walters, Oklahoma

RED GERMAN CABBAGE KRAUT

2 lb. head red cabbage, shredded	1 c. water
1 tart apple, peeled, shredded	2 tbsp. sugar
1 tsp. caraway seed	3 tbsp. cooking oil
Salt to taste	2 tbsp. vinegar
1 c. white wine (optional)	

Cook cabbage, apple, caraway seed and salt in 1 cup water, 20 minutes. Fry onion and sugar in cooking oil, add to the cabbage; add vinegar and wine. Cover and cook over moderate heat 1 hour. Serves 6 to 8.

Mrs. C.H. Wasser
Fort Collins, Colorado

HACIENDA RICE

1 c. long grain rice	1 small can whole Ortega chili
1 c. sour cream	½ lb. cubed Cheddar cheese

Cook rice and mix with sour cream. Place half the rice mixture in a buttered casserole and then place the chili over and the cubed cheese. Add remainder of rice mixture and bake covered at 350° for 40 minutes. Serves four.

Mary Shoop
Ft. Collins, Colorado

RED CABBAGE

1 med. head red cabbage	3-4 whole cloves
½ c. vinegar	1-2 tbsp. sugar
½ c. water	1 med. onion
½ c. salad oil	1 tart apple
⅛ tsp. ground pepper	1 bay leaf

Grate the cabbage. Slice onion and apple. Mix spices, vinegar, oil and water, bring to boil. Add cabbage, onion and apple to above and simmer slowly for about 40 min. or until cabbage is tender.

Rob Brown
R.A. Brown Ranch
Throckmorton, Texas

BARBEQUED ONIONS

1 purple onion per person

Peel onions and quarter ¾ way through. (Do not cut completely through onion.) Set each onion on a piece of aluminum foil large enough to cover completely. Fill each onion half full of barbeque sauce. Seal foil around onion. Place on grill along side meat. Onions are most tender if cooked 1½ hours.

Deseret Land & Livestock Corp.
Woodruff, Utah

ZR FRIJOLES

2 c. dried pintos	1 clove garlic
Water to more than cover	1 tbsp. red chili powder
½ lb. saltpork, ham hock, bacon diced	¼ tsp. ground cumin
1 onion, chopped	½ tsp. ground oregano

Add salt if other than salt pork is used. Soak beans in water overnight. Add salt pork, onion, garlic, chili powder, cumin, oregano and simmer on low heat at least 4 hours.

Background: This recipe came from a ranch wife on a registered cattle ranch in Santa Rosa, New Mexico, and she won a National Cowbelle Cook-Off one year.

Ruth Buchanan
The Buchanan Ranch
Thermopolis, Wyoming

SMORGASBORD CABBAGE ROLLS

1 lb. cooked ham, ground	*½ tsp. pepper*
1½ lbs. ground fresh pork	*1 tbsp. chili powder*
1½ c. cooked rice	*1½ c. sauerkraut*
1 tsp. salt	*1½ c. meat broth (from cooked ham)*

Mix all together. Wilt cabbage leaves for a few minutes in boiling water. Place 1 tbsp. meat mixture on each cabbage leaf. Roll it up and fasten with a toothpick. Place in rectangular shaped pan. Pour ham broth over them. Bake 1½ to 2 hrs. at 375°.

Background: This recipe originated at Duboise, Wyoming, at a Scandinavian Smorgasbord they have had there each year since 1950, originated by Lydia Olson.

The Four Sixes Ranch
Guthrie, Texas

6666

REFRIED BEANS — NEW MEXICO STYLE

1 15-oz. can pinto beans	*1 clove garlic, minced*
without seasonings	*½ tsp. salt*
½ c. chopped onion	*¼ tsp. pepper*
1½ tsps. chili powder	*2 oz. Monterey Jack cheese*
2 tbsp. butter	

Mash beans in electic mixer. Stir in all ingredients except butter. Melt butter in skillet. Add beans and cook, stirring occasionally, until beans have thickened.

Background: A great tasting Southwestern habit.

Marilyn Seiker
Elmwood, Nebraska

FRIED APPLES

6 red apples (unpared) sliced	*½ c. water*
3 tbsp. butter	*1 c. sugar*
½ c. white cooking wine	*1 tbsp. lemon juice*

1 cinnamon stick, 6 inches long

Saute apples in butter for 6-8 minutes in non-stick skillet. Boil wine, water, sugar, cinnamon and lemon juice for 5 minutes. Pour over apples. Cook uncovered until apples are tender. Pour into serving dish. Serve warm or cold. Yield 6 servings. This dish is good with pork.

Background: In 1872 at Hahoore, Germany, Rosina Lichkey composed a "Now or Never" letter and mailed it off to her intended, Leapol Simmerman in Illinois. His reply was "Now". When Rosina packed her trousseau trunk to sail across the Atlantic, she included her mother's recipe for fried apples. 110 years later, in Nebraska, Colorado, Arizona, Minnesota, Florida, and Iowa, Grandmother Liemkey's great, great, great granddaughters continue to prepare this revised version of the original recipe.

Wilma Newman
Dunkirk, Montana

CRISP CUCUMBER SLICES
(Pickles)

4 qts. sliced cucumbers	*2 green peppers, chopped*
6 med. white onions, sliced	*⅓ c. salt*

3 cloves garlic (optional)

Do not pare cucumbers, slice thin, cover with cracked ice, mix and let stand 2 hours or put in refrigerator over night. Drain. Combine:

5 c. sugar	*1½ tsp. celery seed*
1½ tsp. tumeric	*2 tsp. mustard seed*

3 c. vinegar

Pour over cucumber. Mix. Heat just to boiling or until cucumbers start to look yellow. Seal in jars.

SRM   **SOCIETY FOR RANGE MANAGEMENT**

Aunt Pearl Baker
Robbers Roost
Southeast Utah

OUTLAW TRAILS PICKLES

Assemble and cut into strips all about the same size, and four or five inches long: Carrots, celery, red and green bell peppers, yellow and red Hungarian wax peppers, small dill-sized cucumbers quartered lengthwise, tender string beans, dry onions cut into fourths, sixths or eights, depending on size, and little jalapeno peppers, halved. Cauliflower flowerets, dill (fresh if possible), using leaves, stems, and seed heads.

PICKLING SOLUTION: put two quarts best cider vinegar and 4 quarts water into a large kettle—not aluminum. Add a cup of salt and a cup of pickling spices. Bring to a boil and boil a few minutes. Strain out the spices, keep for another batch, adding about ½ cup fresh spice each time. Bring strained liquid to a boil and pour it over the packed jars. It takes one pint of solution to one quart of packed vegetables.

DIRECTIONS: Hold jar in one hand and tilt it on its side. Pack vegetables until the bottom is full. Stand up; it should be about ½ or ¾ full. Add 12 cloves garlic—this sounds like a lot, but this makes the flavor! Press about four halves of jalapenos down the sides of jar, pack full of cauliflower flowerlets and add solution. Wad up about as much dill as would make a pingpong ball and stuff it down in the top of the jar. Seal. Jar may break the seal and leak a little, but seems to ferment, and this is o.k.—there is enough salt and vinegar to discourage the most ambitious salmonella.

Background: My sister Hazel and I grew up at Robbers Roost. I owned and ran the ranch for several years until my children were pretty good sized, then sold it to my sister and her husband, Arthur Ekker in 1939. They raised their family and grandchildren there. The Roost belongs to the Ekker children now, and we all cherish our heritage. This pickling recipe became a hit years ago and I have bottled 100-400 quarts every fall, since!

The Four Sixes Ranch
Guthrie, Texas

6666

HONEY BEAN BAKE

1 lb. dried pinto beans	1 c. honey
½ lb. (8 slices) bacon, diced	1 tsp. salt
1 medium onion, sliced	1 tsp. dry mustard
	1 tsp. ginger

Wash and pick over beans, put in mixing bowl. Cover beans with cold water and soak overnight. Next morning, cook beans in water until skins burst, about 1 hour. Drain and reserve liquid. Place half the bacon and onion in the bottom of 2½ qt. bean pot or casserole dish; add beans and top with remaining bacon and onion. Combine remaining ingredients and 1¾ cups reserved bean liquid; pour over beans. Cover and bake in a 300° oven for 3½ hours. Uncover and bake 1 hour or until beans are of desired consistency. Stir occasionally.

Background: Baked beans with a flavor borrowed from wild Texas honey bees.

Recipe Notes

MEXICAN FOOD

A BILLBOARD ON THE HOOF

A range cow was often a walking billboard of marks from hot irons and sharp knives. These marks could appear almost anywhere on the animal, but the locations shown here were common. From its first owner it often got a hip brand (and a jaw brand if the original was unclear or incorrect). A trail driver later marked its side with a road brand. A subsequent purchaser might mark out (or vent) the old hip brand and burn his own nearby. Since brands were hard to read in herds, cattle also bore knife cuts (wattles, dewlaps or earmarks) on their necks, throats, briskets and ears.

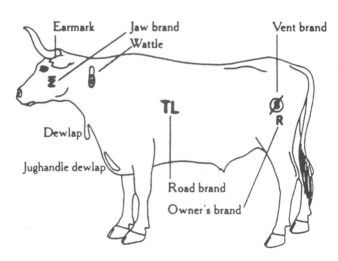

MEXICAN FOOD

Historic Pioneer Mexican Recipe

NIXTAMAL
(Parboiled Corn)

1 gal. water   ⅓ c. unslaked lime
2 qts. (8 cups) whole dry corn (maize)

Mix the water and lime in a galvanized kettle and stir the combination with a wooden spoon. Add the corn kernels and stir until the mixture no longer effervesces. Bring to a boil, then lower the heat to a simmer. Stirring frequently, cook for one hour, then drain the corn and wash the kernels in cold water until all traces of lime taste are removed. Rub the kernels between your hands until they are free of their hulls. The result is a mixture that is very much like hominy, which can now be ground into masa, or moist corn dough. Place on cup of *nixtamal* in a blender or food processor, then reduce it to a medium fine flour. Then add just enough water to keep the mixture moist. Cover with a damp cloth until used. This recipe makes about two dozen tortillas.

Historic Mexican Recipe

TORTILLAS DE MAIZ
(Corn Tortillas)

Break off a small piece of masa and form it into a two-inch ball. Place this ball on a cloth-covered board. Press and pat round and round from the center to the circumference with your fingertips, until the cake is thin and six inches in diameter. Bake both sides on a hot, ungreased griddle until slightly brown and blistered.

Shirley Williamson
Fairfax, Virginia

SQUASH AND GREEN CHILES

6 *medium yellow crooknecked squash*	½ *cup tomato juice*
1 *medium sized onion*	3 *slices bacon*
1 *can chopped green chiles*	4 *crumbled saltines*
	Grated cheese

Slice squash — boil and drain. Brown bacon and mince. Mix all ingredients except cheese and place in a casserole.
Bake at 350⁰ for one hour. Remove from oven and top with cheese. Return to oven until cheese has melted.

Paul S. Brady

MEXICAN CHICKEN

1-3 *lb. chicken, boiled, boned, diced*	½ *to 1 lb. sharp cheese*
1 *can Ro-tel tomatoes (hot)*	2 *pkgs. corn tortillas*
1 *c. chicken broth*	1 *med. onion finely chopped*
1 *can cream mushroom soup*	1 *can cream of chicken soup*
1 *tsp. cumin*	1 *tbsp. chili powder*
	1 *tsp. oregano*

Saute onion in butter. Add soups, spices and tomatoes. Mix, simmer until hot. Grease large baking dish. Line bottom with tortillas which are quartered. Put chicken on top, cover with sauce, sprinkle with cheese. Repeat layering until complete. Place in 350° oven to melt cheese and warm. Serves 8.

Paul S. Brady

MEXICAN STYLE MACARONI

2 *cups elbow macaroni*	1 *c. grated cheese*
1 *medium onion, finely chopped*	2 *tbsp. bacon drippings*
1 *can Ro-tel tomatoes (hot)*	*Salt, & black pepper*
	Garlic powder to taste

Boil macaroni according to package directions. Drain. Saute onion in drippings, add tomatoes, stew a few minutes, season, add macaroni. Remove from fire and add cheese. Serve.

Linda Zimmerman
Seven K Ranching Corp.
Roundmountain, Nevada

ㄱK

CHILI CON CARNE ENCHILADAS

2 pkgs. corn tortillas	1 bell pepper
1 tbsp. chili powder	Garlic salt
½ c. oil	Pepper
3 lbs. hamburger	1 lb. Monterray Jack cheese grated
1 onion diced small	2 15-oz. cans of Chili con Carne

Soften corn tortillas in oil with tablespoon of chili powder, over medium flame, stack on top of each to stay soft. Cook hamburger with bell pepper and ½ onion, add garlic sal   pepper. When done get at 13x9x2 in. pan, put a tortilla with some hamburger, cheese and onion and roll. Set side by side. Will make 2 rows. Heat chili separately, when hot pour over enchiladas. Sprinkle cheese and some onion on top and set in oven for 15 more minutes at 350°. Will serve 12 to 15 people.

Background: This recipe is very popular in the South Texas area. It is easy to make and in 45 minutes you can have a good meal.

Mrs. Monte McPeak
M Hanging 7
Loomis, Washington

M⁊

EASY ENCHILADAS

2 lbs. hamburger	Flour tortillas
1 can Enchilada Sauce (19 oz.)	1 can Refried beans
⅔ c. sour cream	Cheddar cheese
Mozzarilla cheese	

Brown hamburger, add mushrooms, (opt.). Set aside. Mix canned Enchilada sauce and sour cream and heat. Spread refried bean on tortilla. On one each of tortilla spoon on some hamburger, put some cheese (grated) over hamburger, roll up and place in pan. When all are rolled and pan is full, pour Enchilada sauce over them, top with cheese and bake 20 mins. approx. at 350°. (Serve with fresh sour cream optional).

Historic Mexican Recipe

PUCHERO
(A Stew)

1 sun-dried beef or veal knuckle bone	3 dried tomatoes
½ tsp. pepper	2 green chili peppers
2 tsp. salt	1 lb. green string beans
2 lbs. cut-up veal	tied in bunches
2 lbs. cut-up beef	1 bundle turnip leaves
3 ears corn	3 small green pumpkins or
3 sweet potatoes	summer squash
1 c. garbanzos (chick-peas)	1 hard apple
2 whole onions	1 hard pear

Cover the knuckle bone and meat with cold water. Add the pepper and salt. Bring to boil and skim scum from the water. Place all the vegetables and fruit over the meat in the order listed, the corn at the very bottom, the pear at the top. Simmer for three hours. Do not stir. To serve, place the vegetables and fruit on one platter, meat on a second platter and broth in a tureen. Serves 12.

Historic Mexican Recipe

SOPA DE CARNE SECA Y ARROZ
(Jerky-and-Rice Soup)

1 lb. dried beef	1 green chili pepper
1 tbsp. fat	1 onion
½ c. rice	½ tsp. salt
1 ripe tomato	Pepper

Roast the beef at 400° for one hour to soften the dried meat. Then pound it on a wooden block until it shreds. Heat the fat in a kettle and fry the rice, tomato, chili and onion. Season. Add meat, cover with one quart boiling water and simmer 15 minutes or until rice is cooked. Serves six.

Sylvia Rucker
Rucker Herefords
Hilger City, Montana

SOUR CREAM N' CHEESE ENCHILADAS

2 cans cream of chicken soup	1 pkg. flour tortillas
1 small can green chilies (chopped)	1 lb. longhorn cheese
1 c. sour cream	1 lb. hamburger

Fry hamburger. Mix with sour cream and soup. Add green chilies. Grate cheese and roll cheese into tortillas. Place some cream mixture on bottom of pan. Put rolled tortillas on top. Place remaining cream mixture on top of tortillas. Sprinkle with grated cheese. Bake 20 mins. at 350° degrees. Makes 12 tortillas.

Ray Margo
Rancho Margo
Rio Grande City, Texas

MARGO RANCH CASSEROLE

1-3 lb. boneless fryer	½ medium onion (finely chopped)
2 cans chicken soup	18 corn tortillas
1 can mushroom soup	1 lb. grated Cheddar cheese
3 stalks of celery	½ stick margarine
2 c. chopped green chile	

Boil and debone fryer, chop celery and onion saute in ½ stick margarine in a skillet until tender. Add green chile, soups and diced chicken. In a 9x13 pan arrange layer of tortillas, layer of chicken mixture, sprinkle w/grated cheese. Alternate layers, leaving grated cheese layer on top. Bake at 350° for 30 minutes.

Background: This is easy to prepare. It serves 8 people. The orginal recipe did not have the green chile. This was added later from green chile cooking ideas from New Mexico. This ranch is located in North Starr County, Texas. It has been in the Margo family for three generations.

Diana Kessler
Orme Ranch
Mayer, Arizona

CHILI PIE

6 eggs, separated*
⅓ + lb. velvetta, longhorn or
jack cheese
8-10 whole green chilis, fresh
are the best

Garlic salt to taste; about ½ tsp.
2 dashes of sugar
2 tsp. water, maybe more
1½ cubes margarine
* use 10 if eggs for #10 skillet
use 12 eggs for #12 skillet

Melt 1 stick of margarine in –8 iron skillet; leave on very low heat; slice cheese and drain chilis. Separate eggs; beat white until stiff; add to yolks the garlic, salt, sugar, flour and water; beat with same egg beater 'til frothed a little; pour yolk mixture into whites and fold together; tilt skillet to coat all the sides of skillet; pour ½ egg mixture into skillet; layer chilis and cheese; pour remaining eggs mixture; cook on top of stove for 10-15 minutes on low heat, pour ½ stick melted margarine around edges and a little on top; cook until it is done on bottom layer. Bake in oven 400-450⁰ for 10+ or until brown. Can cook in dutch oven, just make sure heat isn't too high.

Background: Easy for large numbers; lazy man's Chili Relleno; also good cooled if crew doesn't arrive at estimated time.
Diana Kessler's husband, Alan, is the manager of the Orme Ranch, farmous for the Orme Ranch School which draws students from all over. However, the ranch is a full-fledged working cow-calf operation, providing a realistic ranch setting for the school. Alan is the son of Wayne Kessler, past president of the SRM, and is an active member of the Arizona Section.

Debra Buchanan
Fairfax, Virginia

CHAMPURRADO
(A Thick Chocolate)

6 tsps. grated chocolate
6 tsps. sugar
1 c. hot water
5 c. milk, scalded

½ c. masa
2 eggs, well beaten
2 tsps. vanilla
Dash of cinnamon

In a double boiler, combine the chocolate and sugar. Add the hot water slowly, stirring until a smooth paste is formed. Add the milk, a little at a time, then the masa, which has been thinned with a little of the hot liquid. Before serving, fold in the eggs, vanilla and cinnamon. Serves four to six.

Dixie Lee Jones
1 mile west of Payson, Utah

SΛ

TAMALE PIE

2 lb. ground beef
1 med. can tomatoes
1 med. onion, chopped
1 glove garlic, chopped

½ tsp. salt
½ tsp. pepper
½ tsp. oragano
½ can green chili (7 oz. diced size)

TOPPING

1 c. grated cheese
½ c. cornmeal
½ c. flour
1 tsp. baking powder

dash salt
2 tbs. oil
2 tsp. sugar (opt.)
½ c. milk

½ can chili, diced

Brown meat in skillet. Add remaining ingredients and simmer 20 min. Pour into a 4 qt. cassarole. Top with cheese. Pour cornmeal mixture over the top. Bake at 375 for 30 minutes (or until topping is done). Serves 8 to 10.

Background: My family does not care for the orginal type of Tamale pie so I came up with this one. I am Past President of the Arizona State Cowbelles. My problem with putting a recipe in writing is because I do not measure, I am a dump and pour cook. The Jones family ranches both below and above the Mogollon Rim (it is Arizona's jumping-off place) on national forest land. Lee and Dixie have been recipients of the Arizona Section Range Manager of the Year Award. Lee has served on the Arizona Section Board.

Mrs Violet Utt
Riverside, Washington

UΛ

UTT RANCH TAMALE PIE

1 lb. hamburger
1 envelope Taco Seasoning

1 can Tomato Sauce (8 oz.)
1 c. whole corn - including juice

1 c. water

Brown hamburger. Stir seasoning in, add tomato sauce, corn and liquid, and water. Bring to a boil. Reduce heat, simmer 10 minutes, stirring once. Pour into a baking dish. Sprinkle ½ cup corn meal over mixture. Very slowly and carefully pour 1 cup water over corn meal.
Bake in 400° oven for 25 minutes.

Ray Margo
Rancho Margo
Rio Grande City, Texas

CARNE GISADA CON PAPAS
(Meat & Potatoes)

3 lbs. round steak	½ tsp. ground pepper
2 lbs. potatoes	½ tsp. ground cumin
1 small can of tomato sauce	1 large clove garlic (smashed)
1½ tsp. salt	Water

Cut round steak into cubes and brown in shortening in heavy skillet or Dutch oven. Peel and cube potatoes (approx. ½" cubes). Once meat is slightly browned add potatoes and continue to brown. (Don't worry if it sticks to the bottom of the skillet) Add tomato sauce, salt, pepper, cumin powder, and garlic. Add approximately ONE cup water and simmer until meat and potatoes are tender. Potatoes will thicken the sauce.

Background: This recipe is commonly prepared at round-up time by Ranch Foreman Daniel Garza, for all the cowboys who are are helping. It can be served with camp bread, or flour tortillas. Serves 5 or more depending on the number of helpings per person.

Mrs. Jane Stevens
Jess Valley Ranch
Jess Valley, California

TAMALE PIE

1 qt. or more of boiled chicken	4 tsp. chili powder
1 qt. chicken broth	5 cloves garlic, cut fine
1 lge. can corn or hominy with juice	1 medium onion
1 can tomatoes	1 tsp. cumin seed
1 can olives, handful raisins (opt.)	Salt to taste
1 c. milk	Cornmeal

Mix well with cornmeal to the consistency of mush. Boil slowly for 15 to 20 minutes, then put in casseroles and bake in slow oven 1 to 1½ hours. It is best to put the casseroles in a pan of water while baking.

Background: This was a recipe used by Mrs. Arthur Flournoy of Likely, California. The Flourney family are old settlers in Modoc and their sons are still big ranchers in the area. (I am the ranch cook for one of them.)

Annaley Redd
LaSal Livestock
AKA Redd Ranches
La Sal, Utah

PRAIRIE FIRE

2 qts. cooked pinto beans
2 small or 1 lrg. ham hock
1 onion (small)
1 tsp. salt
1 lb. butter

1 lb. sharp cheddar cheese, grated
2 hot peppers - chopped fine
½ cup chopped fine onion
2 cloves garlic, chopped very fine
Fresh ground pepper

Soak pinto beans overnite to get 2 quarts soaked beans. Pour off water and add fresh water. Add ham hocks, small onion and salt to beans and cook unitl beans are soft. Remove ham hock and onion. Drain off water, add butter, cheese, peppers, chopped onion, garlic, pepper. Cook over low heat till cheese melts.

Background: Pinto beans served to our banker persuaded him not to foreclose our mortgage. Prairie Fire is served at the Redd Ranch bull sale in rememberance.

Howard and Caroline Borgerding
Courthouse Ranch
Imnaha, Oregon

STORM AT SEA

3 eggs	1 tbsp. butter - no margarine
¼ tsp. salt	⅓ c. shredded Monterey Jack or
5 good shakes Tabasco sauce	Cheddar cheese
1 tbsp. cold water (ice water, if avail.)	½ c. Chili beans

This recipe is for one individual serving. Multiply by the number of servings desired.

In a small bowl, crack eggs, add water, salt, Tabasco sauce. Stir lightly with fork (eggs should be stringy. DO NOT OVERBEAT). Using a heavy omelette fry pan, melt butter over high heat. When the butter is melted and hot, pour in the egg mixture. Working quickly, raise pan off fire and move gently right and left as you use your fork to push the mixture back and forth at right angle to pan movement. The idea it to fluff up the eggs in just a few seconds. Set the pan back on the fire and immediately sprinkle the cheese over the eggs. Then, in a few seconds, when the eggs have begun to firm up, pick up and tip the pan, using the fork to roll up the omelet and at the same time slide it onto a plate. Don't tarry — eat the omelette pronto.

Once you get the hang of it you can be preparing the next omelette while one is cooking. Wrangle up a helper to crack eggs and add the ingredients in a bowl ready for cooking. This is a quick operation — you should be able to turn our at least an omelette a minute if you are doing things right and your pan is hot.

Background: *Storm at Sea* is a meal you can whip up in a hurry if you come in tired at the end of the day, a quick meal at noon at home or out on the range if you have a fire and a pan.

I picked up the omelette recipe and technique in Andorra while serving in the Navy — hence the name. In many ways the sea makes the kind of demands on its sailors that the range does on its cowboys, so this recipe could fit the trail boss' brand of cooking.

Jean Thompson
Scharbauer Cattle Co.
Midland, Texas

5

CHILI-BEEF RELLENOS WON-TON

1 lb. ground lean beef
2 medium onions, chopped
1 clove garlic - chopped fine
4 c. shredded longhorn cheese
24 egg roll wrappers

24 green chilies - fresh roasted &
peeled or canned whole ones
Fat for frying
1½ tsp. salt
½ tsp. ground oregano

½ tsp. ground cumin

Brown beef slowly over low heat. Pour off drippings. Add onions, garlic, salt, oregano and cumin - cook, stirring constantly until onions are golden. Remove from heat, add cheese - stirring to blend. Remove seeds from chilies and pat dry with paper towel. Stuff chilies - using about 2 tbsp. of meat mixture. Place each filled chili diagonally on an egg roll wrapper. Wrap each chili as follows: Place lower triangle flap over chili and tuck the point under the chili. Bring left and right corners toward center and roll up. Seal edge with a few drops of water. Fry in deep fat - 325 ° until golden brown.

I serve these with a taco sauce (homemade or commercial). They may also be served with tomato cups filled with guacamole salad (homemade or commercial) and top with ripe olives. 12 servings.

Since this is a large recipe, they may be cooled and wrapped individually in wax paper, placed in plastic bags and frozen. To serve, place on cookie sheet, cover with foil, heat until heated thoroughly (about 1 hour at 325° if heating several at a time). Open foil for about the last 5 to 8 minutes so that the won-tons will again be as crisp as they were when deep fried.

Background: The son of a German immigrant, Tom Scharbauer learned the cattle trade at his relatives' Eastern ranch. In 1880 he left New York and followed the railways to Texas. He invested in the sheep business and by 1888 owned his first cattle ranch in Midland, where his brothers and their families joined him. Scharbauer Brothers was established in 1892. By the mid-1890s the figure "5" was readily identifiable as the Scharbauer brand. By 1930 the Scharbauer holdings spread over five Texas counties and two counties in New Mexico. Today the Scharbauer ranching operation, headquartered in Midland, Texas is a family partnership consisting of eight cattle ranches in West Texas, the Panhandle and a sheep ranch in southeastern New Mexico.

SRM **SOCIETY FOR RANGE MANAGEMENT**

Joanne Dickenson
Dickenson Ranch
Melrose, New Mexico

TEQUITAS

2 doz. tortillas (corn)
1½-2 lb. hamburger meat
  cooked and drained
1 tbsp. enchilada sauce (dry)

1 tsp. cumin
Salt to taste
2 tbsp. dry chili powder
¼-lb. grated cheese

Toothpicks (round)

SAUCE

1 4-oz. can tomato sauce
1 8-oz. jar hot picante sauce

2 green chiles (cooked canned) or 2 Jalapeno peppers

Mix all seasonings into hot, cooked, drained meat. Stir in cheese until melted. Dip each tortilla in hot oil until soft. Roll up 3 tbsp. of meat mix in tortilla and secure with toothpick. Place in deep hot fat and fry until crips. Dip into sauce.

Ray Margo
Rancho Margo
Rio Grande City, Texas

3

BAR-B-Q "FAJITAS" BEEFSKIRTS

3 lbs. of Beefskirts
½ c. Italian Dressing

Salt and pepper to taste

Remove any skin visible on the beefskirts. Marinate at least 2 hours before cooking. Cook on outdoor Bar-B-Q grille. Mesquite wood is the best wood to Bar-B-Q. Beefskirts are very tender and tasty. They can be found in most meat markets. Serves 6-8 people.

Background: When the slaughtering was done for ranch use, the cowboys would start a fire ahead of time and cook the beefskirts together with the sweetbreads. This was always a real treat, they would snack on while preparing the rest of the meat for packing. They would just throw them over the coals.

Virginia Sellars
Fairfax, Virginia

ENCHILADAS REAL

1 c. black olives, pitted	*6 tbsp. fat*
1 tbsp. olive oil	*½ clove garlic*
1 tsp. salt	*1 tsp. vinegar*
12 red chili peppers	*12 corn tortillas*
3 tbsp. toasted bread crumbs	*½ lb. white cheese, grated*
1 large onion, minced	

Mix the onion with olive oil and salt. Wipe the chilies; stem them; then slit and remove seed veins and seeds, and boil until pulp separates from hulls, producing a puree. Continue simmering. Brown crumbs in 2 tbsps. of fat in a skillet; stir in mashed garlic and vinegar. Add to chili puree and simmer 20 minutes. In another skillet, heat 4 tbsps. of fat, and lightly fry tortillas one at a time. Immerse each in chili sauce, place on warm platter and fill with cheese, onion and olives. Fold in thirds. When all tortillas are filled, cover with the remaining chili sauce, cheese, onion and olives. Place in an oven to keep warm. Serves six.

THE COWBOY'S
SWEET TOOTH

BRANDS

Brands are registered with state or county governments to show ownership of animals. They may be used for generations without modification. In the past it was not uncommon for established ranch brands to be retained by new owners. In the early days of the range livestock industry, many a rancher got his start by securing and putting his mark (brand) on unbranded mavericks. The alteration of brands by unscrupulous would-be ranchers (better known as rustlers) is a colorful part of the development of the range livestock industry.

Brands are sometimes difficult to decipher, and brand reading is an ailing art. Many symbols may be read several ways, depending on the section of the country where they are used. Letters and numbers may be standard and readily discernable, or they may be lazy, open, running, flying, leaning, hanging, backward or reversed. Symbols are often used such as a pilot wheel, ⚙ a spade, ♠ pitchfork, ⴤ wagon wrench, ⲧ or a heart ♡ . The bars may be over, under, between or on either side of the numbers or letters.

We were unable to put proper descriptive terms with many of the symbols we received with our recipes. Following is a list of symbols and what may be or could be the descriptive terms for them. Try your knowledge, expertise, or luck at brand reading. See if you agree with our interpretations. Can you think of additional or alternative ways of expressing the symbols?

KEY TO BRAND NAMES

6666	The Four Sixes	R	R Bar
ꟼS	Lazy Jay S	ʹĹ	(L)
J˙	Two Eyed Jay	⚙	Pilot Wheel
W̶ᵜ	W Cross	Y⊣	Y Lazy T

‾⊢	Bar Cross	38	Thirty Eight
S∧	S Open A	Ɣ	Triangle Tail
∧U	Rafter U	⅁	Lazy Spade
3	Quarter Circle 3	W͛	S Hanging W
K	Seven K	T̅	(TT)
M₇	M Hanging 7	NB	(NB)
5	The Five	∿	Running M
AX	The A X	⅃	L Lazy S
ℐ/	Jay F Slash	Y,V	The Y, The V
ⱧK	Quarter Circle H K	Y̅U	Bar Y U
⅄	The Pine Tree	Z̅	Bar Zee
⅂	Lazy V Jay	–Ƀ–	Bar B Bar
Ⱳ	Running W	FEE	FEE
⊔	Rocking Lazy T	T̅	Bar Tee
Z̲	Bar Z	÷⅄	Dot Bar Spade
♡	Heart Lazy Jay	∧∨	Open AV
ⅅ	(?)	⅄	Triangle Jay
𝝥	Camp Stool	↑	Fleur de lis
W9	(W9)	∪∪	Muleshoe
∧R	(AR)	–T–	Bar T Bar
5̅P	Bar 5 P	ⅉ	Crossed J

DM The Lazy AM

∀ (?)

ΛL Open AL

ᒧ Quarter Circle J

X Slash X

8⟋ The SF

⌒⟩ The Shoe Nail

RO The RO

⌣ Flying U Bar

XXX Triple X

♡♡ Double Heart

MB (MB)

⌒⌣ Sled Runner

⊥ J L Bar

Ⓜ Circle L M

⌒S Crown S

GI Gee One

ᔛ Wagon Wrench

SN (SN)

UA (UA)

⊥ Rocking L

UA The UA

AVA The AVA

♡ The Ace of Hearts

ᒿ The Hayhook

◀⊓ Spear E

HAP H A P

WC W C

ᵞ The Yellow Rose

∠ (?)

ᘐ/ Triangle Jay Slash

V Quarter Circle V Bar

╫╤ (?)

S⊥ (St)

UU Double U

ᙡ (?)

B F BF

JX Jay X Slash

Z II K Seven Bar Eleven

K Bar K

ᑫ⊃ Reverse C Lazy R

N N

247

⋙	Three V's	+́	Cross Slash (?)
P	(?)	l7	(17)
Ψ	(?)	⊃	Seven Jay
◁	Spade	夭	Lazy H Open A
ℛ	Quarter Circle K	N4	The N4
$	Dollar Sign	⊔	The Rocking 4
$	Dollar Sign	∂	Laurel Leaf
Ł	Cross L	H-F	H Bar F
J-Ǝ	Jay Bar Reverse E	EB	The EB
C	Cee	H-J	Quarter Circle H Bar J
Ⅲ	Lazy Ladder	B I X	The B I X
♂	Banjo	G	G Lazy V
⅃℧	Flying AT	⌒AD	Quarter Circle J A D
36	Rafter 36	7H	(7H)
RR	Double R	(ᕭ	(?)

Now that you've taken this quickie course in brand reading, see if you can decipher one we recently ran across:

2∾P

CAKES

Nettie Fuchs
Brush Prairie, Washington

YU

PRUNE CAKE

1 c. strained prunes	*1 tsp. allspice*
1 c. Wesson oil	*1 tsp. salt*
2 c. sifted flour	*1 tsp. soda*
1 c. buttermilk	*1 tsp. nutmeg*
3 eggs	*1 tsp. cinnamon*
1 tsp. vanilla	*1 c. chopped walnuts (optional)*

Measure out flour, add allspice, salt, soda, nutmeg and cinnamon. Sift. Next put prunes, oil and sugar in mixing bowl and beat well. Add eggs, buttermilk and flour. Bake in greased pans, either layer or sheet, 350° for 20-30 minutes, or until done.

The Four Sixes Ranch
Guthrie, Texas

6666

TEXAS PECAN CAKE and GLAZE

6 tbsp. butter	*1½ c. cake flour*
1 c. sugar	*1 tsp. baking soda*
1 egg	*½ tsp. salt*
½ tsp. vanilla	*½ c. milk*
½ c. sourdough starter	

Beat butter, sugar, egg and vanilla together until fluffy. Mix cake flour, baking soda, and salt together and add alternately with sourdough starter, blending after each addition. Blend in milk. Pour into buttered 8½ inch tube pan. Bake at 350° for 35 minutes. Remove from pan and cool.

GLAZE

¾ c. light brown sugar	*6 tbsp. cornstarch*
¼ tsp. salt	*2 tbsp. butter*
¾ c. water	

Combine brown sugar, cornstarch, and salt in saucepan. Stir in ¾ cups water. Cook, stirring constantly, until mixture thickens and boils. Boil one minute. Add butter. Cool mixture until spreadable. Cover with whole pecan halves.

Jeanne Edwards
Saval Ranch
North Fork, Nevada

∿

APPLE CAKE with ICING

3 eggs	1 c. pecans
1½ c. oil	3 c. apples, peeled and diced
2 c. sugar	
3 c flour	ICING:
1 tsp.soda	1 stick oleo
1 tsp. salt	1 c. brown sugar
2 tsp. vanilla	¼ c. milk

Mix ingredients and bake 45 minutes at 350° in oblong pan.
ICING: Cook icing ingredients 2½ minutes and pour over warm cake.

Fran Symms
Idaho

RAW APPLE CAKE

4 c. sliced raw apples, chopped fine	2 tsp. soda
1½ c. sugar	¼ tsp. salt
½ c. vegtable oil	2 tsp. cinnamon
2 eggs well beaten	½ tsp. allspice
1 tsp. vanilla	½ tsp. cloves
2¼ c. flour	1 c. chopped walnuts

Pare and chop apples (may leave peeling on if desired). Pour sugar over apples and let set ½ hour. Mix eggs and oil. Add to apples. Then add sifted dry ingredients and nuts. Bake in 9x13 loaf pan at 350° for 1 hour. Serve warm with ice cream or sprinkle with powdered sugar and serve plain; or ice with plain powdered sugar icing; or caramel frosting; or cream cheese frosting.

Dalice Wolters
Portis, Kansas

LEMON SPONGE

Mix the grated rind of 1 lemon, 1 cup sugar, 2 tbsp. flour. Add 1 cup milk, yolks of 2 eggs, juice of 1 lemon. Fold in the beaten whites of 2 eggs. Set in pan of water and bake in moderate (350° oven) until done.

Lois Eversole
Needmore Ranch
Bitter Creek, Wyoming

NEEDMORE RANCH APPLESAUCE CAKE

1 c. sugar	½ c. shortening
1½ c. applesauce	2 c. flour
1 c. raisins	2 tsp. soda
½ c. nuts	1 tsp. cloves

1 tsp. cinnamon

Cream shortening and sugar together. Mix flour, soda, cloves and cinnamon, and add to sugar. Add raisins and nuts. Stir and pour into well-greased and floured square cake pan and bake at 350° for 35 to 40 minutes. Cool, then frost with caramel or plain vanilla frosting.

Background: This cake was a favorite for lunches taken in the fall as we gathered cattle for shipping. The old ranch has been in the family since 1914. Part of it was homesteaded. An old uncle checked his 3 cows daily with much pride. Their main source of income was from trapping and part-time work on sheep ranches in the area.

Arlene Bohning
No Tenemos Rancho
Yavapai County, Arizona

NO TENEMOS RANCHO APPLESAUCE CAKE

2 c. flour	2 tsp. baking soda
1 c. sugar	1 tsp. baking powder
1 tbsp. corn starch	½ tsp. salt
1 tbsp. cocoa	1 c. nuts
½ tsp. cinnamon	1 c raisins
½ tsp. nutmeg	½ c. oil
½ tsp. cloves	1 tsp. vanilla

3 c. HOT Applesauce

Sift together all the dry ingredients, add nuts and raisins. Stir in the oil, vanilla and hot applesauce. Pour into a 9x13 inch pan. Bake at 350° for 30 to 40 minutes.

Virginia Sellars
Fairfax, Virginia

BLACKBERRY JAM CAKE

½ c. sugar	¼ tsp. ground cloves
¼ c. butter or margarine	¼ tsp. ground nutmeg
2 eggs	⅓ c. buttermilk
1 c. all-purpose flour	½ c. seedless blackberry jam
1 tsp. ground cinnamon	or preserves
½ tsp. baking soda	¼ c. chopped walnuts

Cream together sugar and butter or margarine. Beat in eggs. Stir together flour, cinnamon, soda, cloves, and nutmeg; add to creamed mixture alternately with buttermilk, beating just till blended after each addition. Fold in blackberry jam and nuts, leaving swirls of jam. (Do not overmix.) Turn into a greased and lightly floured 9x9x2-inch baking pan. Bake at 350° till done, about 25 minutes. Cool completely. Frost with Caramel Icing.

CARAMEL ICING

In saucepan melt 2 tbsp. butter or margarine; stir in ½ cup packed brown sugar. Cook stirring constantly, till mixture bubbles; remove from heat. Cool 5 minutes. Stir in 3 tbsp. milk. Blend in 1¾ cups sifted powdered sugar; beat till spreading consistency.

Mrs. Robert M. Case
Toner Ranch
Pagosa Springs, Colorado

BREAD CAKE

⅔ c. lard	2½ c. flour or more
2 c. sugar	3 eggs
2 c. bread sponge	1 c. raisins
½ c. sour milk	1 tsp. cinnamon
1 tsp. soda (level)	1 tsp. nutmeg
⅛ tsp. cloves	

Mix ingredients and let rise in pans for 30 minutes. Bread sponge is water, yeast and approximately one-third of the flour from your favorite hot roll recipe. This will make one large bread pan or two smaller pans. Bake at 375° for about 45 minutes or whatever is right for your altitude and area.

Background: Grandma Toner came west with her family from Pennsylvania due to tuberculosis, and ended up in Gallup, New Mexico. She was a seamstress for Fort Wingate and used to drive her team and buggy out there. After she and Grandpa were married they came to the Piedra River, north of Pagosa Springs and homesteaded. Family members still live on the ranch.

June Schmautz
Fairfax County, Virginia

ANGEL FOOD CAKE

2 c. whipping cream	½ c. fresh lemon juice
1 can Eagle Brand sweetened milk	Grated rind of 1 lemon

Stir lemon juice and rind into milk. Set aside. Whip 2 cups cream. Fold lemon-milk mixture into whipped cream. Slice an Angel food cake into 3 layers. Put above mixture between layers of cake and frost top and sides.

Virginia Sellars
Fairfax, Virginia

APPLE CAKE

2 large eggs	2 tsp. cinnamon
1 tsp. vanilla (optional)	4 c. cubed apples
2 c. flour	ICING:
1 tsp. soda	16-oz. pkg. Philadelphia cream cheese
1 c. oil	6 tbsp. melted butter
1 c. chopped nuts	2 tbsp. vanilla or lemon extract
¼ tsp. salt	1 tbsp. lemon juice
2 c. sugar or 1½ c. honey	2 c. powdered sugar

Mix eggs, oil, sugar well. Add vanilla. Beat until foamy. Sift dry ingredients together; adding to liquid in small amounts. Add apples and nuts. Chop apples as stirring. Fold into greased Dutch oven, which has been floured. Bake at 350° for 1 hour, depending on altitude.
ICING: Cream all ingredients together, using butter knife, and add to cooled cake. Makes a very moist cake.

Bob Papworth

TEXAS SHEET CAKE and FROSTING

2 c. flour	4 tbsp. cocoa
2 c. sugar	½ c. buttermilk
1 stick margarine	2 eggs, well beaten
½ c. shortening	½ tsp. soda
1 c. water	½ tsp. vanilla

Mix flour and sugar in a large bowl. Put margarine, shortening, water and cocoa into a large saucepan and bring to a boil. Pour this over the flour-sugar mixture. Add buttermilk, eggs, soda and vanilla to the batter and mix. Pour onto greased and floured cookie sheet or jelly roll pan 11x17 inches. Bake at 400° for 15-20 minutes.

FROSTING

1 stick margarine	6 tbsp. milk
4 tbsp. cocoa	1 tsp. vanilla
1 box powdered sugar	1 c. chopped nuts

Mix margarine, milk, cocoa, and vanilla. Bring to a boil. Add powdered sugar and chopped nuts. Spread on warm cake.

Dalice Wolters
Portis, Kansas

WACKY CAKE

1½ c. flour	½ tsp. salt
1 c. sugar	1 tsp. vanilla
3 tbsp. cocoa	1 tsp. vinegar
1 tsp. soda	5 tbsp. Wesson oil
1 c. cold water	

Mix flour, sugar, cocoa, soda and salt. Make three wells in flour mixture. In one put vanilla; in another the vinegar; and in the third the Wesson oil. Pour 1 cup cold water over all and stir. No need to beat. Make an 8x8 cake. Bake in 350° oven until it springs back.

Bonita Harris
Walters, Oklahoma

MISSISSIPPI MUD CAKE and ICING

4 eggs	*1 c. coconut*
2 c. sugar	*2 sticks melted margarine*
⅓ c. cocoa	*1 c. pecans*
1½ c. flour	*1 tsp. vanilla*

Mix all ingredients and bake at 350° for 30 minutes. Spread one jar of marshmallow cream on cake while still hot. Mix icing ingredients and spread on top of marshmallow cream.

ICING

⅓ c. cocoa	*1 box powdered sugar*
6 tsp. milk	*1 c. pecans*
1 tsp. vanilla	

Archie Hayden
Hayden Ranch
Lakeview, Montana

POOR MAN'S CAKE

1 c. sugar	*¼ tsp. allspice*
2 c. raisins	*¼ tsp. cloves*
1 c. lard	*Pinch of salt*
1 tsp. cinnamon	

Boil together all ingredients. Add water just to cover raisins until they are tender. Cool. Add 1 tsp. soda and enough flour to make a stiff batter. Bake in moderate oven until cake springs back when touched lightly (about 1 hour at 350°). Serve warm or cold with cream, custard sauce or a powdered sugar frosting. Walnuts may be added to batter just before baking.

Background: Archie Hayden is the grandson of a Pioneer, Samuel Hayden, who came to Alder Gulch in 1863 and settled later in Silver Star. The Lakeview Montana ranch was established in 1889 and was eventually sold to the migratory waterfowl refuge at the Red Rocks Lakes.

Berniece Marts
Double U Hereford Ranch
Post Texas

UU

FRESH STRAWBERRY CAKE and ICING

1 box white cake mix	*1 box strawberry Jello*
½ c. Wesson Oil	*½ c. water*
4 eggs	*½ c. frozen, thawed strawberries*

Mix well the cake mix and strawberry Jello, then add Wesson Oil and water. Mix well 4 eggs, adding 1 at a time and beating well after each egg. Stir in strawberries. Put in 3 waxed-papered pans and bake in 350° oven until done.

ICING

1 box powdered sugar	*1 stick butter*
½ c. strawberries	

Beat until smooth and creamy and spread on cake.

Background: Legend has it that not long after the turn of the century, one of the original owners of the UU stepped off the train and onto Texas soil, taking a good look at this newly purchased land for the first time. So impressed was he with the sprawling open spaces that he dug deep into his pocket and pulled out a shiny silver dollar. Tossing the coin high into the air, he shouted excitedly, "This is where I'm going to **double you**."

Established in 1906 and owned today by the Post-Montgomery joint venture, the Double U Hereford Ranch encompasses some 55,000 acres in Garza, Lynn and Hockley Counties. The ranch is worked from both horseback (for cattle and by pick-up truck (for general chores, such as mending fences). Almost 50 percent of the ranch's water is still generated by windmill, a practical use for the ever-present West Texas wind.

Ann Gates
Corvallis, Oregon

APPLE CAKE SUPREME with LEMON SAUCE

1 c. corn oil	LEMON SAUCE:
2 c. sifted sugar	
3 large eggs, well beaten	1 c. sugar
2 c. self-rising flour, spooned into cup	1 c. hot water
1/8 tsp. salt	3 tbsp. lemon juice
2 heaping tbsp. ground cinnamon	Grated rind of 1/2 lemon
2 tsp. vanilla extract	1/8 tsp. salt
3 c. peeled & chopped raw tart apples	1 tbsp. butter
1 c. pecan pieces	2 tbsp. flour
1/4 c. powdered sugar	1 egg

Blend oil and sugar in a large bowl; add well-beaten eggs and beat until creamy, using medium speed of electric mixer or by hand. Sift flour, salt, and cinnamon into creamed mixture and beat well. Stir in vanilla and apples. Fold in nuts. Spread batter evenly into a greased and floured 13x9x2 inch pan. Bake in preheated oven 350°F on middle shelf for 25 to 30 minutes or until cake tests done. Cook in pan on wire rack; sprinkle with powdered sugar while still hot. Serve plain, warm or cold, for a morning coffee or brunch. Serve hot for a dessert with Lemon Sauce. LEMON SAUCE: Combine all ingredients in top of a double boiler over rapidly boiling water. Cook until mixture begins to thicken, stirring constantly. Make sauce ahead of time and keep refrigerated. Reheat to use.

Bonita Harris
Walters, Oklahoma

ORANGE SPONGE CAKE

6 egg whites (3/4 cup)	6 egg yolks
1 3/4 c. sifted flour	6 tbsp. orange juice
1/2 tsp. salt	1 tbsp. grated orange peel
1 1/2 c. sugar	Confectioners sugar

Sift flour, then measure, filling cup lightly to overflowing. Sift flour with salt and set aside. Beat egg whites until foamy, gradually adding 1/2 cup sugar. Continue beating until stiff peaks stand. Set aside. Beat egg yolks until very stiff. Beat in 1 cup sugar until mixture is smooth. As low speed blend in flour mixture alternately with orange juice. Add peel with whisk, using over-under motion. Fold in egg whites. Pour into 10-inch bundt pan. Bake at 350° for 35-40 minutes. When cool, invert onto serving plate. Sprinkle confectioners sugar over top. Serves 12.

Peggy Brown
R.A. Brown Ranch
Throckmorton, Texas

Y‚V

POUND CAKE

3 sticks butter	1 lb. box powdered sugar
6 eggs	2½ c. sifted flour
1 tbsp. lemon extract	1 tbsp. bourbon whiskey

Have ingredients at room temperature. Cream butter and sugar till fluffy. Add eggs one at a time. Add flour and flavorings. Pour in greased and floured fluted tube pan. Bake at 325° for 1¼-1½ hours. Immediately remove from pan to rack. Prick surface with toothpicks, and spoon or brush the following on it while still very hot. Dissolve by heating — but DO NOT BOIL: the sugar, lemon extract, ½ c. water, and whiskey.

Background: When Robert H. Brown of Fort Worth, a livestock commission company owner, bought land in Throckmorton County in 1900, he not only established a ranch on the land, but he also established a ranching family that is now into the fourth generation.

Today the R.A. Brown Ranch, originally referred to as R.H. Brown & Son operates 3 ranches, totaling 60,000 acres, and is headquartered in Throckmorton County.

R.A. Brown, for whom the ranch is named, was a founder of the American Quarter Horse Association, and served as an officer and director of the association until his death in 1965.

Today R.H.'s grandson, Rob Brown, and his wife, Peggy Donnell Brown, both third generation West Texas ranchers, carry on the 50-year-old breeding tradition. The ranch has consistently ranked among the top 25 breeders of Register of Merit performance horses in the nation.

Ardythe L. "Susie" Body
Body Ranch
Casper, Wyoming

W‚S

MOCK LEMON SAUCE

1 tbsp. butter	¼ c. water
2 tbsp. cornstarch	¼ c. sugar
1½ tbsp. vinegar	

Melt butter. Add cornstarch and water. Mix well. Add boiling water and stir until thick sauce forms. Add sugar and vinegar. Stir well. This is used as a sauce over cake. It is especially good when you have leftover cake that is a little dry.

Bonita Harris
Walters, Oklahoma

FRIENDSHIP CAKE

1 c. butter or margerine, melted	¼ tsp. ground cloves
1¾ c. sugar	¼ tsp. ground nutmeg
3 c. all-purpose flour	2 eggs
1 tsp. soda	2 c. brandied fruit
1 tsp. ground cinnamon	1 c. chopped pecans
½ tsp. salt	¼ c. brandied fruit juice

Combine butter and sugar in large mixing bowl. Beat well. Combine next 6 ingredients. Beat well. Add eggs. Coarse chop brandied fruit and stir in batter. Add pecans and juice. Mix well. Pour batter into well-greased bundt pan. Bake at 350° for 1 hour. Cool in pan 10 minutes, then remove from pan. Makes one 10-inch cake.

BRANDIED FRUIT STARTER

1 15½-oz. can pineapple chunks	1 10-oz. jar Maraschino cherries
1 16-oz. can sliced peaches	1¼ c. sugar
1 17-oz. can apricot halves	1¼ c. brandy

Drain all canned fruit. Combine all ingredients in clean, nonmetallic bowl. Stir gently. Cover and let stand at room temperature for 3 weeks, stirring twice per week. As you use it, replace the amount taken with 1 cup of sugar. Cover and let stand at room temperature 3 days before using again. Yields 6 cups of brandied fruit.

John and Denzel Mills
Charleville, Queensland, Australia

ORANGE SPONGE CAKE, Bush Style

8 eggs	½ c. cornflour
1½ c. sugar	1 tsp. (heaping) cream of tartar
1½ c. S.R. flour	1 tsp. carb soda
Orange flavoring or grated orange peel from 2 oranges	

Mix together eggs, sugar, cream of tartar an carb soda, then sift in the flour and cornflour and mix all together, along with the orange flavoring, gently with a knife. When ready pour mixture into a greased cake tin or in the camp oven. Cook in moderate camp oven for 20-30 minutes.

Wilma Newman
Dunkirk, Montana

CARROT CAKE with ICING

2 c. flour	3 c. shredded carrots
2 c. sugar	1 c. chopped nuts (optional)
1½ c. oil	ICING:
4 eggs	1 8-oz. pkg. cream cheese
1 tsp. salt	3½ c. powdered sugar
2 tsp. baking soda	2 tbsp. vanilla
2 tsp. cinnamon	¼ c. soft butter

Mix ingredients and spread in baking pan. Bake for 350° for 50 minutes or until center is done.

ICING: Blend ingredients and spread over cake. This is enough for 2 cakes. This recipe also freezes well.

Louis and Josie Bell Merrill
Running M Ranch
Midlothian, Texas

CHRISTMAS DATE CAKE

1 lb. dates, cut into small pieces	1 c. sugar
¼ lb. candied cherries, chopped	1 c. flour
¼ lb. candied pineapple, chopped	4 eggs
1 lb. pecans, halves preferred	2 tbsp. baking powder
	1 tsp. vanilla

Combine ½ c. sugar, flour and baking powder. Into mixture of fruit and nuts, stir these dry ingredients (sifted together) until every bit is well floured. Beat eggs well and add ½ cup sugar and vanilla. Combine both mixtures until fruit and nuts are well coated. Pack in greased and floured tube cake pan. Bake at 325° from 45 minutes to one hour. Tip pan for tightly packed fruitcake: After batter has been put into cake pan (and before baking), hold pan a couple of feet above kitchen flour and "drop" pan 3 or 4 times. Padding floor with newspaper is desirable.

Background: Lemuel Pruitt Merrill ranched in Texas with his father before the War between the States and returned to Texas from Georgia after the war. He made six trail drives north from 1868 to 1884 and moved near Glen Rose, Texas in 1872, when he began to use the Running M Brand, now used by Louis Merrill and the XXX Brand used by John Merrill. John, Jr. represents the fifth generation Merrill rancing in Texas and the third generation life member of SRM.

Phyllis Simpson
Alton, Kansas

HOT WATER CHOCOLATE CAKE

2 c. flour	1 c. buttermilk
2 c. sugar	1¼ c. oil
½ c. cocoa	3 eggs
Dash of salt	2 tsp. vanilla
1½ tsp. soda	1 c. boiling water

In a large mixing bowl mix the first five ingredients. Mix the oil and the buttermilk together and stir into the dry mixture. Add the eggs, one at a time, mixing well after each addition. Mix in the vanilla, then stir in the hot water. Stir well. Pour into a 9x13 inch pan and bake at 350° for 35 minutes or until done.

Willis and Betty Orr
Orr Angus Ranch
Lakeside, Nebraska

SOUR CREAM CHOCOLATE CAKE

2 c. sour cream	2 tsp. soda (rounded)
3 eggs	Vanilla
½ c. cocoa	Few drops of red food coloring
1½ c. sugar	2 c. flour

Combine all ingredients except flour in large mixing bowl and blend well. Add the 2 cups of flour, sifted. Blend. Bake at 350° for 30 minutes in 9x13x2 inch pan. If thick separated cream is used, use 1½ cups of cream and ½ cup of hot water. If thinner cream is used, use 2 cups.

FUDGE FROSTING

3 c. white sugar	⅓ c. cocoa
3 tsp. white Karo syrup	2 c. cream

Blend in a large sauce pan and cool to firm ball stage. Remove from fire and add 2 tsp. vanilla. Stir and allow to cook, then beat to desired spreading consistency. Spread on cake. Note: brown sugar may be used and omit the cocoa.

SRM SOCIETY FOR RANGE MANAGEMENT

R.J. and Rita Bell
Pitchfork Ranch
Guthrie, Texas

ψ

FRUIT COCKTAIL CAKE and ICING

2 c. flour	2 tsp. soda
1½ c. sugar	2 eggs
2 c. fruit cocktail	1 pinch salt

Mix and cook at 350° for 40 min. in 9x13-inch pan. Mix by hand.

ICING

1½ c. sugar	½ c. pecans
1½ sticks oleo	½ c. coconut
1 c. canned milk (undiluted)	

Cook sugar, oleo, and milk until thick. Remove from heat and add pecans and coconut. Pour over hot cake.

Background: Boyhood friends from Alabama, Eugene Williams, a sales manager for the St. Louis-based Hamilton Brown Shoe Company, and D.B. Gardner, a Texas surveyor, established the Pitchfork Ranch in the 1870s. Gardner located the prospective property near Guthrie, Texas, and asked Williams to come from St. Louis to take a look at it.

Near Henrietta, Texas, Williams became ill and unable to continue the journey. Before returning to St. Louis, Williams said, "If it's all right with Gardner, it's all right with me. I wouldn't know any more after I looked at the ranch anyway." And on that trust, the deal was made, and the property bought. Williams died shortly afterwards, never having seen the Pitchfork Ranch.

Gardner purchased Hereford cattle from south Texas to begin the ranch. The herd already wore the pitchfork brand, so Gardner simply named the ranch after the cattle.

In 1883, the ranch was incorporated. With the principal stockholders, the Williams family, living in St. Louis, Gardner managed the Pitchfork Land & Cattle Company until his death in 1928.

Although it grew larger and more prosperous, the Pitchfork Land & Cattle Co. never lost the spirit of friendship and trust that Gardner and Williams brought to it. According to local legend, several lost souls found refuge on the ranch.

Quanah Parker often took refuge on the ranch. A white girl kidnapped by Indians before the Civil War, Parker's mother, Cynthia, married an Indian chief. Parker often made camp near an exceedingly clear spring on the ranch. A close friend of Burk Burnett, owner of the Four Sixes, Parker remained in the area after most of his people had moved on.

Today, Jim Humphreys manages the ranch. Expanded considerably since its incorporation, the ranch now holds 202,000 acres in Texas, Wyoming and Kansas. A cow/calf operation is run on a 166,000-acre Texas ranch; a 32,000-acre Wyoming ranch works steers and sheep; and a 4,000-acre Kansas ranch raises steers.

CANDY

Marie Rumburg
Fairfax County, Virginia

BEEF CANDY

2 c. white sugar
1 c. brown sugar
½ c. light karo syrup
½ c. milk

½ c. ground cooked beef
3 tsp. butter
1 tsp. vanilla
½ c. nuts

2 squares chocolate, if desired

Cook to a soft ball stage the sugar, milk, beef, butter, and karo syrup. Cool, and add nuts and vanilla.

Johneta Jackson
Peter V. Jackson Ranch
Harrison, Montana

GRANDMA MCLEAN'S COCONUT FUDGE

2 c. white sugar
2 tbsp. white karo syrup
2 c. sour cream*

2 c. coconut, shredded
1 tsp. vanilla
2 tbsp. butter

*(min 30% butterfat; best if 60% butterfat)

Mix first 4 ingredients in a heavy sauce pan. Begin cooking on medium heat, to keep from scorching, stirring well till all sugar is dissolved. Cook to a soft ball stage. Cool. Add butter and vanilla, beat until thick and creamy. Pour into the pan, cutting into squares. A layer of milk chocolate spread over the squares makes a very good Mounds-type candy.

Background: Pete Jackson's Grandmother Lilla McLean brought this recipe to Virginia City, Mt. as a young bride. She cooked it for Christmas treats. Coconut was a special treat then.

263

Mrs. Charles Terwilliger, Jr.
Fort Collins, Colorado

SOUR CREAM FUDGE

3 c. granulated sugar   1 c. sour cream
⅔ c. dark karo syrup   ¼ tsp. cream of tartar

(increase cream of tartar to ½ tsp. if cream is not really sour)

Mix and stir until smooth and almost dissolved. Cover and boil 5 minutes without stirring. Uncover and cook to 230° (soft ball in cold water). Cook to about 150°. Beat until it loses its gloss and looks creamy. If you like, add nuts and vanilla flavoring just as it starts to lose its gloss. Pour into a buttered pan to cool. Cut into squares.

Shirley Williamson
Fairfax, Virginia

PIONEER POTATO CANDY

½ c. warm unseasoned mashed potatoes   1 lb. confectioners sugar
¼ tsp. salt   ½ lb. chocolate for dipping
1 tsp. vanilla   ½ c. shredded coconut

Combine potatoes, salt, and vanilla in mixing bowl. Sift confectioners sugar over potatoes, stirring and adding about 1 cup at a time. Mixture will liquify when first sugar is added, then begin to thicken. When mixture becomes the consistency of stiff dough, knead it even though all the sugar has not been added (likewise, add more sugar if needed). After kneading, cover with a damp cloth. Chill until a small spoonful can be rolled into a ball. Shape into small ½-inch balls. Dip balls in melted chocolate, then roll in coconut. Makes about 4-doz. balls. For true pioneer candy, omit the chocolate and coconut.

Bonita Harris
Walters, Oklahoma

WESTERN PRALINES

2 c. sugar	⅛ tsp. salt
1 tsp. soda	2 tbsp. butter
1 c. buttermilk	2½ c. pecan halves

In a large sauce pan combine sugar, soda, buttermilk, and salt. Cook over high heat about 5 minutes, stirring and scraping sides of pan (it foams). Add butter and pecans and continue cooking over medium heat, constantly scraping bottom and sides of pan, until it reaches soft ball stage. Remove from heat. Beat with heavy spoon until thick and creamy. Drop from tablespoon onto sheets of aluminum foil or wax paper. Makes about 20-25 pralines.

COOKIES

Nina Turner and Bertha Hofer
Portis Kansas

APPLE KRINKLE

5 or 6 apples	1 c. oatmeal
1 c. white sugar	1 c. flour
4 tbsp. flour	¼ tsp. baking powder
1 tsp. cinnamon	¼ tsp. salt
1 c. boiling water	⅔ c. butter or shortening
1 c. brown sugar	1 tsp. vanilla

Slice apples in large flat baking dish, 8x13 inches, and fill the dish about half full. Mix the white sugar, 4 tbsp. flour, and cinnamon and put over apples. Pour the boiling water over the apples, then cover with the mixture of brown sugar, oatmeal, 1 c. flour, butter, baking powder, salt, and vanilla, that has been well mixed together. Bake at 375° until apples are done—from 45 min to 1 hour.

Ruth Chambers Harrison
George Chambers Ranch
Smithfield, Utah

WC

RAISIN FILLED COOKIES

DOUGH:	*FILLING:*
1 c. shortening	*1 lb. raisins, ground*
¾ c. milk	*2 tbsp. cornstarch*
1 c. sugar	*1 c. sugar*
2 eggs	*1 c. water*
2 tsp. baking powder	
½ tsp. salt	
Flour	

DOUGH: Mix ingredients. Start with 4 cups of flour and add enough to make a dough you can roll out. Roll dough to ⅛-inch thickness. Cut into circles. Place filling on one circle then cover with another, and punch sides together. Bake at 350° for 12 to 15 minutes until light brown. Makes about 5 doz. cookies.
FILLING: Combine ingredients and cook until thickened. Cool mixture.

Marjorie Wolters
Portis, Kansas

PEANUT BUTTER FROSTS

1 c. flour	*½ c. brown sugar*
1 c. quick oats	*½ c. margarine*
½ c. sugar	*⅓ c. peanut butter*
1 beaten egg	

Combine in large bowl the above dry ingredients. Add margarine, peanut butter, and egg. Mix thoroughly. Press in 9x9 pan. Bake at 350° for 20 to 25 minutes until batter begins to pull away from the edge of pan. Cool and frost.

PEANUT BUTTER FROSTING

¼ c. margarine	*¼ c. peanut butter*
Milk	*1 tsp. vanilla*

Mix margarine, peanut butter, vanilla and drops of milk until spreading consistency. Spread on top of cookies.

David R. Heydlauff
Rafter 36 Ranch
Manyberries, Alberta Canada

OVERNIGHT MOLASSES COOKIES

1 c. sugar	3 c. flour
1 scant c. lard	2 tsp. soda
½ c. molasses	½ tsp. ginger
½ c. hot water	

Cream lard and sugar. Add molasses, then water. Next add dry ingredients that have been mixed together. Mold into a roll and let stand overnight in a cool place. Slice and bake.

Background: The Heydlauff Ranch has been using the Rafter-36 brand for about 75 years. My grandfather came to Wild Horse in 1904 and established a horse ranch. Later the ranch was converted to a cattle operation. My two brothers and I still run the ranch. This recipe has been in our family for three generations.

Mrs. Henry A. Pearson
Pineville, Louisiana

HAP

OATMEAL REFRIGERATOR COOKIES

2 sticks margarine	1 tsp. soda
1 c. white sugar	1½ c. flour
1 c. brown sugar	1 tsp. salt
2 eggs	3 c. oatmeal
1 tbsp. vanilla	1 c. finely chopped pecans

Let margarine come to room temperature and cream well. Add white and brown sugar. Add eggs, one at a time, beating after each. Add vanilla. Mix together soda, salt, and flour and add to above mixture. Stir in oatmeal and nuts. Shape into rolls; put each in waxed paper and refrigerate overnight. Slice and bake 8 to 10 minutes at 400°.

Wilma Newman
Dunkirk, Montana

SNICKERDOODLES

1 c. butter	1 tsp. soda
1½ c. sugar	½ tsp. salt
2 eggs	ROLL IN:
2¾ c. flour	2 tbsp. sugar
2 tsp. baking powder	2 tbsp. cinnamon

Cream butter and sugar; add eggs and blend. Combine flour, baking powder, soda, and salt. Mix thoroughly. Chill dough several hours. When ready to bake, roll dough into small balls (a teaspoon of dough). Roll each ball in the sugar/cinnamon mixture. Bake on ungreased pan at 350° for 7 to 8 minutes.

Catherine M. Jameson
Ft. Collins, Colorado

COWBOY COOKIES

2 c. flour, sifted	1 c. shortening
½ tsp. baking powder	2 eggs
1 tsp. baking soda	2 c. quick rolled oats
½ tsp. salt	1 tsp. vanilla
1 c. white sugar	1 large (12-oz. pkg)
1 c. brown sugar	milk chocolate chips

Sift flour, baking soda, baking powder, and salt together. Combine with the rest of the ingredients and drop from a teaspoon on greased baking sheet. Bake at 350° for 15 minutes.

Willis and Betty Orr
Orr Angus Ranch
Lakeside, Nebraska

PRALINE COOKIES and FROSTING

1⅔ c. sifted flour	1 c. butter
1½ tsp. baking powder	1½ firmly packed brown sugar
½ tsp. salt	1 unbeaten egg

1 tsp. vanilla

Sift flour, baking powder, and salt together and set aside. Cream butter and brown sugar. Add egg. Blend well. Add vanilla. Blend and add dry ingredients. Mix well. Drop by teaspoonful on ungreased cookie sheet. Bake at 350° for 10 to 12 minutes.

FROSTING

1 c. pecan halves	½ c. cream (or half & half)
1 c. firmly packed brown sugar	1 c. sifted powdered sugar

Break pecan halves into pieces and put 4 or 5 pieces on top of each cookie. Combine brown sugar and cream in small sauce pan. Bring to a boil, stirring constantly. Boil two minutes, Remove from heat. Blend in sifted powdered sugar and beat until smooth. Drizzle sauce over cookies. Sauce pan may be set in pan of warm water to keep frosting soft enough to cover all cookies.

 **SRM SOCIETY FOR RANGE MANAGEMENT**

Catherine M. Jameson
Fort Collins, Colorado

COLORADO HONEY-PEANUT BUTTER COOKIES

½ c. shortening	½ c. peanut butter
½ c. honey	½ tsp. salt
½ c. brown sugar	2 c. flour
1 egg, well beaten	½ tsp. baking soda

Cream shortening, honey, and sugar together until light and fluffy. Add egg, peanut butter, and salt. Stir in flour and soda, and mix well. Form into small balls; place on greased cookie sheet; press with fork. Bake at 350° for 8 to 10 minutes.

Myrtle Hendee
Bethesda, Maryland

PEANUT BUTTER DELIGHT

¾ c. raisins	¼ c. brown sugar
¾ c. pitted prunes	½ c. dried milk
½ c. other dried fruits	¼ c. Bran cereal
¼ c. wheat germ	1½ c. peanut butter
1 c. honey	

Crush or grind dry ingredients until uniform. Stir in peanut butter and honey. Chill in refrigerator, then shape into cookies. Sprinkle with brown sugar. Bake at 250° for 30 minutes. Wrap in foil and refrigerate until needed.

W. Don and Jean G. Walker
Ardgowan
Dunsandel, Canterbury, New Zealand

PAVLOVA
(A typical New Zealand dessert)

8 oz. sugar	*1 tsp. vanilla*
4 egg whites	*1 tsp. vinegar*
½ tsp. salt	

Beat egg whites (room temperature) until stiff. Add sugar gradually and continue beating. Add vanilla and vinegar, beating until very stiff. Must form peaks when beater is raised. Mark a ring about 8 or 9 inches across on grease-proof paper which has been run under the tap or on aluminum foil. Empty mixture on paper or foil and form inside the ring. Bake 15 minutes at 300-325°, then reduce to 275° and bake for another hour. Leave to cool, then turn out onto a plate. Cover with whipped cream and decorate with sliced fruit. Slices of kiwi fruit on top make an especially attractive dish. Serves 6-8.

Background: The Walkers are gracious hosts to many Americans who visit their home. They are retired stockraisers — sheep and cattle.

Marjorie Wolters
Portis, Kansas

CARAMEL BROWNIES

1 pkg. German chocolate cake mix
¾ c. margarine, melted
⅓ c. evaporated milk
1 c. chopped nuts
1 c. chocolate chips

30-40 caramels
⅓ c. evaporated milk
4 tbsp. margarine

Mix first column of ingredients together, except for chocolate chips, set aside. Melt caramels, milk and margarine (second column). Spread ½ cake mixture in 9x13 inch greased pan. Bake 8 minutes at 350°. Sprinkle 1 cup chocolate chips over pan. Pour caramel mixture over the chips. Spread on other half of cake mix. Bake 18 minutes at 350°.

Phyllis Simpson
Alkton, Kansas

COTTAGE CHEESE ROLLS

12-oz. creamed cottage cheese
(small curd)
2 sticks margarine

⅓ c. sugar
Dash salt
2 c. flour

Cream thoroughly. Stir in 2 cups flour. Divide into 3 balls and chill several hours or overnight. Roll each ball out like a pizza. Cut into 12 wedges. Roll each wedge, starting at the big end. Bake on a cookie sheet 30 minutes at 350°, or until lightly browned. Frost with butter cream frosting.

COBBLERS, CUSTARDS, DUMPLINGS, PIES & PUDDINGS

Guy Goen & Sons
Goen Ranch
Dickens County, Texas

PEACH OR APPLE COBBLER

1 gal. peaches or apples,
   peeled & quartered
8 c. white sugar
1 stick margarine
1 c. cornstarch

dash of salt
2 boxes Duncan Hines white cake mix
3 c. brown sugar
cooking oil
1 can Coke or Dr. Pepper

Put peaches or apples in 16" dutch oven. Add white sugar, margarine, cornstarch, dash of salt, ¾ box of cake mix, and one (6. oz.) can of Coke. Put dutch oven on fire and stir constantly until the ingredients boil and thicken. You may need to add water. Remove from the fire. Put the remaining cake mix (1 to 1-¼ box) on top for the crust. It should be about 3/8" thick. Try to get the top moistened with juice from the cobbler. Sprinkle cooking oil over top of crust, then sprinkle the brown sugar on top of crust. Put lid on dutch oven. Set it over a small amount of fire and cover lid with coals until cobbler boils lightly. Remove oven from coals and let crust brown. This pot cobbler will take the wrinkles out of 25 to 30 hungry bellies.

Ted V. Russell
Ogden, Utah

QUICK MADE COBBLER

¾ stick butter or margarine
1 c. flour
1 c. sugar

2 tsp. baking powder
¾ c. milk
pinch salt

1 can fruit (cherries, peaches, etc.)

Melt the butter in a baking dish and set aside. Mix remaining ingredients (except fruit) together. Pour batter into butter and top with fruit, do not stir. Bake in 375° oven for 30 minutes. Good served with ice cream on top.

John & Denzil Mills
Charleville, Queensland, Australia

CREAMY CUSTARD

3 tbsp. custard powder	*1 c. Sunshine powdered milk*
½ c. sugar	*vanilla essence*

Mix custard powder, sugar and Sunshine milk together with a little water until you have a fine texture. Place saucepan on coals with water in and bring to the boil. When boiling, pour in the prepared mixture slowly, stirring all the time until you have a creamy custard. Now add the vanilla essence. Serve hot or cold. Cooking time: 10 to 15 minutes.

Phillis Simpson
Alton, Kansas

APPLE DUMPLINGS

DOUGH—SIFT:
  2 c. flour
2 tsp. baking powder
  1 tsp. salt

CUT IN:
1-½ sticks butter or ¾ c. margarine till crumbly.

ADD:
½ c. sweet milk—stir well
(Will be a soft dough. Chill while making syrup)

SYRUP:
  2 c. sugar
  2 c. water
3 tbsp. red hots
  ¼ tsp. nutmeg
  ½ stick margarine
(Stir over low heat until all red hots are dissolved)

Peel 8 apples and core. Roll dough thin and cut in square big enough to fit apple. Set apple in center of dough square and fill hole in apple with sugar-cinnamon mixture. Press dough up around apples. Set in bake dish and pour syrup over them. Bake in 350° oven for 45 minutes.

Virginia L. Jackson
Heart J Salers Ranch
Harrison, Montana

HIGHPOCKETS VINEGAR COBBLER

4 c. sugar	*¼ lb. butter*
2-½ c. water	*nutmeg to suit*
¾ c. vinegar	*dash salt*

Put all ingredients in pan you are going to bake in—a bread pan if cooking on a stove or a dutch oven if cooking on open fire. Let mixture boil while you make pie dough (enough for two regular crusts). Roll pie dough out thin and cut into strips. Crisscross on top of hot vinegar solution. Bake in medium oven until crust is brown. If pie is thin, that is the way it should be. This is not a custard pie. It is best baked in a dutch oven over a camp fire. Sourdough dumplings can be used instead of pie crust. Best eaten while fresh; it begins to taste vinegary if left too long.

Four Sixes Ranch
Guthrie, Texas

6666

SUNDAY COBBLER

¾ c. all purpose flour	*¼ c. butter*
½ c. brown sugar	*½ c. chopped pecans*
½ c. sugar	*¼ c. sourdough starter*
½ tsp. cinnamon	*1 1-lb., 5-oz. can cherry pie filling*
½ c. seedless raisins	

Combine flour, sugars, and cinnamon; cut in butter. Stir in pecans and starter. Combine pie filling and raisins in an 8" round baking dish. Spoon first mixture over the top. Bake in 425° oven for 25 minutes or until hot and brown. Serves 6.

Niels L. Martin
Range Specialist LCRD Project/Lesotho
Masery, Lesotho Southern Africa

FRUIT DUMPLINGS

MIX TOGETHER THE FOLLOWING:

2 c. flour	¼ c. sugar ½ tsp. cinnamon (optional)
2 heaping tsp. baking powder	½ c. dry milk powder (or use fresh
¼ tsp. salt	milk instead of the water)
¼ c. oil or shortening	water to make a moist dough

Drop by spoonful into boiling fruit. Cook until the interior of the dumplings are not sticky. Serve warm.

Prepare fruit (I have used anything from mangoes to berries to fruit cocktail) by boiling with sugar to make sweet stewed fruit. Canned fruits usually have enough liquid and sweetening already. Just dump in the pot and bring to a boil. Dried fruits need a little extra time boiling to rehydrate.

Background: This is a recipe I have used in range camps in the U.S. and in Africa. It was a favorite of my Malian counterparts when I was camp cook in that country.

James Newland
Greenwood Ranches
Belle Fourche, South Dakota

W
+

Air Pie

1 bottom crust	3 c. fresh sliced peaches
1 c. sugar or less	1 tbsp. cinnamon
2 tbsp. butter	

MERINGUE:

½ c. sugar	2 egg whites
dash salt	

Fill unbaked crust with fruit which has been stewed until tender. Add cinnamon and butter plus optional salt. Bake until fruit is tender at 350° about one hour. Check after 45 minutes. Can be kept in refrigerator for several days.

When ready, make meringue by beating egg whites stiff and gradually add sugar. Spoon big dollops of meringue to cover entire pie, do not spread. Bake in 425° oven until meringue is meduum brown. If you prefer a firmer, thicker pie, add a tbsp. of cornstarch.

Dalice Wolters
Portis, Kansas

PEACH CREAM PIE

1 unbaked pie shell   *3 level tbsp. flour*
3 med. peaches (enough to fill shell)   *3 c. coffee cream or half-and-half*
½ tsp. cinnamon (more if desired)

Peel peaches, cut in half and remove stones. Arrange halves, cut-side down in pie shell. Mix sugar, flour and cinnamon with cream to make a paste. Pour over peaches. Place in hot oven (450°). Bake 10 minutes or until shell begins to brown. Reduce heat to moderate oven (350°). Continue baking for 30 minutes or until peaches are done. Serve cold.

Historic Western Recipe

DEEP-DISH PLUM PIE

5 c. halved, pitted, fresh purple plums,   *dash ground nutmeg*
(2 lbs.)   *dash salt*
¾ c. packed brown sugar   *1 tbsp. butter or margarine*
2 tsp. quick-cooking tapioca   *pastry for 1 crust 9" pie*
¼ tsp. ground cinnamon   *light cream or ice cream*

In a large bowl combine the purple plums, brown sugar, tapioca, cinnamon, nutmeg, and salt. Let stand 15 minutes. Turn mixture into an 8 x 1-½" round baking dish. Dot with butter. Roll pastry to a 9" circle. Place over filling. Trim; flute edges to seal. Cut slits for escape of steam. Using pastry trimmings, garnish top of pie with pastry cutouts, if desired. Bake at 375° for 40-45 minutes. Serve warm with light cream or ice cream.

Background: On early frontier homesteads, before the crops had been harvested, the pioneers depended heavily on the wide assortment of fruits and nuts that grew wild. Plums, strawberries, blueberries, raspberries, blackberries, grapes, currants, and elderberries were gathered and either used fresh as in this recipe for Deep-Dish Plum Pie, or carefully preserved. Some fruits were preserved by drying in the sun and others were made into jellies, jams, or sauces. The jellies and jams were served on bread or used in recipes. Nuts, including hickory nuts, walnuts, pecans, butternuts, and hazel nuts, were dried and eventually found their way into all sorts of breads, cakes, and pies.

Janice Grover
Springfield, Virginia

MOIST APPLE PIE

Sift together 1-⅓ c. sifted all purpose flour, 1-½ tsp. sugar and ½ tsp. salt. Place in 9" pie plate. With fork, whip together ½ c. salad oil and 2 tbsp. milk. Pour over flour mixture. Mix all the above until the flour is moist. Press dough against bottom and sides of pie plate to form a crust.

FILLING:

4 c. (tart) apples	*1 c. sugar*
1 c. sour cream	*½ tsp. lemon juice*
1 tsp. cinnamon	

Mix these ingredients together and pour in pie shell.

CREME TOPPING:

⅓ c. flour	*⅓ c. sugar*
2 tbsp. (room temp.) butter or margarine	

Combine with fork until flaky and then sprinkle over pie. Bake at 425° for 10 minutes. Reduce heat to 350° and continue to bake for 45 minutes or until crust is done. Line plate because the juice drips over the pan.

James Newland
Greenwood Ranches
Belle Fourche, South Dakota

W
t

BLUEBERRY CREAM PIE

1 10" pie shell, pre-baked	*2 c. sugar*
5 c. fresh blueberries	*3½ tbsp. cornstarch*
2 c. water	*2 c. heavy cream, whipped*

Wash blueberries; remove stems and green berries. Place four cups drained berries in pie shell. In saucepan, bring water and sugar to a boil and add one cup blueberries and cornstarch, mixed with 2 tbsp. cold water. Bring to a boil. Simmer two minutes, stirring until sauce is thickened. Pour sauce over blueberries and cool pie. Top with whipped cream. Frozen or canned berries can be used.

HICKORY NUT CUSTARD PIE

1 c. sugar	*4 slightly beaten eggs*
2 tbsp. cornstarch	*1 tsp. vanilla*
¼ tsp. salt	*1 unbaked 9" pastry shell*
1 c. water	*¾ c. coarsely broken hickory nuts*
½ c. molasses	*whipped cream*

In a medium saucepan combine the sugar, cornstarch, and salt. Stir in the water and molasses. Cook and stir till thickened and bubbly. Gradually stir the hot mixture into the eggs. Add vanilla. Bake unpricked pie shell at 350° for 5 minutes. Remove from oven. Pour in egg mixture; top with nuts. Return pie to oven. Bake at 350° until a knife inserted just off-center comes out clean, about 30 minutes. Cool. To serve, top the pie with whipped cream. Pecans can be substituted for hickory nuts.

Mrs. Frances Voigt
Voigt Hereford Ranch
Shields, North Dakota

MINCEMEAT PIE

4 lbs. lean beaf	*2 c. molasses*
10 lbs. tart apples, coarsely ground	*2 oranges, rind & juice*
2 lbs. beef suet, coarsely ground	*1-½ qts. cider*
3 lbs. sugar	*1 glass currant jelly*
3 lbs. currants	*1 tbsp. cinnamon*
3 lbs. seeded raisins	*1 tbsp. nutmeg*
½ lb. citron, cut fine	*1 tsp. allspice*

salt to season

Put meat in a large kettle, cover with water and let simmer until tender, about 1-½ hours. Allow to cool. Remove meat from broth and grind. Cook broth down to one cup and mix with meat and other ingredients. Heat gradually, and simmer one hour to blend flavors. Seal in hot sterilized jars and process 30 minutes in boiling water bath. Yields 10 quarts. For a 2-crust, 9" pie, use 1 qt. of mincemeat. Bake in hot oven (400°) for 35 minutes.

CIDER PIE

1 unbaked 8" pastry shell
1 6-oz. can frozen apple juice
    concentrate, thawed
3 eggs
ground nutmeg

½ c. packed brown sugar
2 tbsp. butter or margarine, melted
¼ tsp. salt

Bake unpricked pastry shell at 450° for 4 minutes. Remove from oven; reduce oven temperature to 350°. Meanwhile, beat together concentrate, eggs, sugar, butter, and salt. Pour into pastry shell. Sprinkle with nutmeg. Bake at 350° till knife inserted just off-center comes out clean, 25 to 30 minutes.

Background: In the old West, homemakers made Cider Pie by boiling apple cider down until it was very thick, Today frozen apple juice concentrate is a convenient substitute for boiled cider.

James Newland
Greenwood Ranches
Bell Fourche, South Dakota

W
+

GOOSEBERRY PIE

4 c. gooseberries
4 tbsp. flour (or 2-⅔ tbsp. tapioca)
¾ c. sugar

½ tsp. cinnamon, ginger, or nutmeg
1-½ tbsp. butter
pie crust

Preheat oven to 450°. Line a 9" pie pan with any pie crust. Pick over and hull gooseberries.

Thicken gooseberries with flour (or tapioca) and sugar. An alternate method uses 2 tbsp. cornstarch dissolved in ¼ c. water. Let the mixture stand for 15 minutes. Spice your mixture with cinnamon, ginger or nugmeg.

When the fruit is in the pie shell, dot with butter. Cover with a top crust or lattice and bake at 450° for 10 minutes. Reduce heat and bake 40-45 minutes.

Mrs. Gene McCormick
Mcnoken, North Dakota

MOTHER McCORMICK'S MINCEMEAT

6 lbs. lean fresh neck meat, boiled
until tender. When cold, chop fine
1 lb. ground beef suet
6 lbs. ground seeded raisins
dishpan full (5 lbs.) of chopped apples,
(Johothan or a good juicy apple)
2 lbs. currants
2 tbsp. cinnamon

1 tbsp. nutmeg
1 tbsp. cloves
1 tbsp. mace
1 tbsp. allspice
1 tbsp. fine salt
2 lbs brown sugar
½ c. lemon juice
½ gal. apple cider

wine glass of brandy is an improvement

Mix all ingredients together; simmer and bring to boiling point. Seal in sterilized jars. Will keep for months in cellar. I process this for 30 minutes.

Background: This recipe was Mrs. Mary Johnston McCormick's. She and her husband William Patrick McCormick homesteaded in Frances Township in 1878.

Harold F. Heady
Berkeley, California

BRANDY SAUCE
(For Mince Pie)

1 c. water
½ c. sugar
2 tbsp. cornstarch

1 tsp. nutmeg
2 tbsp. butter
¼ c. brandy

1 tsp. vanilla

Mix dry ingredients and then add them while stirring into cup of boiling water. Boil for 5 minutes and then add butter, brandy, and vanilla. Serve hot over mince pie.

Susie Fee
Fee Ranch, Inc.
Ft. Bidwell, California

FEE

FEE RANCH MINCEMEAT

½ lb. butter (cut into tiny chunks)
2-½ lbs. brown sugar
3 lbs. boiled beef neck,
stripped off & ground
2-½ lbs. white sugar
2 tbsp. each of:
cinnamon
nutmeg
allspice
mace
common salt

juice & rind (grated) of 3 lemons
1 lb. ground citron
1-½ lbs. ground beef suet
3 lbs. seeded raisins
3 lbs. seedless raisins
8 lbs. apples, peeled & ground
½ gallon cider
1 pint brandy
1 pint sherry
1 tbsp. almond extract

Cook meat the night before making mincemeat. Grind all ingredients to be ground. Mix all ingredients in a very large container as follows, and in this order: meat, apples, raisins, currants, citron, butter, suet, spices, cider, sherry, brandy. This recipe makes nearly 50 lbs. of mincemeat. It can be stored in a cool place in large covered crocks, or canned in canning jars and sealed, like any fruit. If stored in crocks, it must be "watered" about every two weeks. To water, pour brandy, sherry, or cider over the mincemeat and re-mix. Amount of the liquid to use depends on how dry the mincemeat gets, and the taste of the user.

Mrs. C. H. Wasser
Fort Collins, Colorado

MYSTERY PUDDING

1 c. flour
1 c. sugar
1 tsp. soda
dash of salt
1 egg, slightly beaten

1 can (no. 2) fruit cocktail & syrup
¾ c. brown sugar
½ c. chopped nuts
whipped cream
Maraschino cherries

Sift together flour, sugar and soda. Combine flour mixture with egg, fruit cocktail and syrup from fruit cocktail. Mix thoroughly. Spoon batter into greased pan, 8½ x 8½". Combine brown sugar and nuts and sprinkle over batte. Bake at 350° for 45 minutes or until wooden pick inserted in center comes out clean. Garnish with whipped cream and maraschino cherries. Serves 9.

Jeanne Edwards
Saval Ranch
North Fork, Nevada

∧L

I'M NOT ON A DIET PIE

3 eggs	½ c. butter (melted)
1-½ c. sugar	½ c. buttermilk
1-½ tbsp. flour	1 tsp. vanilla

unbaked pie shell

Beat eggs until fluffy, add dry ingredients, buttermilk and vanilla. Pour into unbaked pie shell. Bake one hour in 300° oven.

Bonita Harris
Walters, Oklahoma

HARRIS PIE CRUST

5 lbs. flour	½ c. white Karo syrup
3 lb. can Crisco	3-½ c. water

2 tbsp. salt

Mix flour, Crisco, and salt. Mix Karo syrup and water in Crisco can, then add to the flour-Crisco mixture. Mix well. Pinch off balls of dough the size of an orange, put in a plastic bag, flatten and put in freezer. Makes about 25 pie crusts.

Phyllis Simpson
Alton, Kansas

NEVER FAIL PIE CRUST

4-¾ c. flour	2 c. Crisco
¾ c. water	3 tsp. salt

Mix ¾ c. of the flour and the water. Set aside while you mix the remaining 4 c. of flour, Crisco, and salt. Then mix all together. May be used immediately or stored in refrigerator. Keeps in refrigerator three weeks.

Dalice Wolters
Portis, Kansas

APPLE PUDDING

CREAM:

½ c. shortening   1 c. sugar

ADD:

1 beaten egg   1 tsp. nutmeg
1 c. flour   1 tsp. soda
1 tsp. cinnamon   2 c. apples, diced very fine
½ c. nuts

Batter will be quite stiff. Bake in 8 x 8" pan at 350° for 30 to 40 minutes.

Watt R. Matthews
Lambshead Ranch
Albany, Texas

BREAD PUDDING

2-½ c. bread crumbs   1 tsp. nutmeg
1 c. sugar   2 c. milk
1 tsp. vanilla   1 c. raisins (optional)
1 tsp. cinnamon   ½ stick margarine

Warm milk, melt margarine. Mix all ingredients. Pour into baking pan and bake at 425° for 20 to 25 minutes, or until top is brown.

Background: Provided by John White, cook on the 42,377-acre Lambshead Ranch for over 20 years. He usually feeds 10-20 people.

Watt R. Matthews
Lambshead Ranch
15 miles N.W. of Albany, Texas

Ω℧

RICE PUDDING

2 c. leftover cooked rice	1 tsp. vanilla
1 c. sugar	2 c. milk
1 tsp. cinnamon	3 eggs

1 tsp. nutmeg

Heat milk to boiling. Slightly beat eggs, sugar and vanilla. Add heated milk. Stir until smooth. Add remaining ingredients. Pour into baking pan and bake at 375° for 25 minutes until knife inserted comes out clean.

Background: Provided by John White, cook on the 42,377-acre Lambshead Ranch for over 20 years. He usually feeds 10-20 people for lunch.

Historic Ranch and Trail Drive Recipe

SON-OF-A-GUN-IN-A-SACK

2 c. all-purpose flour	¼ tsp. ground nutmeg
1-½ c. soft bread crumbs	1 c. raisins
½ c. packed brown sugar	1 c. ground suet (5 oz.)
1 tbsp. baking soda	½ c. chopped nuts
1 tsp. salt	1 5-⅓-oz. can evaporated milk (⅔ c.)
1 tsp. ground cinnamon	½ c. light molasses
¼ tsp. ground cloves	sweetened whipped cream (optional)

In mixing bowl combine flour, breadcrumbs, sugar, soda, salt, cinnamon, cloves, and nutmeg. Stir in raisins, suet, and nuts. Stir in milk and molasses; mix well. Arrange layers of cheesecloth to form a 16" square about 1/8" thick; set in a 1-quart bowl. Fill cheesecloth with pudding mixture; bring up sides of cheesecloth allowing room for expansion of the pudding; tie tightly with string. Place the "sack" in a colander. Place colander in kettle; add enough boiling water to cover the sack. Cover; boil gently for 2 hours. Remove colander from pan; remove cheesecloth from around pudding at once. Turn pudding, rounded side up, on plate. Let stand 30 minutes before serving. Serve warm with whipped cream, if desired. Serves 10-12.

Background: When the ranch cook wanted to be especially nice to the cowhands he made a boiled pudding sometimes called Son-of-a-Gun-in-a Sack. Raisins or dried apples and suet were added to a soft dough. Following the old colonial method, the mass was placed in a cloth sack and boiled in a big kettle of water until done. Perhaps it got its name because it was so much trouble to make.

Mrs. William Cruse Sweeney
Bozeman, Montana

SUET PUDDING & ENGLISH SAUCE

2 or 3 eggs, well-beaten　　　　1 pkg. dates, cut fine (floured)
1 lge. spoon molasses　　　　　　1 c. suet, ground
1 c. sugar (scant)　　　　　　　　1 c. nuts, cut
1 c. rich sour milk　　　　　　　　1 c. dry bread crumbs
½ pkg. raisins (floured)　　　　　1 level tsp. baking soda
flour to make real stiff

Mix baking soda with flour. Steam 2-½ to 3 hours. Serve with the following sauce.

SAUCE:

2 tbsp. butter　　　　　　　　　　　　　　½ c. sugar
1 tbsp. (small) flour

Mix and add 1 c. boiling water. Boil until thick. Add vanilla, brandy or what-have-you.

Background: This recipe was brought from England by William Skelton in 1883. He walked when a young boy from New York to Sioux City, where he got work and then walked on to Montana, arriving at Fort Benton. He was an Indian Scout for the army, later rode the range with Charlie Russell. He was successful in ranching, sheep and cattle.

Ivy Peart
Peart Ranch
Randolph, Utah

SOUR CREAM PIE

1-½ c. sour cream　　　　　　　　　1 c. sugar
2 eggs　　　　　　　　　　　　1 tbsp. b. flour (heaping)
½ tsp. cinnamon　　　　　　　　　½ tsp. nutmeg
1-½ c. raisins　　　　　　　　½ c. nuts (cut medium fine)

Mix flour, spices, and sugar. Add lightly beaten eggs, sour cream, raisins and nuts; Pour into one 9" unbaked pie shell, and bake for 30 minutes in a moderate oven (375°).

Use white of one of the eggs for meringue, brown slightly.

Background: In the early 1900's, Mother milked about 18 cows by hand, morning and night. Father would find part-time employment to help pay for the ranch. They had a hand separator and would separate the milk both morning and night, so they had a lot of cream. She had many recipes using cream, very rich, but very good.

Nancy Reagan
Washington, D.C.

PUMPKIN PECAN PIE

4 slightly beaten eggs
2 c. canned or mashed,
   cooked pumpkin
1 c. sugar
1 c. chopped pecans
         2 cups milk

½ tsp. cinnamon
¼ tsp. salt
1 unbaked 9-inch pie shell
½ c. dark corn syrup
1 tsp. vanilla

Combine ingredients except pecans. Pour into pie shell—top with pecans. Bake at 350° for 40 minutes, or until set.

Historical Pioneer Trail Recipe

DRIED APPLE PIE

Soak 2 cups dried apples in water overnight. Drain off the water and mix apples with ½ cup sugar and 1 teaspoon each of allspice and cinnamon. Line an 8-inch pie pan with a crust, add the apple mixture, dot with 3 tablespoons of butter and cover with a second crust. Make a few slashes in the top for ventilation and bake in a 350° oven for about 1 hour, until the crust is golden brown.

John and Denzil Mills
Charleville, Queensland, Australia

PIE MELON AND RICE SWEETS

½ or ¼ melon
         2 c. rice

1 c. sugar

Dice up melon. Take out seeds and stew until tender with sugar added. Put into dish and let cool. Boil the rice, when cooked wash off starch and cool. Cooking time: approximately 15 minutes. Serve pie melon with rice. Very tasty.

Arthur T. Williams
Malad, Idaho

ɣ

PUMPKIN PUDDING OR PIE FILLING

1 c. pumpkin or squash,   ½ c. sugar
    cooked & mashed   pinch of salt
    1 c. milk   1 heaping tbsp. flour
        pumpkin seasoning to taste

Combine first four ingredients and heat in a saucepan. Gradually add flour and cook until thick. May be used as pudding with whipped cream on it, or may be poured into a cooked pie shell and used as pie filling with whipped cream on top.

Background: Ranch headquarters is a Historic rest stop & park. This recipe is over 80 years old.

Doug Sellars
Historic Ranch Recipe
Society for Range Management
Washington, D.C.

RED BEAN PIE

1 c. cooked, mashed pinto beans   1 c. milk
    1 c. sugar   1 tsp. vanilla
    3 egg yolks, beaten   1 tsp. nutmeg

Combine ingredients and place in uncooked pie crust. Bake at 350° for 30 minutes or until set. Make meringue with the leftover egg whites; spread on pie and brown in oven.

VINEGAR PIE

1 c. sugar   5 tbsp. vinegar
    2 tbsp. flour   2½ tbsp. butter
    1 c. cold water   4 eggs, beaten

Combine sugar and flour. Add the rest of the ingredients and place in a saucepan. Cook until thick and pour into a prepared pie crust. Bake in a 375° oven until crust is brown.

JAMS and JELLIES

Wilma Newman
Dunkirk, Montana

APPLE BUTTER

1 peck (approx. 12 lbs.) apples   1 tsp. cloves
          6 c. sugar   1 tsp. allspice
               1 tbsp. cinnamon, or more to taste

Wash, drain, and slice apples. Cook in small amount of water until soft. Press through seive, add sugar and spices. Put in large pan (aluminum dishpan or large roaster). Place in oven at 250° until thick, which will take 6 to 10 hours. Stir ever half hour to 45 minutes. Have canning jars and lids sterilized. Put apple butter in jars. Seal while hot.

Guy Goen and Sons
Goen Ranch
Dickens County, Texas

HEN BUTTER

1 qt. syrup, preferably cane flavored   1 c. Duncan Hines white cake mix
          1 qt. sugar   Pinch of salt
        1 stick margarine   8 eggs
                    1 c. Coca Cola

Mix syrup, sugar, margarine, cake mix and salt in a large Dutch oven. With a heavy spatula stir constantly until the mixture boils for 3 or 4 minutes. After it has boiled for 3 or 4 minutes, set it off the fire and let the ingredients cool thoroughly. Beat up eggs. Put Dutch oven back on the fire. Start stirring and pouring in eggs. Mix eggs well before the contents start to boil. Then let the mixture boil until big bubbles come to the top. Let boil for 3 or 4 minutes. Then add 1 cup of Coca Cola. It is now ready to eat. Hen butter makes a good dessert with hot biscuits. It will keep in the refrigerator a long time.

Background: The wagon cook at the Pitchfork Ranch made this dessert around the turn of the century and gave it its name.

Joe J. McEntire and Joe B. Norris
Abilene, Texas

AGRITO JELLY

5 c. juice from Agrito fruit
5-7 c. sugar
1 pkg. Sure-Jell

Cover agrito fruit with water and boil until skins burst. Strain juice to remove impurities. Mix juice and Sure-Jell. Bring to a hard boil for 1 to 2 minutes. Remove from heat. Skim foam. Pour into scalded jars. Seal immediately.

Background: Agrito, sometimes called Algertio, is an evergreen shrub. It is a low growing native plant rarely over 12 feet high. The shrub has small yellow flowers in early spring and produces a red fruit by summer. The reddish fruit is about the size of a pea and is used today for jelly and wine making. This plant has compound leaves with 3 leaflets. They are stiff and have sharp needles on the margin of the bluish-green leaves. The woody portion was used by Indians to make small wooden-ware articles. The roots were used to prepare a tonic and also a yellow dye. Young tender leaves are grazed by goats and deer and many small wildlife eat the fruit.

Texas Section, SRM
Texas

PLUM JELLY

5 c. plum juice
5 to 7 c. sugar
1 pkg. Sure-Jell

Cover the fruit with water and boil until skins burst. Strain juice to remove impurities. Mix plum juice and Sure-Jell. Bring to a hard boil for 1 to 2 minutes. Remove from heat. Skim foam. Pour into scalded jars. Seal immediately.

Background: Wild plums are shrubs which often form dense thickets. These shrubs are seldom more than 6 feet tall. The clustered white flowers emerge in early spring before the leaves appear. The fruit, a round plum, ripens in mid-summer to a red or yellow color. The fruit of the wild plum makes excellent preserves and jelly and is widely used for that purpose throughout the state. Wild plum thickets make excellent cover for wildlife. The leaves and twigs are utilized by deer and the fruit is valuable as a food for turkey and many other types of birds and wildlife.

Texas Section, SRM
Texas

PRICKLY PEAR JELLY

3½ c. prickly pear fruit juice   1 box Sure-Jell
 ½ c. lemon juice   5½ c. sugar

Singe stickers off pear apples. Wash and cut fruit into 2 or 3 pieces. Put enough water in fruit so that it can be seen through the fruit in the pan. Cook about 45 minutes or until partially tender, then strain off juice. Juice will be thick, syrupy, and stringy. Measure 3½ cups of juice and add the lemon juice and Sure-Jell. Boil 3 or 4 minutes. Add the sugar and boil again for about 25 to 30 minutes. Test with a spoon. Add red food coloring if needed.

Background: The spiny Prickly Pear cactus plants are usually low growing but some reach a height of 12 feet. They are evergreen and have many flat, succulent "pads" sometimes called leaves. Flowers appear in late spring and are usually yellow to red in color. The fruit or "pear" ripens in late summer and is usually red to purple in color with many small seeds inside the flesh covering. Indians and early day settlers used the plant extensively for food. The fruit may be eaten raw or made into a preserve. The "pods" when young and tender may be cooked and served with a dressing and seasoning. They are also made into candy. Some Indians believe that a tea made from the fruit would cure ailments caused by gallstones. Commercial alcohol has been made from the sap. The juice of the pods is boiled with tallow in candle making to increase the hardness of the candles. Cattle eat the pear as an emergency feed during droughts after the spines have been burned off. Many small animals and birds feed on the fruit.

Rosa Lee Hamilton
Reed Hamilton Ranch, Inc.
Thedford, Nebraska

DUTCH HONEY
(Topping for pancakes & biscuits)

1 c. brown sugar
1 c. cream (or half and half)
1 c. white syrup

Mix together in pan. Heat only until mixture is hot — not boiling. Our family prefers this caramel-like toping to the regular pancake and waffle syrups.

Background: This ranch is being operated by third and fourth generations. Mr. Hamilton's grandfather T.P. Hamilton homesteaded here in 1897.

Mrs. Harlan DeGarmo
Elmwood, Nebraska

EGG BUTTER

1 pt. sorgum molasses	*3 well beaten eggs*
1 tsp. nutmeg	*Lump of butter, size of a walnut*

Bring molasses to a boil over medium heat. Add eggs slowly, stirring constantly. Cook until thick. Serve on hot biscuits fresh from the oven.

Background: Grandfather Jonnie R. Rice was one of the first homesteaders of Pratt County, Kansas. He came with his young bride to farm the Kansas Prairie. They lived in a dugout while waiting for their 12 room, two story house to be built.

Mrs. Robert M. Case
Pagosa Springs, Colorado

BLACK KETTLE APPLE BUTTER

10 gal. quartered apples	*20 lbs. sugar*
7 qts. water for cooking	*1 qt. vinegar*
4 tbsp. cinnamon	

Boil apples about 3 hours, stirring frequently. Cook apples about 1 hour before adding sugar. Add cinnamon when apple butter is nearly done. May be canned or kept in large stone jar. The original recipe as done by Grandma and Granpa Toner was made in a large black kettle in the back yard.

John and Denzil Mills
Charleville, Queensland, Australia

ALBERT NUNN'S STOCK CAMP STAND-BY

12 slices of bread	*BATTER:*
Butter	*2 c. flour*
Jam	*1 egg*
Oil	*Milk*
	Pinch of salt

To make batter place flour, salt and egg in bowl. Add a little milk at a time and mix well together, until you have a smooth paste. Now make six jam sandwiches and cut into quarters. Put the oil in the camp oven and get it hot. When ready dip each quarter piece of sandwich into the batter and then drop into hot oil. Cook until brown, about 4-5 minutes. When ready place on paper and sprinkle with sugar. Cooking time: 5 minutes.

Joe J. McEntire and Joe B. Norris
Abilene, Texas

MESQUITE JELLY

5 c. juice from Mesquite bean	*⅓ c. lemon juice*
7½ c. sugar	*1 box Sure-Jell*

Pick mesquite bean when first ripe (turning from green to reddish). Make sure the beans are insect-free. Boil to yield 5 cups of juice. Mix mesquite bean juice and lemon juice and bring to a boil. Add Sure-Jell and bring to a hard boil that can't be stirred down. Add sugar and bring to boil. Cook 10 to 15 minutes.

Background: Honey Mesquite—this thorny shrub or small tree may grow up to 30 feet tall and is a member of the legume family. It has pinnately bi-compound leaves with 12 to 20 leaflets. The leaflets are smooth, green and about 2 inches long. A small yellowish green flower is produced in the spring or early summer. The fruit, a bean or pod, ripens in late summer or fall and may be from 4 to 9 inches long, usually containing 10 to 20 seeds.

Mesquite beans are eaten by most kinds of wildlife and livestock, however, under some conditions they are poisonous. The pods or beans contain about 30% sugar and were used to make meal for bread by Indians of the Southwest. Also the gum produced on larger trees was used to make candy. The wood is valued as firewood and it will take an excellent polish. It is also used extensively for fence post. Mesquite is a common invader on abused Texas rangelands and is a troublesome pest throughout most of Texas except the northern Panhandle.

SWEETS

Fran Symms
Idaho

ROSY CINNAMON APPLES

2 c. water   2 c. sugar
½ c. red hot cinnamon drops

Make a syrup with equal parts sugar and water. Heat to melt cinnamon candies. Peel and core apples. If desired slice them crossways or leave them whole. Cook apples a few at a time, adding red food coloring if you like. These apples are very good served with meat or, if left whole, filled with cream cheese mixed with mayonnaise and served as a salad.

Mrs. A.T. Hibbard
Sieben Livestock Company
Helena, Montana

CARAMEL ICE CREAM

1 qt. milk   2 eggs
1½ c. sugar   1 qt. whipped cream
2 level tbsp. flour   1 tsp. vanilla
1 pinch salt   Caramel

Scald milk. Add 1 cup sugar, flour and salt. Mix thoroughly. Beat eggs and add above mixture gradually. Cook until mixture clings to spoon. When cold, add 1 quart of cream, whipped, and ½ cup sugar, caramel to taste, and 1 teaspoon vanilla. Serves 15.

Background: Henry Sieben born in Abenheim, Darmstadt, Germany, in February, 1847, came to the United States with his family in June, 1852, and to Montana exactly twelve years later. Here he first worked in overland freighting, but in 1869 entered the livestock business, first establishing headquarters on the Missouri River near the present location of Cascade and near where he later established the Sieben Livestock Company ranch which continues in the family operation. Alberta Sieben, the originator of this recipe, was born in Wisconsin in 1864.

James Newland
Greenwood Ranches
Bell Fourche, South Dakota

INDIAN ICE CREAM
(Whipped Berry Dessert)

4 c. berries   *½ c. honey or sugar*

This is a simple dessert and you can very the amount of berries and the sweetening to your taste. Mash the berries. (Northwest Indians use huckleberries. I have to use raspberries.) Add honey or sugar. Obviously huckleberries would need more sweetening. Whip with beater or by hand. Chill before serving. You may enjoy this more if you top it with real whipped cream.

Historic Pioneer Recipe

BLACK WALNUT & HONEY ICE CREAM

In saucepan blend 2 cups milk into ¾ cup honey. Cook and stir till hot (*do not boil*). Remove from heat. Stir moderate amount of hot mixture into 3 beaten eggs; return to saucepan. Cook and stir 2 minutes longer. Cool to room temperature. Blend in 2 cups whipping cream and 1 tsp. vanilla. Stir in 1 cup coarsely chopped black walnuts. Freeze mixture in ice cream freezer according to manufacturer's directions. Makes 2 quarts.

Mrs. Joe Rogers
Caddo, Texas

STRAWBERRY MOLD

1 lb. butter	*1 c. pecans*
2½ c. sugar	*2 egg whites, stiffly beaten*
1 qt. strawberries	*1 box Vanilla wafers*
	1 c. whipped cream

Cream butter well. Add sugar slowly and cream well. Add strawberries (halved or quartered if desired) and pecans. Fold in egg whites. Line dish (9x9 inches) with broken Vanilla wafers. Add a layer of strawberry mixture. Continue to alternate layers until dish is full, with wafers on top. Chill. Cut into squares and serve with whipped cream or Cool Whip.

June Schmautz
Fairfax County, Virginia

RASPBERRY FLAMBE

1 pkg. (10-oz.) frozen raspberries	*1 tbsp. cornstarch*
½ c. orange juice	*⅓ c. brandy*

Thaw raspberries, drain and reserve liquid. Combine liquid and cornstarch in saucepan. Add orange juice. Bring to a boil, stirring. Boil 2 to 3 minutes. Add raspberries, stirring gently. In a small pan heat brandy until bubbles form around edge of pan. Ingnite with match and pour over raspberry sauce. Serve the flaming sauce over ice cream. Makes 6 servings. Goes nicely with cookies at holiday time.

John and Denzil Mills
Charleville, Queensland, Australia

BOILED JAM ROLL

2½ c. flour	*3 tbsp. drippings or butter*
1½ tsp. baking powder	*1 tsp. sugar*
	Pinch of salt

Mix all ingredients to a stiff dough. Roll out neatly square onto a clean tea-towel. Spread dough thinly with a little of your favorite jam. Roll up in a tea towel and fasten with a safety pin or pins. Drop into boiling water and boil for 1½-2 hours. Serve with cream.

Mr. & Mrs. Arthur L. Mudge
Mudge Ranch
Kimble County, Junction, Texas

AMERICAN CREAM

1 qt. milk	*4 eggs*
2 envelopes plain gelatin	*1½ c. sugar*
1 tsp. vanilla	

Dissolve gelatin and half of the sugar in milk on a SLOW fire. Separate eggs. Beat yolks, add milk, and cook only until mixture thickens on the spoon. Remove from heat at once. Stand saucepan on a wet dish rag and fold in stiffly beaten egg whites, remaining sugar, and vanilla. Pour into wet mold. Refrigerate until firm. Unmold and serve with whipped cream.

Background: American Cream is a delightful dessert that has been served at the Mudge Ranch since the late 1880's. A fourth generation of Mudges on the same ranch still enjoy it topped with whipped cream. When it is made properly, it separates and has a perfectly clear gelatin on the bottom. Although at times, it doesn't separate and is all the same color as a custard. (It taste great, either way!)

W
+

James Newland
Greenwood Ranches
Bell Fourche, South Dakota

LUMPY DICK

1 egg	*¾ c. flour*
2½ c. milk (divided)	*Salt (optional)*
Sweetener	

Break egg into flour. Stir with a fork until lumpy. Add enough milk so that the mixture could be poured but leave the lumps. Add salt if desired. Pour the egg, flour and milk mixture into boiling milk. Cook for 15 minutes or until a toothpick inserted into the center comes out clean. Serve Lumpy Dick in sauce dishes with the rest of the milk and a "bit of sweetener" such as honey, molasses or sugar.

Background: Whenthe weather got bad, the old cow gave little milk and the chickens laid only an occasional egg, it was time for Lumpy Dick. No exact measurements of ingredients were made because the size of the egg and the available milk varied.

Mrs. Robert M. Case
Case Ranch
Pagosa Springs, Colorado

COWBOYS CREAM

1 c. sugar	*1 tbsp. flour*
Shake of nutmeg	*1 pt. water*

Lump of butter

Mix thoroughly and bring to boil to thicken. To be used in place of cream, when not available.

Background: Grandpa Toner moved to New Mexico from Iowa. First he ran a Zuni Indian Trading Post. Then he was in partnership with a big cattle Barron in Arizona. While freighting from Gallup, New Mexico to Durango, Colorado he fell in love with the area and homesteaded on the Upper Piedra River out of Pagosa Springs, Colorado. He used to mix this Cowboy's Cream up to serve on his puddings or sweetbreads. My daughter used the recipe in Safari Camps in Botswana, Africa because she didn't have any cream.

John and Denzil Mills
Charleville, Queensland, Australia

SPOTTED DOG

4 c. S.R. flour	*½ c. sugar*
1 dessertspoon drippings	*1 tsp. nutmeg*

1 lb. currants

Dissolve the drippings in a pint of hot water. Mix the flour, nutmeg, currants and sugar altogether then add the hot water mixture. Add enough more water as to make a sloppy mix, but not runny. When all mixed put into a cloth, like Christmas pudding and boil for 3 hours. Place a saucer in the bottom of the pot to stop the pudding from burning on the bottom. Make sure the water is boiling before you place the pudding in. Serve with custard.

Background: This is a magnificent recipe and to see it sitting in the middle of a table is really something. It looks wonderful served with custard or cream. It is also very nice fried with butter in a camp oven for breakfast.

SRM SOCIETY FOR RANGE MANAGEMENT

Conversion Charts

METRIC EQUIVALENTS
FOR U.S. VOLUME MEASURES

U.S. Volume Measure	Metric Equivalent
⅛ teaspoon	0.5 milliliter
¼ teaspoon	1 milliliter
½ teaspoon	2 milliliters
1 teaspoon	5 milliliters
½ tablespoon	7 milliliters
1 tablespoon (3 teaspoons)	15 milliliters
2 tablespoons (1 fluid ounce)	30 milliliters
¼ cup (4 tablespoons)	60 milliliters
⅓ cup	80 milliliters
½ cup (4 fluid ounces)	125 milliliters
⅔ cup	160 milliliters
¾ cup (6 fluid ounces)	180 milliliters
1 cup (16 tablespoons)	250 milliliters
1 pint (2 cups)	500 milliliters
1 quart (4 cups)	1 Liter

METRIC EQUIVALENTS
FOR U.S. WEIGHT MEASURES

U.S. Weight Measure	Metric Equivalent
½ ounce	15 grams
1 ounce	30 grams
2 ounces	60 grams
3 ounces	85 grams
¼ pound (4 ounces)	115 grams
½ pound (8 ounces)	225 grams
¾ pound (12 ounces)	340 grams
1 pound (16 ounces)	450 grams

METRIC EQUIVALENTS
FOR TEMPERATURES

Degrees Fahrenheit	Degrees Celsius
200°F	100°C
250°F	120°C
275ºF	140°C
300°F	150°C
325°F	160°C
350°F	180°C
375°F	190°C
400°F	200°C
425°F	220°C
450°F	230°C

Note: All metric equivalents are approximate; they have been rounded to the nearest metric equivalent.

Abbreviations
Commonly used for Recipes

tsp. – teaspoon

tbsp. – tablespoon

c. – cup

pt. – pint

qt. – quart

gal. – gallon

g. – gram

oz. – ounce

lb. – pound

pk. – peck

bu. – bushel

min. – minute

hr. – hour

List of Contributors

SRM wishes to thank all who submitted recipes for this book. We received a lot of good recipes. It was not possible to include every recipe submitted due to volume and duplication. If a contribution was not printed precisely as submitted, it is due to editorial changes made for clarity and an effort to stay within the number of pages allowed.

(continued)

Range Management Today

Range Management today presents greater challenges than ever. We are striving to improve and increase rangeland productivity with increased research. Range management educational programs seek to provide the general public with greater appreciation for, and knowledge of, this vast, renewable natural resource so that rangeland productivity can be maintained and improved for future generations.

The Society for Range Management will use the proceeds from this book to support and promote the art and science of good range management.

Since SRM is a non-profit organization, part of the funds given for this book are tax-deductible in the U.S. Thanks for your support. We hope you enjoy The Trail Boss's Cowboy Cookbook!

Index of Recipes

TRAIL BOSS'S COWBOY COOKBOOK
ORDER FORM

Name_____

Address_____

City_____State_____Zip_____

Please send me _____ copies at $16.95 per copy plus
$4.00 for postage and handling in the U.S. The total amount
enclosed is_____.
Call (303) 355-7070 for postage rates on multiple copies.

Send check or money order to:
TRAIL BOSS'S COWBOY COOKBOOK
1839 York Street, Denver, Colorado 80206

- -

TRAIL BOSS'S COWBOY COOKBOOK
ORDER FORM

Name_____

Address_____

City_____State_____Zip_____

Please send me _____ copies at $16.95 per copy plus
$4.00 for postage and handling in the U.S. The total amount
enclosed is_____.
Call (303) 355-7070 for postage rates on multiple copies.

Send check or money order to:
TRAIL BOSS'S COWBOY COOKBOOK
1839 York Street, Denver, Colorado 80206

Recipe Notes

Recipe Notes

Recipe Notes

Recipe Notes